RHODODENDRONS
CAMELLIAS & MAGNOLIAS
2018

A ROYAL HORTICULTURAL SOCIETY GROUP

SHARING THE BEST IN GARDENING

Published in 2018 by the Royal Horticultural Society,
80 Vincent Square, London SW1P 2PE

ISBN 978 1 907057 85 4

Designed for the RHS by SHARON CLUETT
Edited for the RHS by SIMON MAUGHAN

Editor for the Rhododendron,
Camellia and Magnolia Group
BARRY HASELTINE

Opinions expressed by the authors are not necessarily those of the Royal Horticultural
Society or the Rhododendron, Camellia and Magnolia Group

The Rhododendron, Camellia and Magnolia Group is a Charitable Incorporated
Organisation, Registered Number 1161254

Printed by Page Bros, Norfolk

COVER ILLUSTRATIONS
FRONT COVER: *Rhododendron* 'Azuma-kagami' (Wilson's no 16) (Polly Cooke)
BACK COVER (*LEFT*): *Camellia* 'Augusto Leal de Gouveia Pinto' (Jim Stephens)
BACK COVER (*RIGHT*): *Magnolia* 'Princess Margaret' (Vaughan Gallavan)

SHARING THE BEST IN GARDENING

CONTENTS

Chairman's Foreword

This yearbook begins a new era following Pam Hayward's outstanding ten year tenure as Editor. I was told a number of times that she was irreplaceable, but hopefully this edition will prove otherwise. By the time it is published, Pam will have been presented with the prestigious RHS Loder Cup to acknowledge her huge contribution to the world of rhododendrons in helping to educate all our members and the wider community. The Committee was unanimous in nominating her for the RHS award, and of course this reflects not just rhododendrons but also the articles on camellias and magnolias which she balanced in successive yearbooks.

Numerous appeals for another editor produced little response, but we could not allow our esteemed publication to wither after all these years, so the Committee established four commissioning editors covering rhododendrons, azaleas, camellias and magnolias, to obtain and edit suitable articles from leading authors around the world. But we still needed someone to coordinate all the authors and liaise with Simon Maughan who has produced the yearbook on behalf of the RHS for many years. Step forward the remarkable Barry Haseltine who has grasped the task needed and has led it to fruition, in much the same way as he helped to sort out our constitution when we separated from the RHS a few years ago. I don't think Barry will mind me quietly telling you that he is well into his eighties, so his contribution to the Group is all the more remarkable. No doubt the yearbook will have a slightly different feel to it, but we are fortunate that we can use the same successful format and layout that Pam has created, even though she has distanced herself from future editions. If Barry can work so hard on our behalf, then so can you, and your committee needs and welcomes offers of help to keep this charity progressing.

The most recent offers have been from Mark Bobbin and Nick Butler, who are instigating our new Outstanding Gardens Scheme. This is an exciting new project to raise the standards of curation, conservation and labelling in gardens open to the public, and in return the Group will help raise publicity and inform the public of the best gardens to visit that specialise in plants of our genera. The scheme follows a very similar format to the Gardens of Excellence scheme devised by the International Camellia Society. With their permission and great co-operation between the two organisations, we will publicise their scheme for Camellias, and operate our own Outstanding Gardens Scheme for rhododendrons and magnolias. Camellia gardens that meet the criteria and standards required by the ICS are reporting increased visitor numbers, and the plants and gardens themselves are in better shape. If we can do the same for rhododendrons and magnolias then we are into a win-win situation.

Thanks to the generosity of members, friends and a bit of Gift Aid, the Centenary Fund raised more than £7000 to enable rare and endangered plants to be propagated and planted in secure garden trusts around the country. The first donations included some additional large leaved species rhododendrons to supplement the collection at Abbotsbury Gardens in Dorset. The next donation is the Amos Pickard magnolia collection to be planted in the grounds of Canterbury Cathedral. Amos Pickard was a local nurseryman, who raised and registered a number of important magnolias in the 1960's, the best known being *Magnolia* 'Pickard's Schmetterling'. Many of his hybrids were hybrids of *M.* × *soulangeana* 'Picture' and are strong growing plants which seem surprisingly cold tolerant, and flower prolifically with flowers of good substance in March and April, when grown where light levels are good. Scions of these increasingly rare varieties have been obtained from a number of sources, and these have been grafted and grown on by specialists, prior to planting out. It will be good to help establish a reference collection of these choice plants in such a prestigious location where they can be enjoyed by future generations for years to come. Discussions are ongoing with gardens in the

CAMELLIA 'ANNETTE CAROL'

JIM STEPHENS

North of the country to establish other collections of plants that deserve to be better preserved and displayed.

The plant shows and competitions around the country continue to go from strength to strength. This is due to the good working relationship we have with the RHS, and in particular Georgina Barter in the Shows department who manages the construction of the shows, the printing of the schedules and the management of the cups and silverware on the day. Recently the competitions have been held at RHS venues, but with the huge developments and construction projects at Wisley, the decision was taken to move the 2017 Early Rhododendron Show to Savill Gardens where Keeper of the Gardens John Anderson, and his team treated us especially well in such a great location. Unfortunately the weather was against us as far as exhibiting rhododendrons was concerned, but there were some excellent camellias, and perhaps the highlight of the show was the wonderful display of ornamental shrubs, competing for the new Charles Eley Centenary Bowl, kindly presented by our membership secretary Rupert Eley. The two Rosemoor Shows go from strength to strength, while the Harlow Carr Show gains a late daffodil show at the same time. The addition of daffodils and ornamental shrubs has helped bring a new audience to our shows, and can save the day after frosty weather, though we may struggle for space in a good flowering year! The show at Wisley in May, with the theme of the Wilson 50 azaleas, was not a competition but was a real public facing event in a marquee on the lawns outside the restaurant. This was one of their peak weekends when 8000-10000 people could be expected, so it was excellent to 'fly the flag' for all our genera that were represented at this colourful show at peak season, and to gain some new members. None of these shows or competitions can take place without the dedication of exhibitors staging their flowers, and volunteers manning our stand, for which we are all really grateful. Do please get involved, and meet and talk to other like-minded enthusiasts to expand your own interest and knowledge!

MAGNOLIA X *SOULANGEANA* 'PICKARD'S SCHMETTERLING'   DAVID MILLAIS

Editorial

After the remarkable period of 30 years when the Group has only had three editors of the Yearbook, it was time for change, and unfortunately, no-one from our membership felt able to take on the task of editing the Yearbook, our most prestigious publication. It is interesting to note that the thirty years were evenly split into 10 year periods, firstly Cynthia Postan, for whom there is an appreciation later in this edition, Philip Evans and Pam Hayward.

Philip made use of an editorial Panel when he first became the Editor, and that is the route that we have followed this year to tap enough members to produce the 2018 edition and to lessen the load for any one individual.

The Panel consists of 4 commissioning editors, Polly Cooke, John Marston, David Millais and Stephen Lyus, with Peter Furneaux to give a link to the Bulletin, and me. Initially we hoped to get the articles and simply pass them to our layout specialist, Simon Maughan, and so arrive at the Yearbook – but life is not so simple! So that we could progress, I offered to act as leader of the Editorial panel, so in effect to become the Editor. I can assure the membership that there will not be a 10 year period before the next editor is required, so offers to assist are needed, as David points out.

The last two Yearbooks have been larger than was our normal size, because of the Centenary and the follow up to it; this issue is back to our usual size, and, hopefully, just as interesting as past ones. We are most grateful to our contributors who have given us a wide selection of interesting articles, yet again. We have probably a first this year in that Ted Brabin's son, Charles, is a barrister, and has had cause to give an opinion on the Nagoya Treaty situation. So we have a specialist report for the yearbook in the 'The Nagoya Protocol: Legal Framework and Challenges Ahead'. I must say that having read the article, it seems likely to be a very long time before the dust has settled sufficiently for much seed collection to restart, but I hope that I am wrong. Magnolias feature quite strongly this year with three articles about them. The Magnolias of Brooklyn Botanic Garden are seemingly fabulous, although I do not know them, but the article about them illustrates how important the work of the Brooklyn Botanic garden in hybridising has been. All those lovely yellow magnolias.

The wonderful gardens at Borde Hill are famous for many things, not just magnolias, but Jim Gardener has written a detailed history of magnolias there and gives an insight into just how long a history the property has had. There was an injection of 50 magnolias into the garden in 2015 to celebrate 50 years of the garden being open to the public, but yet more colour is to be added now by the addition of 60 magnolias, selected by Jim, as a start to making a new magnolia field or dell; the first planting was this spring.

New Zealander Vance Hooper has spent his life hybridising magnolias, starting at one of the major nurseries and moving through working for Mark Jury to setting up Magnolia Grove, a large thriving magnolia propagator on the North Island. He seems to have noticed early on in his breeding programme that gardens were getting smaller and so the plants needed to be smaller as well, hence a lot of introductions of smaller trees. The pictures are always mouth watering. I was particularly struck by the photograph of seed collected from his plants – kilograms of them!

Azaleas are not so often featured in the Yearbook, but this year we have a special group of articles on them, including a feature from Japan. Polly Cooke, our Group Secretary, is very interested in the Shimane Project: a study of traditional Japanese Tsutsuji cultivars, Tsutsuji (evergreen azaleas). The project is a world-wide one in which the RHS was asked to participate for the UK, and it has asked our Group to be the principle UK collaborator with Polly being at the forefront. Just before we finalised this Yearbook, the news came through that the Stanley Smith Horticultural Trust has given a substantial grant to the Group to help fund the work. Linked to Polly's

SEED COLLECTING, see the Nagoya Protocol article (p.84) KEITH RUSHFORTH

work on the Shimane Project is a translation of a Japanese paper on the Kirishima azaleas, recommended to the Group by our International Branch Chairman Rama Lopez-Rivera.

Jim Inskip is very well known for his work with Azaleas over many years He takes us, as he puts it, on a magical mystery tour of deciduous Azaleas of the far east.

Colin Mugridge, the winner of the Crosfield cup at last year's main Rhododendron Competition for the best three hybrid trusses raised by the exhibitor, shares some of his secrets about hybridising rhododendrons with us. He is a prolific hybridiser and shows us some fine examples of his work.

Camellias receive good coverage in this edition. Well-known camellia expert Jennifer Trehane has fallen in love with Oshima Island, Japan and shares some of the reasons for her love with us. It is not difficult to see why she is so fond of the island, judging by the stories and photographs that she shows.

The contrast with Oshima Island is obvious when it is compared with the hot and humid conditions of Vietnam which presented an unusual starting point for an article on collecting new camellias. George Orel has written about those conditions in 'Selected Notes on Camellia Hunting in South-East Asia

and China, 1999–2017'. The illustrations show camellias as many of us will not know them; they are very beautiful. George Orel tells a disappointing tale, however, about the difficulties of getting good photographs in the conditions, including losing a camera in a ravine!

A further contrast in background between Oshima Island and Vietnam is provided by an old book – Stephen Lyus has written an interesting article after coming across an old book in a private library – it was by Englebert Kaempfer and had been published in 1712. Stephen knew from his knowledge of Camellias that Kaempfer had a place in the early Camellia Story, so he has given us an article describing it, illustrated with photographs of the drawings in the original book.

We have the usual pieces towards the end; there is an Appreciation of Lady Cynthia Postan, 1918–2017, followed by Notes from the International Rhododendron Register 2017 by Dr Alan Leslie, who, to many people's surprise, retires this summer!

The Exceptional Plants article has usually been written by Pam Hayward, but we have persuaded Russell Beeson to do a similar job this year, but with a wider remit to suit his views and interests. We are most grateful for the enormous effort he has made.

Finally, I have put together the list of Challenge Cups that were awarded through 2017.

It has been quite a challenge to take the efforts of the Commissioning Editors, together with all the other 'bits and pieces', and to weld them into a book that I hope is worthy of the title Yearbook of the Rhododendron Camellia and Magnolia Group. Thanks are, of course, due to the many authors and collaborators without whom there would not be anything to edit.

I hope that you enjoy our product.

The Magnolias of Brooklyn Botanic Garden

MAGNOLIA PLAZA WITH VISITOR CENTRE
REBECCA BULLENE, COURTESY OF BROOKLYN BOTANIC GARDEN

Brooklyn Botanic Garden (BBG) is famous in horticultural circles for introducing the yellow-flowering magnolia to the world, but the Garden's magnolia breeding programme has a deep history that is not as well known, even to gardeners who may have planted one of the trees in their own garden.

In 1932, BBG unveiled Magnolia Plaza, then called Laboratory Plaza for its adjacency to the Laboratory building that now houses our administration. Eighty magnolias were planted, formalising a collection of magnolias that would join our systematics collection a year later. The systematics collection looks at plant evolution and interrelationships, now greatly enhanced by DNA analysis. Yulans (*Magnolia denudata*), star magnolias (*M. stellata*), and various saucer magnolias (*M.* × *soulangeana*) from the plaza's opening are still standing today, and their extravagant blooms are among the showiest signs of spring.

Our collection has since evolved to showcase a number of important magnolias bred by BBG's own breeding programme. *Magnolia* × 'Elizabeth' and '*Magnolia* × 'Judy Zuk', now mainstays in magnolia and horticulture circles, were developed by this small but important programme begun in the early 1950s. The general goal at that time was to develop hardy cultivars of the most prominent woody ornamental species. However, having had the most success with magnolias, the programme eventually narrowed its focus more specifically on this genus.

In 1956, BBG acquired 90 hectares (223 acres) of woodland in Ossining, New York, through the generosity of the Van Brunt family. The magnolia breeding programme soon relocated there and become part of BBG's new field research centre, known as Kitchawan. At Kitchawan, the magnolia programme occupied approximately two acres, and its move upstate was spearheaded by Dr Evamaria Sperber, the influential breeder who helped found the programme and was also responsible for the initial hybridisation work.

M. 'ELIZABETH'   BLANCA BEGERT, COURTESY OF BROOKLYN BOTANIC GARDEN

In 1954, a cross made between the northeastern American native cucumber tree (*M. acuminata*) and the Asian mulan (*M. liliiflora*) resulted in the hybrid group × *brooklynensis,* with a type clone selected and named 'Evamaria' after its hybridiser. Not only was this the first successful cross of an American and Asian species, but it also brought the modest cucumber tree into the consciousness of magnolia breeders far and wide. Demonstrating that the cucumber tree was a compatible partner for the showier Asian species was a major coup; it contributed increased hardiness and an expanded colour range previously unseen in magnolias.

Flowers of the hybrid group × *brooklynensis* have six tepals with a unique combination of purples, oranges, yellows and greens in varying degrees and tinges. 'Evamaria' has a predominantly purple-pink flower, with hints of orange, yellow, and green emanating from the base of its tepals. Its flowers do not open widely and reach about 9.5cm in width. Bloom times typically occur a week or so after the saucer magnolias (*M.* × *soulangeana*) and about three weeks after the star magnolias (*M. stellata*). This later bloom time generally protects its flowers from late-season frosts, but arguably diminishes the display compared with its precocious counterparts. The tree reaches 4.5–6m tall (15–20ft), with a 3–4.5m (10–15ft) spread. 'Evamaria' was officially introduced in 1972.

But with BBG's second hybrid introduction the horticulture and plant worlds really took notice.

In 1977, Dr Lola Koerting, then director of BBG's breeding programme, presented at the Magnolia Society's annual meeting in Washington D.C. images of precocious, yellow-flowering magnolias. Nothing like this had been seen before. Many contemporary magnolia breeders of the time were in attendance, and everyone was completely awestruck.

The precocious yellow magnolias were the result of crosses Dr Sperber made between the cucumber tree (*M. acuminata*) and the yulan (*M. denudata*) in 1956. The most well known of BBG's magnolia hybrids, 'Elizabeth', introduced in 1977, was selected from these crosses, mostly for its uniform yellow coloration, floriferous nature and ideal pyramidal habit. It is generally considered the first precocious yellow-flowering magnolia. Its flowers are a pale, buttery yellow with six to nine tepals that vary from 7–9 cm in length and 2.5–5cm in width. 'Elizabeth' blooms late April to early May, about a week after the saucer magnolias and two to three weeks after the star magnolias. 'Elizabeth' reaches 6–8m (20–30ft) tall and 4.5–6m (15–20ft) wide. Its name honours Elizabeth Van Brunt, who donated the land for the Kitchawan site.

The yellow-blooming magnolias, from which 'Elizabeth' originated, had first been observed in 1972. Their novelty and potential led BBG to focus more research and development on them. Following 'Elizabeth' was *Magnolia* × 'Yellow Bird', the result of a backcross of *M.* × *brooklynensis* 'Evamaria' with *M. acuminata*

M. 'LOIS' BLANCA BEGERT. COURTESY OF BROOKLYN BOTANIC GARDEN

blooms as the leaves unfurl — like most × *brooklynensis* hybrids — after the saucer magnolias bloom and after the threat of late frosts. It is named for Hattie Carthan, a Brooklyn environmentalist and community activist who was instrumental in preserving a near-century-old *Magnolia grandiflora* in her neighbourhood of Bedford-Stuyvesant. 'Hattie Carthan' was named and introduced in 1984, mere months after her passing.

Of course, BBG's magnolia breeding programme did not concentrate exclusively on producing yellow magnolias. An early cross between *M. liliiflora* 'Nigra' and *M. kobus,* made by Dr Sperber in 1954, yielded *Magnolia* × 'Marillyn', which has a dark magenta-rose flower. Very similar to the Kosar or "Little Girl" hybrids developed by the National Arboretum in Washington D.C., 'Marillyn' is a small multi-stemmed tree that reaches 3–4.5m (10–15ft) tall and 5–6m (8–12ft) wide. Its tepals usually come in sixes and are approximately 12cm long and 4–6 cm wide. 'Marillyn' has proven to be extremely hardy, up to USDA Zone 4, more so than some of the garden's other hybrid introductions. Its name honours Marillyn Wilson, a benefactor of BBG. It was introduced in 1989, the last introduction before the magnolia breeding programme was discontinued and Kitchawan closed in 1991.

Luckily, before operations ceased, several original test hybrids that showed promise were passed on to other locations and institutions, including the grounds at Brooklyn Botanic Garden. While some trees disappeared into obscurity, others — known by their test plot numbers from Kitchawan or some other unofficial naming — were developed with great fanfare and propagated in the ornamental plant world. Three hybrids of note have come out from this bunch.

Magnolia × 'Lois' was known merely as *Magnolia* BBG No.1160 until its official naming and registration in 1998. Another addition to BBG's yellow flowering magnolias, 'Lois' is a

var. *subcordata*. The hybridisation work was done by Doris Stone in 1967, and 'Yellow Bird' was officially introduced in 1981. This magnolia's blooms are deeper yellow and smaller than those of 'Elizabeth'. It flowers one to two weeks later, and the blooms appear simultaneously with its leaves. This lack of precociousness does make for a less dramatic show, but 'Yellow Bird' is much more dependable since it blooms after most frosts. 'Yellow Bird' grows from 6–9m (25–40ft) tall and 3–6m (10–20ft) wide.

The traits of *M.* × *brooklynensis* hybrids vary considerably due to the complex genetic make up of the parent *M. liliiflora*. It is also very fertile, making *M.* × *brooklynensis* a valuable species for hybridisation work. In 1965, Stone cross-pollinated several *M.* × *brooklynensis* hybrids with one another. One effort crossed *M.* × 'Evamaria' with an unnamed *M.* × *brooklynensis* hybrid (No.209). While 'Evamaria' has a predominantly purplish-pink flower, *M* × *brooklynensis* No.209 had a flower described as a "washed-out yellow" with purple-magenta veins. The result became *Magnolia* × 'Hattie Carthan', which has a bright yellow flower with magenta-rose veins ascending from the base of its tepals. As the flowers begin to unfurl, the outer tepals display a green tinge. The tepals are 10–12cm in length and 2.5–3cm in width. The tree itself reaches 3–4.5m (10–15ft) tall and 2–3.5m (6–8ft) wide.

Considered a second-generation × *brooklynensis*, 'Hattie Carthan' nonetheless

M. 'JUDY ZUK'   BLANCA BEGERT, COURTESY OF BROOKLYN BOTANIC GARDEN

director of the Scott Arboretum of Swarthmore College. Both institutions still have specimens from the time they were known as *Magnolia* BBG No.1164.

Magnolia × brooklynensis 'Black Beauty' is universally recognized as a BBG introduction, but it has in fact never been registered or officially named. Originally known as *Magnolia × brooklynensis* No.204, its history is not well documented. The 'Black Beauty' name first appeared in the spring 2001 catalogue of Fairweather Garden's nursery in New Jersey. The name stuck, and it continues to be offered around the world as such. A selection from crossing *M. acuminata* and *M. liliiflora*, 'Black Beauty' was presumably named for its unusually dark, purple flower. This is in contrast to the pale white interiors of its tepals. Extremely hardy (to Zone 4), 'Black Beauty' will reach 5–7.5m (15–25 ft) tall and 3–4.5m (10–15ft) wide.

Since 2017, all eight of BBG's magnolia introductions have been once again in full view on the garden's Magnolia Plaza. Specimens of 'Evamaria', 'Elizabeth', 'Yellow Bird', 'Hattie Carthan', 'Lois', and 'Judy Zuk' at BBG came

backcross of an unnamed 'Elizabeth' sibling (Magnolia BBG No.850) to its seed parent *M. acuminata*. The hybridisation work was done by Dr Koerting in 1980. 'Lois' first bloomed in 1987, exhibiting a darker yellow flower than 'Elizabeth' but blooming later, when 'Elizabeth' is reaching the end of flowering, and just as its leaves begin to emerge. Its flowers are erect and cup-shaped with nine tepals, each 6–9cm long and 2.5–5cm wide. 'Lois' can reach up to 8–10m (25–30ft) tall, and 5–8m (15–20 ft) wide. Its name honours Lois Carswell, a former chairperson of BBG's Board of Trustees and co-chair of BBG's annual Plant Sale. 'Lois' was planted at BBG in 1991, as No.1160, directly from Kitchawan and still stands today in Magnolia Plaza.

Magnolia × 'Judy Zuk' was known as *Magnolia* BBG No.1164 until its official naming and registration in 2007. 'Judy Zuk' is a rather complex cross between *M. acuminata* and an unnamed BBG hybrid of *M. acuminata, M. liliiflora*, and *M. stellata* (BBG #491). Its fragrant flower is dark yellow, bordering on orange, with a slight pink blush at the base of its five to six tepals. The tepals are 8 to 10 cm long and 4 to 5.5 cm wide. 'Judy Zuk' blooms about a week after 'Elizabeth' has finished, just as its leaves are emerging. An upright-branching tree, it appears rather columnar early on and becomes more oval with age. It reaches 6–8m (20–25ft) tall and 2.5–3m (8–10ft) wide. Its name honours Judith Zuk, a magnolia lover and former president of Brooklyn Botanic Garden and

M. 'YELLOW BIRD'
BLANCA BEGERT, COURTESY OF BROOKLYN BOTANIC GARDEN

PLAZA MAGNOLIAS

REBECCA BULLENE, COURTESY OF BROOKLYN BOTANIC GARDEN

directly from Kitchawan and represent some of the oldest trees of their kind. Other specimens in the collection have been replaced through various nurseries that fortunately continue BBG's legacy in magnolia breeding. As our hybrids stand next to their species counterparts (*M. denudata, M. kobus, M. stellata,* etc), the future of our collection puts special emphasis on representing the parentage of our BBG hybrids, of which most are seminal. How BBG's personal story fits within the larger development of the genus *Magnolia* and its hybrids will then become clearer as time passes.

Outside the confines of the BBG, the legacy of its magnolia breeding programme lives on. Breeders worldwide have incorporated and continue to build on BBG's work. The introduction of *M. × brooklynensis* and *M. ×* 'Elizabeth' demonstrated the hybridisation possibilities of *M. acuminata.* This has resulted in exciting hybrid introductions like *M. × brooklynensis* 'Woodsman' (1975), *M. ×* 'Butterflies' (1989), and *M. ×* 'Yellow Lantern' (1989). Breeders similarly have used BBG hybrids as parents for more complex crosses to produce second-generation hybrids, such as *M. ×* 'Sunsation' (*M. × brooklynensis* 'Woodsman' × *M. ×* 'Elizabeth'), introduced in 2000; *M. ×* 'Blushing Belle' (*M. ×* 'Yellow Bird' × *M. ×* 'Caerhays Belle'), introduced in 2001; and *M. ×* 'Ambrosia' (*M. × brooklynensis* 'Evamaria' × *M. × brooklynensis* No.143), introduced in 2004.

As public opinion and favourites ebb and flow, the BBG hybrids continue to make their presence on the market known. They help keep BBG's pioneering breeding work in the public's consciousness. While each hybrid has its own unique story and unique traits that run the gamut from the sure and nuanced to the bold and precocious, the collective story is greater than the sum of its parts.

WAYKEN SHAW
is the Gardener/Curator of Lily Pool Terrace & Judith D. Zuk Magnolia Plaza Brooklyn Botanic Garden, New York

Asian Species Deciduous Azaleas

RHODODENDRON WADANUM

As a collector, conserver and propagator of rare deciduous azalea hybrids and species for 30 years, I thought that an article on the species of deciduous azaleas from the Far East would be of interest. These azalea species are native to Japan, China, Korea and Taiwan. They are difficult to propagate from cuttings or grafts and are usually propagated from seed. These are mostly hardy shrubs and many have spectacular leaves with truly wonderful autumn colour. The species are from two distinct subgenera, **Pentanthera** and **Tsutsusi** and I have grouped them accordingly. Amongst the species covered are the well known *R. molle, R. reticulatum* and *R. schlippenbachii.* The remainder are less well known and indeed some of them are very rare. In a way, it is these lesser known species that persuaded me to write this and draw them to your attention.

The RHS accepts the names of all species included, fully or tentatively, with the exception of *R. viscistylum,* which is not recognised. This species is recognised in many books and texts and therefore, I feel, deserves inclusion. In writing this I will attempt to give a little of the history of each species and a brief description of it, accompanied by at least one photograph.

RHODODENDRON PENTANTHERA

Rhododendron albrechtii was named after Michael Albrecht, a physician working at the Russian Consulate in Hakodate, on the island of Hokkaido, Japan. Albrecht discovered this species growing around Hakodate in 1860. It was first described by the Russian botanist Maximowicz in 1870. Its natural range is from central Honshu to Hokkaido at altitudes between 750 and 2,000m. Charles Sargent collected and sent seed to The Arnold Arboretum in 1892. Ernest H Wilson also collected seed in 1914 which was distributed by The Arnold Arboretum.

R. albrechtii is a deciduous azalea of loose habit growing 1–1.5m tall in the wild but taller in cultivation. Its leaves are arranged in clusters of five at the end of the branch. They are dark green, obovate to oblanceolate, bristle-toothed on the margin and between 4 and 10cm long.

RHODODENDRON ALBRECHTII   **SALLY PERKINS**

The predominantly pink flowers open in late April to early May in clusters of three to five. The flower colour can vary from rose pink to reddish purple but is generally described as bright purplish rose, spotted with green on the upper lobes. R. albrechtii received an Award of Merit on the 13th April 1943. The clone 'Michael McLaren' was awarded a FCC when shown from Bodnant on 1st May 1962. This species is commercially grown in the UK.

Rhododendron molle ssp. japonicum is a deciduous bush, of rounded habit, 1.3–2.8m high with erect branches. Its leaves are narrowly oval or obovate 4–10cm long. It bears six to ten flowers in a cluster in May. The flowers are in

RHODODENDRON MOLLE SSP. *JAPONICUM*

SALLY PERKINS

various shades of soft rose, salmon red and orange-red, with a large orange blotch.

R. molle ssp. japonicum is native to Japan and grows from Kyushu to Hokkaido in scrub and on open grassland at altitudes up to 2,100 m. Ernest H Wilson observed that it never grows in woods or dense thickets. It was introduced into Europe in the 1830s and to the UK in the 1860s and was commonly called *Azalea japonica*. When compared with its American relatives in the section *pentanthera*, this sub species is tolerant of less acid soil.

Rhododendron molle ssp. molle is a sub species closely related to R. molle ssp. japonicum. The most obvious difference between the two is that the leaves of R. molle ssp. molle are coated

RHODODENDRON MOLLE SSP. *MOLLE*
Royal Botanic Garden Stockholm   **HAROLD GREER**

beneath with a dense felt of soft down and the buds too are conspicuously downy. This species was once better known as *Azalea sinensis*, *Azalea mollis* or the 'Chinese Azalea'. It is common in Eastern China especially on the mountains of Chekiang province. It makes a small shrub growing 0.6 to 1.5m tall. The flowers are always a shade of yellow.

The British Nursery, Loddiges, received seed in 1823. The Earl of Liverpool's gardener, Smith, raised some fine azaleodendrons in the 1830s and 1840s, described as the Norbiton Group. *R. ponticum* or a hybrid *R. ponticum* × *R. maximum* was the seed parent; *R. molle* ssp. *molle* was the pollen parent. Examples of these plants are 'Ochraleucum', 'Smithii Aureum' and 'Broughtonii Aureum'.

This species is particularly interesting, as plants raised from it were used by Lionel de Rothschild in breeding the Exbury strain of the Knap Hill azaleas.

RHODODENDRON NIPPONICUM   COEN ZONNEFELD

Rhododendron nipponicum is a little known Japanese species confined to the mountains of North Hondo. It is the only species in the section *Viscidula* of the subgenus *Pentanthera*. First described by Matsumura in 1899, its foliage looks similar to *R. schlippenbachii* but the similarity ends there. It is a very distinct species with its papery, cinnamon brown bark which shreds off, leaving polished brown stems and branches. No other species with deciduous leaves has such attractive bark. It forms a bushy shrub from 1 to 2m tall. Its white tubular bell

shaped flowers can be disappointing as they are small and are often hidden by the leaves and young new growth. The foliage is one of the finest in the autumn turning brilliant orange with crimson tints. Twenty first century scientific examination has suggested that *R. nipponicum* may be better placed in section Tsutsusi.

RHODODENDRON PENTAPHYLLUM   CHRIS KLAPWIJK

The deciduous species, **Rhododendron pentaphyllum**, commonly called the Five-Leaf Azalea, is found growing in woodland, from the extreme south of Kyushu through Shikoku and Hondo to the Nikko region of Japan. It was first described by Maximowicz in 1887. Ernest H Wilson saw it in the wild and wrote of its beauty both in flower and its autumn colour when it changes from rich orange to crimson.

RHODODENDRON PENTAPHYLLUM white form
HANS EIBERG

A deciduous shrub or tree growing to 6.5m in height in the wild, but it is much smaller in cultivation. It has leaves in whorls of five, oval to oval-lanceolate in shape and 2–5cm long. The flowers are bright pink rose, opening in April and May. A specimen of *R. pentaphyllum* was shown by Lord Aberconway on April 14th 1942 and received an Award of Merit. A rare white form is known.

The 'Cork Azalea', ***Rhododendron quinquefolium***, is native to the Japanese islands of Honshu and Shikoku and was first introduced from Japan in 1896. In the wild it grows to 4.5–6m but is smaller in cultivation, reaching 2.5–3.5m. It bears white flowers with green spotting in late April to early May, after the leaves have opened. It has whorls of 4 or 5 leaves and each leaf has a

RHODODENDRON QUINQUEFOLIUM   **CHRIS KLAPWIJK**

RHODODENDRON QUINQUEFOLIUM showing pink-edged leaves   **SALLY PERKINS**

pink to reddish edge, which is stunning. In autumn the leaves turn a rich ruby red.

In a ceremony on 7 December 2001, the Japanese Crown Prince Naruhito and Crown Princess Masaka established the Goyo or Five-leaf Azalea *Rhododendron quinquefolium* as the symbol of their new-born child the Princess Aiko, who had been born on the first day of the month. The whiteness of the flowers represents the pure heart of the Princess.

There is an excellent example growing at Exbury Gardens with the clonal name 'Five Arrows'. *R. quinquefolium* received an Award of Garden Merit in 1993.

Rhododendron schlippenbachii is a common shrub in Korea and just crosses the border into north eastern Manchuria on the shores of Possiet Bay. In Japan it is known only in two localities in North Hondo. This species was discovered by Baron A. Von Schlippenbach of the Russian Navy in North East Korea in 1854 and was first described by Maximowicz in 1871. James II Veitch saw it in a garden in Japan and sent it to the UK in 1893. This year was its first appearance in the West.

R. schlippenbachii was exhibited in 1896 by Veitch at Chelsea, gaining an Award of Merit. Since then it has received 2 FCCs, the first in 1942 for a specimen from Bodnant; the second,

RHODODENDRON SCHLIPPENBACHII

    SALLY PERKINS

from Leonardslee, in 1965 with the clonal name 'Prince Charming' whose flowers have deep crimson spotting. This deciduous azalea grows from 1 to 4.5m tall. It bears fragrant pale pink to rose pink and occasionally white flowers which usually open as the leaves begin to unfold. Within its group it has the second largest leaves and the most beautiful flowers. This species is worthy of a place in every garden. It is also known as 'The Royal Azalea'.

RHODODENDRON TSUTSUSI BRACHYCALYX

The species deciduous azaleas in the section *Rhododendron Tsutsusi Brachycalyx* are all very closely related to each other. Separating them out or combining them together is a job for the taxonomists. Insufficient research has been done, to date, for this to be achieved.

Rhododendron amagianum is native to Mount Amagi on the Japanese island of Honshu. This upright deciduous shrub was first described by Makino in 1930. It has a slightly spreading shape; the rounded leaves are a very interesting shape and it is late flowering.

Whorled clusters of three rounded rhombus shaped, dark green leaves are found at the end of branches. In early summer, clusters of one to three non-fragrant blooms appear on the branch ends above the leaves. The flowers are orange red but can be pure red. *R. amagianum* was given an Award of Merit in 1948. This species is currently in commercial propagation in the UK.

RHODODENDRON DECANDRUM
Grown from seed from H. Suzuki   **DAVID MILLAIS**

Rhododendron decandrum is very similar to *R. dilatatum* in many respects. The obvious difference is that *R. decandrum* has 10 stamens, while *R. dilatatum* only has 5 stamens. This species was first described by Makino in 1917 and is native to southern Honshu and Shikoko in Japan. The flowers vary in colour from pale to dark pink. Good examples of this species can be seen at the Royal Botanic Garden, Edinburgh.

Rhododendron dilatatum is found at about 900m in the mountains, on the Japanese island of Honshu and grows both terrestrially and epiphytically. Growing up to about 5.5m in height, it is a deciduous bush or a small tree. The flowers are purple or white, opening in mid May. *R. dilatatum* is a beautiful azalea, with very

RHODODENDRON AMAGIANUM   **HANK HELM**

RHODODENDRON DILATUM   **HANK HELM**

RHODODENDRON FARRERAE growing on Mount Tahashan, Pintung County, Taiwan   CHIEN-FAN CHING

attractive flowers and good autumn colours; it is said to be heat tolerant. *R. dilatatum* was discovered by Siebold early in the 19th century. It was described by Miquel in 1863 from plants growing on the mountains of Okayama and Hakone, in South Honshu, Japan. This species is very similar to *R. reticulatum,* particularly the leaf shape and size and the flower shape, size and colour. It is readily distinguished from its ally by the 5 stamens and the densely, or moderately glandular pedicel and calyx. The plant was first introduced by Veitch in 1883.

Rhododendron farrerae is a low densely branched or medium-sized shrub, with shiny brown branches, that grows 2–3m tall. Its young shoots are strigose but later become glabrous. The leaves are deciduous or semi-evergreen, usually in whorls of 3 at the ends of the branchlets. *R. farrerae* bears 1-2 flowers opening before the leaves. The corolla is rotate-funnel shaped, pale to deep rose in colour, with red/purple spots on the upper lobes; the tube is short and narrow.

This plant is native to Hong Kong and the Guangdong and Guanxi provinces of mainland China. *R. farrerae* is a distinct species and cannot be confused with the other members of its subseries. Its remarkable features are the small, ovate subcoriaceous or coriaceous leaves, the short petiole and the 8-10 stamens which are shorter than the corolla. This species was introduced by Captain Farrer of The East India Company in 1829 and named after Captain Farrer's wife. *R. farrerae* is tender (H1-2) and rare in cultivation.

Rhododendron hidakanum is a very rare shrub. It is appropriate to include taxonomic details, as it seems that a complete description is not available in the reference books that we normally use.

This is a shrub growing to 3m in height, with young shoots that are greyish in colour. Its leaves are broadly rhombic-ovate with a short cuspidate apex and a broadly cuneate base; their upper surface is sparsely glandular but at first they are covered with long white hairs, later becoming

RHODODENDRON HIDAKANUM　　　HANS EIBERG

RHODODENDRON KIYOSUMENSE　　　DAVID MILLAIS

glabrescent, with persistent hair bases. The lower surface of the leaf is pale, with adpressed hairs or glabrous, though with minute papillate glands and long hairs on the leaves; the petioles are 5–12mm and glandular. The inflorescence has 1–3 flowers; the pedicels are between 10–15mm, glandular and pilose below. The calyx is 3mm, glandular and sometimes ciliate, with a funnel-campanulate magenta corolla of 25–30mm; the lobes are 17mm, oblong-obovate. There are ten stamens which are purple and unequal, filaments that are glabrous. The ovary is shortly stipitate-glandular, with scattered pilose hairs; the style is glabrous and the capsule 9–11 × 3mm.

R. hidakanum is closely related to *R. decandrum* due to its glandular ovary. The most significant differences appear to be in the larger calyx and less hairy leaves of *R. hidakanum*. It has a more northerly distribution than *R. decandrum* and is found in southern Hokkaido.

Rhododendron kiyosumense has two synonyms attributed to it; *R. shimidzuanum* and *R. dilatatum* var. *kiyosumense*. It was first described by Makino in 1931.

This Japanese deciduous shrub grows up to 1.2m in height. Its purple to red violet flowers open in April–May. The flower stalk is smooth and the blade stalk is almost smooth.

Rhododendron mariesii is distributed from Fokien and Chekiang provinces of Eastern China westward to south eastern Szechuan. It has pink to rose coloured flowers which open before the leaves unfold, in late April to May. It is an upright shrub 1–3m tall with ovate-lanceolate leaves.

This Chinese plant was discovered by Robert Fortune and later found again in the Lushan mountains behind Kiukiang in the spring of 1878 by Charles Maries, a collector for Veitch. It was introduced to the Royal Botanic Garden Kew, in 1886, by Augustine Henry who sent seed. In 1900, Ernest H Wilson sent seed from south of Ichang to the Veitch Nursery. This species azalea is named after Charles Maries. It flowered for the first time at Kew, in the temperate house, in April 1907.

RHODODENDRON MARIESII　　　ELAINE SEDLACK
University of California Botanic Gardens

FLOWER BUDS OF *RHODODENDRON NUDIPES*

SALLY PERKINS

RHODODENDRON RETICULATUM flowers (*above*) and leaves (*below*) in The Isabella Plantation, Richmond Park April 2017

BARRY COOKE

Rhododendron nudipes is a deciduous shrub found in Honshu and Kyushu, Japan and was first described by Nakai in 1926. It grows in mountain forests at a height of 200–1000m. It forms a shrub or small tree. Young shoots, leaves and flowers are covered with brown hairs. The rhombic shaped leaves, up to 6.5cm long, are borne in whorls of three at the ends of branches. The funnel-campanulate shaped flowers are usually borne in pairs before the leaves unfold. The 5–7.5 cm flowers are rose purple to deep pink with purple spots.

RHODODENDRON NUDIPES   SALLY PERKINS

Rhododendron reticulatum is a deciduous species azalea that grows from 1m to 6m tall and produces an abundance of rose to red-purple or rich magenta coloured flowers. The deepest colours are on plants in the open but they are much paler in dense shade. Its leaves tend towards a rhombic shape and vary to broad-ovate. *R. reticulatum* was first introduced into the UK in 1832–1833 according to G Don but subsequently lost. It was introduced into the Arnold Arboretum by Professor Sargent who sent seeds from the Nikko region in 1892. There is apparently a very rare white variety of *R. reticulatum, R. reticulatum* var. *albiflorum* but it is uncommon in Western gardens.

Rhododendron sanctum can be a deciduous or a semi-evergreen azalea found in Honshu, Japan. It was first described by Nakai in 1932. The flowers vary from deep pink red to rose purple opening in May to June and are up to 4cm across.

RHODODENDRON SANCTUM

SALLY PERKINS

RHODODENDRON TASHIROI white form
Hiroshima Botanical Garden

YUKIKO SHIMADA

Its leaves are broadly rhombic, in whorls of three at the ends of branches. *R. sanctum* is a medium sized shrub in cultivation but a small tree in the wild. Its name is derived from where it was found, within the sacred area at the Great Shrine of Ise.

Recent taxonomic studies have placed *R. sanctum* in with *R. amagianum* but it is different. *R. sanctum* has long brown hairs and the leaves are larger. It has wonderful autumn colour.

It grows in the southern part of Japan, including the Kawanabe Islands, Yakushima Island, Tanegashima, Riukiu and also SW Taiwan. It can grow up to 4.25m in height on Yakushima Island, up to elevations of 1800m. A hybrid with *R. tashiroi* as a parent was given the name 'Tashiroi Pink Pearl' by Koichiro Wada of Yokohama, Japan.

R. tashiroi in Japan resembles some members of the subsection *Triflora*.

AUTUMN COLOUR OF *RHODODENDRON SANCTUM*

HANS EIBERG

RHODODENDRON VISCISTYLUM

HANK HELM

Rhododendron tashiroi is known in Japan as 'The Cherry Azalea', it is a rare species in cultivation. It is considered by botanists a linking species between section Tsutsusi and section Brachycalyx. It has deep glossy evergreen leaves 3.5cm to 5cm long, with brown flattened hairs on the leaves. The flowers are white, pale pink to pink 5–6.5cm across opening at the end of April.

Rhododendron viscistylum is a deciduous shrub that grows up to 3m tall. It flowers in June with reddish-violet to purple blooms with darker spots. First described by Nakai in 1935, *R. viscistylum* is found in the southern areas of Kyushu, Japan. This species is characterised by the sticky glands on its style and also, occasionally, on the underside of its leaves.

RHODODENDRON WADANUM new growth

SALLY PERKINS

RHODODENDRON WEYRICHII VAR. *ALBUM*

SALLY PERKINS

Rhododendron wadanum grows in ridge lines on mountains to a height of 2–4m. This is a deciduous species azalea from South East Honshu, in Japan, with rhombic, almost heart shaped leaves in whorls of three. The corolla is a wide funnel shape and the flowers are normally rose pink to purple in colour. A white-flowered variant, *R. wadanum* 'Album' is known and is now being commercially grown in the UK.

RHODODENDRON WADANUM 'ALBUM'   DAVID MILLAIS

Rhododendron weyrichii is a little known species azalea with a strange distribution. On the Japanese island of Shikoku it is common around Ochi in the province of Tosa but does not grow on the mainland of Kyushu. It is found on the islands of Amakusa and Goto south and west of Nagasaki. It

also grows on the Korean island of Quelpaert. This species was discovered on the Goto Islands by Dr Heinrich Weyrich, a surgeon on the Russian warship 'Vostock' and is named after him.

R. weyrichii is a vigorous shrub that grows from 1–5m tall with distinctly petiolate, chartaceous, shiny green leaves. They vary from broad-ovate to semi orbicular or rhombic in shape and turn from green to purple in the autumn. The corolla is rotate funnel-shaped, bright, almost brick red, spotted within the back of the short narrow tube. There are 6–10 stamens and calyx-lobes are persistent.

This species was first introduced by Ernest H Wilson, who sent seeds from Shikoku in 1914 to the Arnold Arboretum and then to the UK. It was

RHODODENDRON WEYRICHII VAR. *MURESAKI*   HANK HELM

RHODODENDRON TASHIROI, R. MARIESII AND *R. SCHLIPPENBACHII*   WILLIAM C MILLER III

reintroduced by him as seeds from the island of Quelpaert in 1917. Seed was sent to the Royal Botanic Garden Edinburgh, on several occasions from various sources.

IN CONCLUSION

Although not all of the species in either subgenus are included here, it is my hope that you have enjoyed a magical mystery tour through Asia with these species deciduous azaleas. Many of them look similar and indeed are taxonomically close to each other, but there is great confusion over the taxonomy and nomenclature of this plant group at present. I am not a taxonomist and I leave this to the experts. Clearly, a good deal more field and laboratory research is needed to establish precisely where each species fits.

There is also confusion about stamens and I haven't mentioned much about those. The reason is that while I have said in a few places, 5 or 10 stamens, I know that some species have been seen with flowers having both 5 and 10 stamens on the same specimen. Despite the confusion I would encourage you all to seek out these fantastic azaleas as they make wonderful garden plants and it is well worth the effort in finding them.

Above you will see a great photograph illustrating the differing flower sizes and colour of three of the species we have travelled with in this article. Obviously, *R. schlippenbachii* wins hands down for flower size.

My thanks go to Polly and Barry Cooke for their support with this article and to all of the photographers credited in this article that have generously shared their photographs with me and made our journey possible.

JIM INSKIP
is a member of the RCMG Wessex Branch Committee and the recent RHS review panel for deciduous azalea AGMs. He is also a member of the Azalea Society and the American Rhododendron Society. Jim's study of deciduous azaleas is focussed largely but not exclusively on the Ghent hybrids

Oshima: Island of Camellias

The image of a Pacific island that springs to mind for many of us is of sun-kissed beaches, palm trees and coral reefs with nubile figures basking in the sun. I've visited a few of these islands in the South Pacific, but my favourite is further north just off the coast of Japan. It's Oshima, part of the Izu chain of volcanic islands with its own, thankfully dormant for the time being, volcano, Mount Mihara.

Oshima is the largest of the Izu chain, 91 km² in area with a resident population of about 8,000, boosted by many visitors in summer. It is 100km from Tokyo and administered by the Tokyo Metropolitan Authority.

The human population is far outnumbered by its native population of *Camellia japonica*. Nobody knows when they arrived on the island but many of the camellia trees in the forests, numbering about 3 million, are between 40 and 60 feet high and estimated to be hundreds of years old. Where the under-

TSUBAKI SENNJU   J. TREHANE

storey of shrubs and vines has been cleared and selected thinning of spindly trees has taken place there is way-marked access for the public to wander; it's rather like walking in our native British woodlands and there are even sites for picnics.

Several individual trees on the island are singled out for attention, notably the ancient tree 'Sennju' which is a popular stopping point on island tours. Estimated to be at least 300 years old, it has medium sized dark red flowers with typically 5 petals and a definite 'presence' as many of these old camellias do have.

In the spring, red petals cover the road under the 'tunnel of camellias' and camellias line the road as street trees especially on the road near Moto-machi, the main town, with imported varieties of *C. sasanqua,* Japan's other native camellia, featured in the autumn.

Native camellias have been used as wind-breaks around island properties for hundreds of years, due to their resistance to salt laden

CAMELLIA FOREST SCENE   J. TREHANE

WINDBREAK AT TSUBAKI FARM   J. TREHANE

winds and gales and even the occasional typhoons experienced in winter. Many can be seen surrounding land enclosed for farming, particularly in the flatter coastal areas.

With all this camellia bounty it's not surprising that a range of activity surrounds Oshima's camellias. The first to be noticed as you arrive, are the Anko dancers who are prominent ambassadors for Oshima, first seen manning their shop at the ferry port, but they really come into their own when they perform their folk dances, with images of camellia blooms prominent on their costumes. The group was founded over 90 years ago and was inspired by the peasant women in the countryside. The dancers still feature the bundles of firewood, or wooden buckets once used to carry water, on their heads.

These still feature in their graceful dances are performed at many island events and during the annual Camellia Festival based at the Tokyo Oshima Park between January and the end of March.

Tokyo Metropolitan Oshima Park covers a large area that is open to the public and includes a very impressive information centre,

rebuilt since I first visited. In 2010 I was there at peak camellia blooming time and a dramatic feature was a row of over 100 small vases showing visitors a number of freshly cut blooms of different varieties, each with its own card with variety name and other information-all frustratingly in Japanese text at that time. Very few visitors from outside Japan visited Oshima then.

My next visit was during October 2014 and there was a brand new very spacious building with modern display facilities. Preserved, (not dried), blooms, cut during the previous March, were artfully displayed in glass vases.

There is a mass of information and many displays show-case almost every aspect of camellia history, cultivation, commerce and activity on the island including its much treasured fossilised camellia leaf. This is valued as evidence that Oshima is a place of origin for *Camellia japonica*, of which they are very proud. This visitor centre is a good place to start, especially as much more is translated into English, now.

Outside, the park's 3000 camellias, comprising up to 1,000 species, varieties and cultivars are claimed to be the largest collection in Japan. They are grouped into specific areas, so for example one can see a

ANKO DANCERS READY TO PERFORM AT OSHIMA PARK

J. TREHANE

OSHIMA PARK

J. TREHANE

large group of historic Japanese-bred camellias, with American-bred ones in another area, whilst others are grouped according to colour. I found the modern sturdy labels very impressive and watched as the park supervisor demonstrated how his iphone scanned the QR code on one and then showed me how a photo of the flower and other information appeared on the screen. I'm a dinosaur in this digital age but the use of satellites for labelling these and other camellias on this small island is impressive.

Following some problems due to injudicious pruning and lack of nutrition, which have been corrected, the plants now look healthy and happy, and the garden has been awarded an International Camellia Society "Garden of Excellence" certificate.

This scheme was designed to encourage owners of reasonably large gardens, containing at least 200 different varieties and/or cultivars of camellia, not only to promote

the genus but also to give status to their gardens; this helps with promotion and publicity in addition to assuring the public about the quality of a garden's camellia collection.

The certificate is renewable every 10 years which gives encouragement to continue high

FOSSIL OF CAMELLIA LEAF

J. TREHANE

standards of cultivation and maintenance of plants and labels, amongst other things. A well-maintained database, available to visitors, is another criterion, with most gardens using a digital system whilst a few have typed lists available on paper.

There are two more International Camellia Society "Gardens of Excellence" on the island, an exceptional achievement for such a small area and it is good to see the friendly co-operation between the three gardens that has evolved as a result.

Tokyo Metropolitan Oshima Senior High School, to give its full name, is very proud of its certificate. This is a school that fully embraces the 'camellia' heritage of the island. A camellia specimen garden was founded in 1977 for the education of students and now contains over 1000 plants of more than 370 cultivars and species. The collection is used in a variety of ways: honing digital labelling and recording computer skills and developing horticultural, manufacturing, business and marketing skills by producing camellia oil, made from seeds that are harvested each September.

Yuu Kaneko, the teacher in charge of camellia culture, an apparently self-effacing man on first acquaintance, has an all embracing attitude that extends to his teaching and is a real inspiration to his pupils and their attitude to camellias. Their activities include welcoming groups of tourists to their camellia collection, where visitors are shown around and are proudly given information about camellias. I enjoy their regular reports on Facebook, whilst their computers are also used for recording information which is valuable for the maintenance of their collection. It was in Yuu Kaneko's classroom that I learned how the two sheep from the school farm are used as grass controllers in the plantation, much more sensible than mechanical mowers here.

CAMELLIAS IN FLOWER IN SPRING

J. TREHANE

IN THE SCHOOL COMPUTER LAB   J. TREHANE

The pupils learn about Oshima's wild camellia forest and its history and help with the practical maintenance, joining the adult volunteers when possible when maintenance work needs to be done.

A group of pupils in a classroom was being taught about camellia propagation using branches cut from their garden and some strange knives that seemed to have a heritage derived from the Samurai warriors.

Then I watched as they were shown how to plant a young camellia, correctly, in their plantation, with a sturdy label securely inserted beside it and a wire netting cage to keep the school's two grass-cutting sheep at bay.

My visit was a week after the main seed harvest in their plantation, but they had kept a tree for me, so we watched as camellia fruits were gathered by a variety of methods and I later received a bottle of oil produced from this harvest.

THE TSUBAKI-HANA GARDEN

Owned by Takashi Yamashita, this is a well landscaped garden of about 17 acres, created in 1970 by Mr Yamashita and still run almost entirely by this very energetic and enthusiastic man. His main philosophy has

FROM THE SCHOOL'S PLANTATION, HARVESTING SEEDS   J. TREHANE

been to select from clones in the wild *C. japonica* forests that bloom extra early, and to propagate and then breed from the selected seedlings with the result that he has bushes that are covered in red blooms in mid-October. He has made a feature of these around the edge of a large grassy area that overlooks the sea, with Mount Fuji in the distance; especially impressive when this famous mountain has its capping of snow.

I was fortunate enough to see a rehearsal for a production of Verdi's opera, "La Traviata", (La Dame aux Camelias), sponsored by Mr Hihara's Tsubaki Oil Company, one October, on this lawn. It was extra special because it was a clear fine evening and our heroine breathed her last breath in the arms of her lover, just as the sun set over the sea in a golden glow. Magical!

Mr Yamashita has a collection of about 2,000 camellias of 400 cultivars and species, including his range of selected wild japonicas from Oshima forests, but he also includes a good range of Japanese cultivars, plus some from Europe and America. I particularly like

the way he considers the natural habit of each variety when pruning, giving each plant space to grow into a bush that is not spoilt by injudicious management. His choice of site for each plant shows that his knowledge of camellias is extensive.

The entrance to the garden is welcoming, with a modern covered area designed to provide information and there is a big splash of colour from a wall covered with Mr Yamashita's own photographs of blooms. It's spacious enough for large groups of visitors. In areas fairly close to this, paths radiate out to reveal beds of camellias with the soil swept clean and labels easy to read.

In another area we were shown some circular pits about 2m across and just over a meter deep, sited amongst groups of youngish camellia bushes. The idea is that all twigs, flowers and leaves from the camellias and overhead trees are swept into the pits. As these rot down to form humus, they provide nutrients for the surrounding camellias. Mr Yamashita scraped away some of the surface soil to reveal a network of young camellia

TSUBAKI-HANA GARDEN

TAKASHI YAMASHITA

roots snaking their way towards one of these pits; evidence of the success of his theory. It's an interesting idea.

It's gratifying to learn that translation into English has recently been carried out for all signs and labels throughout this garden. Mr Yamashita is leading the way with this and in other ways too. He has taken over from the late Mr Ogawa, 'the elder statesman of camellias' on Oshima as the leading authority and offers work experience and advice to the High School and other enthusiasts on the island as well as chairing a newly formed committee to promote Oshima as a 'Camellia Island'.

OSHIMA'S CAMELLIA INDUSTRIES

My first introduction to Oshima in 2010 was when I was editor of the International Camellia Society Journal and, as it happened, I was due to be in Japan for an ICS Congress in Kurume, so it was possible to make a diversion to Oshima and spend a few days with Mr Hihara and his PA. Mr Hihara owns a small factory on the island producing high quality camellia oil,

for use in cosmetics, from camellia seeds. Traditionally seeds have been crushed, heated by steam and then pressed to extract the oil, but Mr Hihara uses a 'cold-pressing' method. He asked for a whole page to advertise his company in the Journal. I was 'hooked' by the camellia sights on the island and have returned to this camellia paradise several times since.

In addition to the camellia forest and gardens there are other industries that depend on camellias, most notably tourism in the spring flowering period, and the production of camellia oil from seeds; there are still four artisan factories that use the 'hot' method method, with wooden buckets, felt covers and clunking machinery. Other products are made using camellia flowers, seeds and wood.

THE OSHIMA-TSUBAKI CORPORATION

This is owned by Ichiro Okada, the dynamic, youngish descendant of a family that owns large tracts of forest and which has been producing oil for generations. He is moving with the times and had just bought some

MOUNT FUJI SEEN FROM THE TSUBAKI-HANA   TAKASHI YAMASHITA

MR OKADA WITH HIS NEW PRESSING MACHINERY   J. TREHANE

brand new equipment when we visited. His oil and the cosmetic products using it are packaged in bright red and yellow cartons, popular with tourists and on-line.

The family also owns a retail shop with museum pieces on display as well as many products for sale. It is good to learn that he is very conscious of the need to conserve the forest, as he and his staff carry out a programme of maintenance work each winter.

THE TSUBAKI OIL COMPANY LTD

This is owned by Mr Hihara and managed by Mr Fukui, who is a chemical engineering graduate; so this is a technically innovative small factory with a very ethical philosophy inspired by Shinto teachings. There is a Shinto shrine up on the wall and each day starts with a reading of the Company philosophy from a poster beside it.

Camellia seeds are bought from all over Oshima and from other islands in the Izu

MR OKADA'S FOREST MAINTENANCE   J. TREHANE

DISPLAY INSIDE THE OKADA FAMILY'S 90 YEAR OLD SHOP J. TREHANE

chain and pressed using the modern 'cold pressing' method. They have designed their own methods and unique machinery and their

THE TSUBAKI OIL COMPANY'S SHINTO SHRINE AND
COMPANY PHILOSOPHY J. TREHANE

oil and cosmetic products that include it are sold as premium quality products as far afield as Paris as well as on-line.

Waste seed cases are used for mulching in the company's nursery where grafted plants from selected clones from high yielding trees are propagated and grown for use in new plantations. The nursery is on the site of an old farm, surrounded by camellias that were originally planted as windbreaks, a common practice on this island as on many others such as the Goto islands in the far south of Japan as well as far away in the Azores.

Camellia wood is a very hard wood, ideal for making charcoal which is sold for barbecues. Ash from the charcoal burners' fires is also used to give unique colour and texture to the pottery mugs and other wares made on the island.

PRESSED SEED WITH 'CAKE' OF EMPTY SEED CASES
EMERGING, OIL TRICKLING DOWN   J. TREHANE

TORAO FUJII IN HIS WORKSHOP

J. TREHANE

TORAO FUJII'S WORKSHOP

A visit to this workshop was really inspiring. He is a multi-talented craftsman, tall, quietly spoken with an aura of calm old-world courtesy. He specialises in making wooden figures using wood from the forests, mostly camellia, but also the slightly softer Box wood (*Buxus*).

Each figure carries either a water barrel or a bundle of firewood on his or her head and each has an individual facial expression. He showed us one modelled on his wife. Tourists are invited to sit at his work bench and watch him at work, then to have a go at carving and painting a small doll themselves. We 'had a go'. Much hilarity ensues! His potter's wheel was nearby and a collection of his popular mugs, painted with camellia flowers, was displayed together with some beautiful bowls glazed grey or light brown by using camellia wood ash from a charcoal burner.

FROZEN CAMELLIA PETALS READY FOR USE IN DYEING
J. TREHANE

DYEING WITH CAMELLIA PETALS

J. TREHANE

CAMELLIA PRODUCTS FROM OSHIMA

J. TREHANE

Later we found him sitting out in the sunshine sorting seeds from camellia trees and from the native *Prunus* trees ready for threading into necklaces after painting them in bright colours.

HIROKO KANEKO WORKSHOP
We were invited to the small workshop, where Mamiko and I were shown how to use red camellia petals that she had gathered the previous spring and kept in her freezer, to make a dye to colour plain white silk scarves. Mine is a clear shade of pink, very warm and soft, which is a lovely memento of the visit, especially when teamed with one of Mr Fujii's necklaces.

It is amazing to find an island so steeped in camellias and using them in such constructive ways. Not only is the next generation of youngsters being taught about them and their maintenance, but tourists and other visitors to the island are able to learn about them and to take home a whole range of artefacts made from camellia wood, flowers and seeds. They are also able to take away with them many memories of a unique ancient camellia forest, three International Camellia Society "Gardens of Excellence", a modern Museum/Information Centre, and exceptionally friendly people who take pride in their island and are generous about sharing its many assets.

JENNIFER TREHANE
helped her father David Trehane create Trehane Camellia Nursery near Wimborne in Dorset and became active in the International Camellia Society, leading to world-wide travelling learning about camellias. Jennifer writes for gardening magazines in the UK and overseas. Published books include 'Camellias, the Gardeners' Encyclopedia'

The Shimane Azalea Project:
a study of traditional Japanese Tsutsuji cultivars

RHODODENDRON 'HON- KIRISHIMA'   YUJI KURASHIGE

Articles published in our Yearbook are normally historical in nature, about the people, plants or gardens associated with our three genera. Equally the author's name is normally familiar to you. This article breaks with tradition in both respects. Most of you will probably not know me and this article looks to the future. My husband, Barry, and I have been members of RCMG since the mid eighties but our active involvement began early in 2016, when we started to go on Branch visits. Barry and I were asked to run the RCMG show at Wisley in 2017, quite a daunting prospect but the theme of Wilson's Fifty azaleas was irresistible to us. I have a great interest in this collection and indeed for all evergreen azaleas, with over 120 in our garden. I became the Group Secretary after

the Wisley Show and was recently asked to become the co-ordinator for our Group's involvement with The Shimane Azalea Project. This article gives further details about the project that I introduced in the March 2018 Bulletin.

The RHS received an invitation from Professor Nobuo Kobayashi to collaborate in a project concerned with azaleas or Tsutsuji as they are known in Japan and specifically to do with those belonging to *Rhododendron* subsection *Tsutsusi*. The University of Turin in Italy and the Institute for Agricultural and Fisheries Research (ILVO) in Belgium have already agreed to participate. Feeling that the project itself would be valuable to UK horticulture, the RHS asked our Group to be the principal UK collaborator. The following paraphrases the letter received by us from Professor Kobayashi and continues to give full details in the Professor's own words:

Professor Kobayashi works at the Shimane University in the Life and Environmental Sciences Faculty. He has been investigating Japanese cultivars of *Rhododendron* subsection *Tsutsusi* to determine their relationships with wild species, and thus their parentages and origins. In addition to classical taxonomic, DNA and other laboratory-based studies, there is an historical dimension to his work. This entails examining old records and horticultural texts to discover how, when and where cultivars were selected and, in some cases, to establish their original names. For example, he and his team have been able to confirm that a significant number of the cultivars published in the work *Kinshū-makura* (1692) are still in cultivation in Japan today. In summary, the team's aims are to determine lineages and trends in breeding; to identify the parentages of cultivar groups and thus to assess their extent and coherence; to clarify issues of cultivar nomenclature and ascription; to restore, where adequately published and evidenced, original names to cultivars; to articulate the horticultural history of Japanese *Tsutsusi*; to conserve historic cultivars and promote their cultivation.

1. Phases of the proposed study

i. Using textual sources, establish a list, from the 17th century (?) to the present, of all documented subsection *Tsutsusi* (species and cultivars) of Japanese origin introduced to British cultivation. Secondarily, establish a list of members of subsection *Tsutsusi* of Japanese origin or with Japanese plants in their ancestry that are currently cultivated in Britain, indicating if possible, where grown and by whom; to include nurseries, institutional collections and private gardens.

ii. Collect small sample specimens of these Azaleas from British sources. These would be subject to DNA analysis using SSR (simple sequence repeat) marker (AZA 002-008) (No.1). Aspects of gross morphology will also be critical to our studies - namely, corolla form and colour; calyx form; configuration of pistil and stamens; trichomes; leaf shape and pubescence; plant habit.

iii. Using the aforementioned studies, compare specimens, collected in the West, of cultivars of Japanese origin with those that are grown in Japan. Where appropriate, revise nomenclature in the light of the results of the comparison.

iv. Evaluate the genetic influence of these cultivars in breeding, reconstructing their origins/lineages and identifying characteristics of potential value in future breeding.

v. Reintroduce to Japanese cultivation any taxa thought extinct but rediscovered in Western cultivation. Set priorities and strategies for conservation of historic cultivars.

2. Period of proposed study: 2018-2020

3. Main Japanese participants in study

Nobuo Kobayashi, Professor, Faculty of Life and Environmental Sciences, Shimane University (project leader, responsible for identification, registration, etc); Akira Nakatsuka, Associate Professor, Faculty of Life and Environmental Sciences, Shimane University (responsible for DNA-marker analysis); Yoko Otsuki, Japanese

advisor to RHS international cultivated plant registration authorities (responsible for project in the West and for liaison with British collaborators); Yūji Kurashige, Deputy Curator of Ni'igata prefectural botanical garden (responsible for documentary research, plant identification). The DNA and other studies will be undertaken at Shimane University. Professor Kobayashi plans to visit Great Britain once a year as the project advances, to meet collaborators and to examine plants in situ. At other times, Yoko Otsuki will represent him and act as the link between Britain and Japan.

GROUP INVOLVEMENT

The RHS kindly hosted our first meeting with Yoko Otsuki, the Japanese botanist who is based in Oxford and is Professor Kobayashi's representative in this country for the Project. Our meeting provided a template within which we will all be working. The Professor has provided a letter to accompany our invitations to participate in the project.

Our first task will be to invite gardens, both public and private, and growers to participate in the project. Those that accept will be asked to provide records of all evergreen azaleas in their collections, with details of the origin of each plant, if available. The Professor will then select the plants of interest to the project. He will come to the UK to personally take samples of those plants for DNA analysis. At the same time we will be taking voucher specimens, in accordance with RHS guide-lines, for the Herbarium at Wisley, so that they can document every stage of the project. Any plants found to be rare or endangered will be propagated, with the permission of their owners, to conserve them.

The verification and naming of azaleas of Japanese origin is an important aspect of this collaboration, especially where the original Japanese name has been retained but misspelled by us in the West. Also of interest are cultivars of Japanese origin that Westerners have named, such as *Rhododendron* 'Pink Pancake' or re-named, such as *Rhododendron* 'Amoenum'

R. 'Pink Pancake' is a cross made by Dr Rokujo in Tokyo in 1960. He sent seeds to Polly Hill of North Tisbury, Massachusetts, who raised, named and introduced it. *R.* 'Amoenum' is an old

RHODODENDRON 'PINK PANCAKE'   **DAVID MILLAIS**

RHODODENDRON 'AMOENUM'   **POLLY COOKE**

Kirishima cultivar from Kyushu, Japan, where it was known as 'Kocho-no-mai' (dance of the butterflies). It was sent by Robert Fortune from Shanghai to England and renamed *Azalea amoena* by John Lindley in 1852.

Dr Alan Leslie, the RHS International Registrar for *Rhododendron*, will be involved with the project, as information about naming comes to light.

Aspects of this project dovetail with our Group's aim to assist with and promote the conservation of rare and endangered plants of our three genera. The project also links well with existing research into the Wilson's Fifty azalea collection (RHS) and translation of descriptions from the Japanese Encyclopaedia of Satsuki Azaleas for the International Register (Yoko Otsuki and Alan Leslie).

There have always been difficulties with the record keeping of evergreen Azaleas, if only because as young plants they are small and labels are easily lost to the weather and the activities of wildlife, especially over a long time span. This project will enable us to check the naming of azaleas in gardens, and we would be pleased to hear from members who have good collections of early introductions who would be interested in joining this venture. Professor Kobayashi intends to give a booklet featuring wonderful photographs of Kirishima Azaleas to all participants. This booklet was written by Professor Kobayashi and his co-researcher Yuji Kurashige. As a thank you for our participation, the Professor aims to introduce to the UK, Kirishima Azalea cultivars that are not presently growing in the West.

Professor Kobayashi has co-authored nearly 40 published research papers concerning evergreen azaleas. These are scientific articles which I find fascinating. I am not daunted by the scientific terms, as 'before children' I worked as an analytical chemist. To those of you without a science background, please don't be put off by these unfamiliar terms, do read the articles.

There follows an article by Yuji Kurashige and Nobuo Kobayashi, previously published only in Japanese (with a short English summary). Thanks go to Yoko Otsuki for translating this article into English and to Rama Lopez Rivera for recommending the article to us for its first full publication in English

There will be brief updates about the project in future editions of our Bulletin and a full report in a future Yearbook.

A post-script, in case you are wondering about names and definitions: Tsutsuji is Japanese for azalea. The most famous and popular Japanese azaleas belong, in terms of botanical classification, to *Rhododendron* subsection *Tsutsusi*. They are mostly compact evergreen or semi-evergreen shrubs with vivid flowers; they include species such as *R. kaempferi* and *R. indicum* and great cultivar groups such as the Kirishima, Kurume and Satsuki azaleas. These are in the parentages of many hardy evergreen cultivars bred in the West.

POLLY COOKE
is Secretary of the Rhododendron Camellia and Magnolia Group and has a particular interest in evergreen azaleas; she gardens with her husband Barry in Surrey

YUJI KURASHIGE & NOBUO KOBAYASHI

An investigation of old Edo-Kirishima azalea specimens in the Noto District of Japan's Ishikawa Prefecture

Translated from the original Japanese by Yoko Otsuki   © Yoko Otsuki 2018

This research paper was written by Yuji Kurashige of the Niigata Prefectural Botanical Garden Kanadzu, Akiha, Niigata 956-0845, Japan and Nobuo Kobayashi of the Faculty of Life and Environmental Sciences, Shimane University, Matsue, Shimane 690-8504, Japan. It was originally published in *Horticultural Research (Japan)*, 8 (3): 267–271, 2009 in Japanese, with a short English abstract.

INTRODUCTION

In the Enpō Era (1661-1681) of Japan's Edo Period, Tsutsuji (in this context, the evergreen and semi evergreen azaleas that belong to *Rhododendron* subsection *Tsutsusi*) became popular in cultivation and numerous cultivars were developed (Itō 1692, 1695; Mizuno 1681). Notable among these were the Kirishima Azaleas, so-called because their wild parents hailed from the group of volcanic peaks collectively known as Mount Kirishima, which lies in what was then the Satsuma domain and is now Kagoshima Prefecture in Kyushu. In 1656, some of these plants were sent via Osaka to Edo (present-day Tokyo), which was the capital of the nation's executive ruler, the Shogun (Itō 1733). These selections were judged remarkable and praiseworthy for their vivid red flowers. Together with their offspring, they became known as the Edo-Kirishima azaleas, although early authors tended to name the individual cultivars concerned using the '-Kirishima' suffix without the 'Edo' modifier. *Kadan Kōmoku,* Japan's oldest known horticultural book (Mizuno, 1681), includes 147 Tsutsuji cultivars,

15 of which were given the '-Kirishima' suffix. The earliest Japanese monograph on Tsutsuji, *Kinshū-makura* (Itō, 1692), contains 337 cultivars, 19 of which were given the '-Kirishima' suffix. Some of these are Edo-Kirishima azaleas. Moreover, it is conceivable that the original Kirishima introductions spawned cultivars in addition to these documented examples after their transportation to Edo.

Evergreen Tsutsuji cultivars with this background are now classed as the Edo-Kirishima Group (Akabane et al., 1979); they include cultivars such as 'Nijun-Kirishima'. Between the Taishō period and the early Shōwa period (1912-1930), these fell from horticultural favour as Kurume and other kinds of azalea became popular. Their commercial production declined correspondingly (Kurashige/Kobayashi, 2008). In consequence, only a few Edo-Kirishima cultivars survive to this day, chiefly as old plants in gardens. It used to be believed that these were mainly in the Kanto region, for example at Tsutsujigaoka Park in Gunma Prefecture and Rikigi-en in Tokyo (Kobayashi et al. 2003).

However, in addition to the Kanto region, the Noto district of Ishikawa Prefecture has now been identified as an important repository of Edo-Kirishima azaleas. Over 286 specimens, estimated to be more than a century old, have been located in gardens there. Their conservation and propagation have been undertaken by the Noto-Kirishima-Tsutsuji Liaison Council. Nonetheless, and surprisingly, they remain little-known outside the area. In this paper we would like to introduce these venerable specimens of Edo-Kirishima azaleas that survive in the Noto district and, by presenting new information, to report on the cultivars concerned and their history in cultivation.

MATERIALS AND METHODS
Distribution and Diversity of Cultivars

The Noto district of Ishikawa Prefecture consists of Nanao City, Wajima City, Suzu City, Shika Town, Nakanoto City, Anamizu Town and Noto Town (see Plate 1). A local group of plant-lovers had already begun recording its Edo-Kirishima azaleas (Bonyū-kai, Yanagida village, Hōzu county 1994). Using this as a basis, we conducted extensive surveys in 2006-2007, sending out questionnaires to the owners of specimens judged to be more than 100 years-old. Based on the results, we chose 49 individuals that were of particular interest in that they exhibited significant variations in flower size, form and colour. On-site investigations followed in the flowering seasons of 2006 and 2007. In these, we used the Japan Horticultural Standard Colour Chart for describing cultivars and the classification of Akabane et al. (1979) for identifying them.

PLATE 1: MUNICIPALITIES IN THE NOTO PENINSULA, JAPAN, INVESTIGATED IN THIS STUDY

Cultivar Comparison using the RAPD Method
(RAPD is pronounced rapid and the acronym means Random Amplification of Polymorphic DNA)

Of the antique Edo-Kirishima azaleas extant in the Noto district, the most widespread is 'Hon-Kirishima', one of the oldest surviving cultivars in this group, if not the oldest, and the standard by which others are measured. Eleven individuals of 'Hon-Kirishima' were compared using the RAPD method. All DNA was isolated by the modified CTAB method (Kobayashi et al., 1998), from new leaves which were cryopreserved after collection, and provided for RAPD analysis. Conditions of detailed analysis followed Kobayashi et al. (1995). Using two types of primers, OPK-19 (5'-CACAGGCGGA -3') and OPK-20 (5'-GTGTCGCGAG-3'), by which clear polymorphisms had been detected in evergreen Tsutsuji cultivar identification in the report of Kobayashi et al. (1995), we compared the band patterns of specimens of 'Hon-Kirishima' from the Noto district with those of specimens of what was said to be the same cultivar collected from Tsutsujigaoka Park in Tatebayashi City in Gunma Prefecture.

Examination of old written and printed sources

To determine the original sources and transportation routes of Edo Kirishima azaleas in the Noto district, we consulted the Museum of Modern History at the Tamagawa Library, Kanazawa City. With the Museum's cooperation, we located and examined old textual sources on Tsutsuji - mainly those that referred to the Kaga domain, to which the Noto district belonged in the Edo Period (1603-1868).

RESULTS
1) Distribution and Diversity of Cultivars

From the questionnaires that we sent out and the survey of old Kirishima Tsutsuji conducted by Yanagida village Bonyū-kai (Yanagida village Bonyū-kai, Hōzu county 1994), it became clear that Noto district in Ishikawa Prefecture contained 286 specimens of Edo-Kirishima azaleas estimated to be more than 100 years-old (see Table 1). Notable individuals include an example of the cultivar 'Hon-

MUNICIPALITIES	NUMBER OF SPECIMENS	VIVID SCARLET 0707*			MAGENTA 9706*	VERMILION 0406*			BRIGHT CRIMSON 9206*		UNIDENTIFIED FLORAL MORPHOLOGY
		SINGLE	INCOMPLETE HOSE IN HOSE	HOSE IN HOSE	SINGLE	SINGLE	INCOMPLETE HOSE IN HOSE	HOSE IN HOSE	SINGLE	HOSE IN HOSE	
NANAO CITY	11	6	0	0	0	0	1	0	2	0	2
WAJIMA CITY	51	20	7	2	0	2	1	7	2	1	9
SUZU CITY	65	22	7	5	0	0	1	7	2	0	21
SHIKA TOWN	13	6	0	2	0	0	0	0	0	0	5
NAKANOTO TOWN	7	6	0	0	0	1	0	0	0	0	0
ANAMIZU TOWN	40	23	0	0	1	3	1	2	2	0	8
NOTOTOWN	99	28	9	6	1	6	0	8	5	1	35
Total	286	111	23	15	2	12	4	24	13	2	80

TABLE 1: NUMBER OF EXTANT SPECIMENS IN THE NOTO DISTRICT OF EDO-KIRISHIMA AZALEAS ESTIMATED TO BE OVER 100 YEARS-OLD AND THEIR FLORAL MORPHOLOGY
*The numbers given here (0707, 0406, 9706, 9206) relate to the Japan Horticultural Standard Colour Chart

PLATE 2: OLD EDO-KIRISHIMA AZALEA SPECIMENS IN THE NOTO DISTRICT
TOP LEFT AND RIGHT: 'HON-KIRISHIMA' IN ŌTANI, SUZU CITY (4M HIGH, 5.1M ACROSS), DESIGNATED A NATURAL TREASURE OF ISHIKAWA PREFECTURE
CENTRE RIGHT: 'MURASAKI-KIRISHIMA' IN NOTO TOWN (1.3M HIGH, 2.4M ACROSS), DESIGNATED A NATURAL TREASURE OF ISHIKAWA PREFECTURE
BOTTOM: UNIDENTIFIED BRIGHT CRIMSON, HOSE-IN-HOSE SPECIMEN OF THE KERA-SHŌ CATEGORY (4.5M HIGH, 6M ACROSS) IN WAJIMA CITY

Kirishima' in Ōtani, Suzu City, that is 4m high and 5.1m across, and a plant of 'Murasaki-Kirishima' in Ikari, Noto Town, that is 1.3m tall and 2.4m wide. In Soriji Town, Wajima City, there is a specimen, 4.5m high and 6m across, of an unidentified cultivar with bright red, hose-in-hose flowers. It belongs to what is termed the Kera-shō or Kera-Kirishima, a category of Edo-Kirishima azaleas with smaller and less brilliant flowers than the most esteemed cultivars. The photographs show old Edo-Kirishima azaleas specimens in the Noto district. One remarkable individual no longer survives, however – a Kirishima azalea that the Natural Treasure Survey of 1923 (Ishikawa prefecture, 1924) reported as growing in Akasaki Town, Wajima City, and being 9m high and 11m wide.

In terms of their distribution by municipality, the highest number of these old azalea speci-mens is 99 in Noto Town. Next, there are 65 in Suzu City, 7 in Nakanoto Town, and 11 in Nanao City. Their concentration increases as one moves into the Noto Peninsula and towards its apex, where Noto Town and Suzu City lie. Our survey showed that most of these antique plants were growing in long-established family gardens, conserved by cultivation down the generations.

The flowers of these azaleas vary widely according to cultivar. In colour, they may be vivid scarlet, vermilion, bright crimson or magenta. In form, they range from single to full hose-in-hose via intermediate forms. Morphological examin-ation identified seven cultivars with known names (shown in Table 2). In addition to these, there were unidentified cultivars with red flowers which, depending on the plant, fell into one of three kinds: single, i.e. a 'normal' corolla; incomplete hose-in-hose, i.e. with the calyx

COLOUR (Japan Horticultural Colour Chart)	FORMS AND OTHER CHARACTERISTICS	DEDUCED CV. EPITHETS
Vivid scarlet 0707	single	Hon-Kırıshıma
Vivid scarlet 0707	incomplete hose-in-hose	Mino-Kirishima
Vivid scarlet 0707	incomplete hose-in-hose, calyx white at first then becoming same colour as corolla	Nijun-Kirishima
Vivid scarlet 0707	hose-in-hose	Yae-Kirishima
Vermilion 0406	single	unidentified
Vermilion 0406	incomplete hose-in-hose	unidentified
Vermilion 0406	hose-in-hose	unidentified
Vermilion 0406	single, repeat flowering	Shikizaki-Kirishima
Bright crimson 9206	single	Beni-Kirishima
Magenta 9706	single	Murasaki-Kirishima

TABLE 2: FLORAL CHARACTERS OF EDO-KIRISHIMA AZALEAS EXTANT IN THE NOTO DISTRICT AND THEIR CULTIVAR EPITHETS AS DEDUCED FROM THEM

NAME OF CULTIVAR	CHARACTERISTICS FROM AKABANE ET AL. (1979)	CHARACTERISTICS OF SIMILAR BUT DISTINCT UNIDENTIFIED SPECIMEN FROM THE NOTO DISTRICT
Inaka-gera	• Corolla single • Corolla slightly smaller than 'Hon-Kirishima' • Petals slightly pointed at the tip • Flowering time approximately a week earlier than 'Hon-Kirishima'	• Corolla single • Corolla larger than 'Hon-Kirishima' • Tips of petals not pointed • Flowering time roughly the same as 'Hon-Kirishima'
Mino-gera	• Corolla with incomplete petaloid calyx • Corolla slightly smaller than 'Hon-Kirishima' • Petals slightly pointed at the tip • Flowering time approximately 1 week earlier than 'Hon-Kirishima	• Corolla with incomplete petaloid calyx • Corolla larger than 'Hon-Kirishima' • Tips of petals not pointed • Flowering time roughly the same as 'Hon-Kirishima'
Yae-gera	• Corolla with complete petaloid calyx, hose-in-hose • Flowers deep and obscure vermilion-crimson • Flowering time approximately 10 days later than 'Hon-Kirishima'	• Corolla with petaloid calyx • Flowers bright red and clear • Flowering time roughly the same as 'Hon-Kirishima'

TABLE 3: THE THREE STANDARD KERA-SHŌ-TYPE EDO-KIRISHIMA CULTIVARS

segments somewhat more enlarged and colourful (more petaloid) than is normal; and full hose-in-hose, in which the corolla sits within, and is replicated by, a funnel-shaped petaloid calyx. Three of these unidentified cultivars bear some resemblance to the variants 'Inaka-gera', 'Mino-gera' and 'Yae-gera' as described in Akabane et al., 1979. Since, however, they differed from those taxa in flower shape and size and blooming time, we have treated them as distinct and as-yet unidentified cultivars (see Table 3).

2) Cultivar Comparison by RAPD Method

By means of RAPD analysis, different band patterns were detected between 'Hon-Kirishima' from Tsutsujigaoka Park (Gunma Prefecture) and specimens from the Noto District (Ishikawa Prefecture) when two primers of OPK-19 and OPK-20 were employed. Thus it became clear that these plants were not clones of the same cultivar.

The same methods revealed no such differing patterns among specimens of 'Hon-Kirishima' from the Noto District (Plate 3).

3) Evidence from Historical Texts

The oldest record of Edo-Kirishima cultivation in this region occurs in *Gunpō Sanbutsu-chō Hakui-gun Kashima-gun* ('Produce Book of Hakui and Kaishima Districts', author anonymous, 1783), an inventory of plants grown in the Kaga domain which was made as

Primer OPK-19

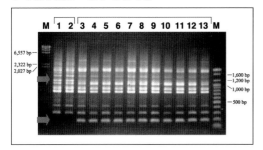

Primer OPK-20

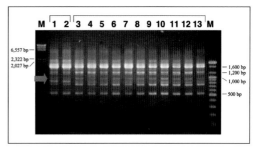

PLATE 3: POLYMORPHISM SHOWN IN SPECIMENS OF 'HON-KIRISHIMA' FROM TSUTSUJIGAOKA PARK AND FROM THE NOTO DISTRICT WHEN COMPARED BY THE RAPD METHOD (ARROWS INDICATE PARTICULAR BANDS WHICH EMERGE OR FADE; *ABOVE LEFT*: PRIMER OPK-19 (5'-CACAGGCGGA-3'); *ABOVE RIGHT*: PRIMER OPK-20 (5'-GTGTCGCGAG-3'); M = MOLECULAR.

1: INDIVIDUAL IDENTIFICATION NO. 1794, TSUTSUJIGAOKA PARK; 2: INDIVIDUAL IDENTIFICATION NO. 1582, TSUTSUJIGAOKA PARK; 3: YANAGIDA, NOTO TOWN A; 4: AKIYOSHI NOTO TOWN A; 5: AKIYOSHI NOTO TOWN B; 6: KOIJI, NOTO TOWN A; 7: WAKAYAMA SUZU CITY A; 8: ŌTANI, SUZU CITY A; 9: KAMINAKA, ANAMIZU TOWN A; 10: KAMINAKA, ANAMIZU TOWN B; 11: AKASAKI, WAJIMA CITY A; 12: AKASAKI, WAJIMA CITY B; 13: YANAGIDA BOTANICAL GARDEN, NOTO TOWN A.

part of a nationwide survey of produce commissioned by the Government in Edo. It mentions 'Kirishima' azaleas. As for how these cultivars arrived in the region, *Sangoku Meibutsu-shi* ('The Journal of Three Districts' Famous Produce', Sakamoto, 1804-1818) states, 'Kirishima are planted in gardens [in this region]. Those brought from the East [Edo] are superior; those from Kansai [Osaka and environs] are inferior', so indicating that Kirishima azaleas came to the Noto district from both Edo and Kansai.

OBSERVATIONS

Original Transportation to Noto and Present Day Distribution there

A cultivar at first known simply as 'Kirishima' in the Edo Period is thought to be the same as the plant subsequently called 'Hon-Kirishima' (Miyazawa, 1940). Having originated from Mount Kirishima, it was transported from Kyushu to Edo via Ōsaka in 1656 (Itō, 1733; Kikuoka, 1735). In Edo, it gave rise to further cultivars, and, with them, was carried to gardens throughout the provinces (Akabane et al., 1979). Together, they became known as Edo-Kirishima azaleas. It used to be thought that few, if any, specimens of these cultivars

survived that were more than 100 years-old (Akabane et al., 1979). However, the investigation introduced in the present paper has so far identified as many as 286 extant individuals of that age in the Noto district. [More have been found since this paper was published. The total of known examples in the Noto district is said to exceed 500 in *Noto-Kirishima-Tsutsuji Guidebook* by Kobayashi and Kurashige (Shimane University, 2015, introduction p. 1). YO.]

The latest date by which they began to arrive in the Noto district can be determined from the incidence of the name 'Kirishima' in *Gunpō Sanbutsu-chō Hakui-gun Kashima-gun* (author anonymous, 1738). From this we can deduce that 'Hon-Kirishima' was introduced to Hakui county (present-day Hakui City, Nanao City, Hakui county, Shika Town, and Hōdatsushimizu Town) by 1738. As stated above, *Sangoku Meibutsu-shi* (Sakamoto, 1804-1818) indicates that they were transported not only from Edo but also from the Kansai area. Today, the greatest concentration of these plants is found in municipalities near the tip of Noto Peninsula, i.e. in that part of the region most remote from Edo (Tokyo), as shown in Table 1. Two possibilities may account for this distribution: 1). These azaleas may first have been introduced to gardens further inland in the Noto district. Having been propagated there, some were subsequently transported to the peninsula's tip. The latter area then became a refuge for them in that it was less affected by urbanization than the more inland areas, and so its old gardens and cultivated plants persisted.

2). In addition to being transported over-land, these azaleas arrived on the coasts of the peninsula's tip, carried by the Kitamae-bune (north-bound ships), which formed a very important shipping route in the Edo period, connecting Osaka, Hokuriku and Hokkaido.

Mass-planted, old specimens of Edo-Kirishima azaleas can be seen elsewhere in Japan in historic gardens that are mostly now public or institutional. However, it is unique to the Noto district that such plants have survived as solitary individuals or just a few together in smaller private gardens throughout so extensive an area. Promoted chiefly by samurai and town-dwellers, the Edo Period fashion for horticulture was a phenomenon not only of the great metropolitan areas of Edo and Osaka but also of provincial towns such as Higo and Ise (Nakao, 1986). The Noto district's old Edo-Kirishima azaleas show that this culture of collecting and appreciating cultivars could flourish among a wide range of gardeners even in a remote region.

Diversity of Cultivars

On the basis of floral morphology, it can be confirmed that seven identifiable Edo-Kirishima cultivars exist in the Noto district (Table 2). Close to these plants but traditionally considered inferior to them are the cultivars collectively called Kera-shō or Kera-Kirishima. In parentage and history, these, too, are Edo-Kirishima azaleas, although, informally, they constitute a separate group. Their flowers are less shapely and vividly colourful than in 'Hon-Kirishima', the cultivar that is the beau idéal of the Edo-Kirishima azalea (hon means 'true'). The Kera-shō category is said to comprise 3 cultivars: 'Inaka-gera', with 'normal' single flowers; 'Mino-gera', in which the calyx shows incomplete petaloid develop-

ment; and 'Yae-gera', in which the calyx is completely petaloid, giving hose-in-hose flowers (Akabane et al., 1979; Komatsu, 1918; Noma, 1928; gera is the same word as kera, the 'k' hardens to 'g' after a vowel).

Examining the Kera-shō azaleas of the Noto district, we found several individuals in which the flowers exhibited the defining character of one or other of these three cultivars - single, incomplete hose-in-hose, and fully hose-in-hose (Table 3). However, these plants appeared to be distinct entities in that they differed from the three described Kera-shō cultivars in aspects such as leaf morphology, flower colour and shape, and time of flowering. In consequence, they could not be identified. Moreover, close examination of specimens from different locations in the Noto district revealed further variations in corolla colour and lobe-width among individuals which, due to their superficial similarity, had previously been considered to be the same taxon. We intend to carry out a detailed investigation to establish the status of these plants, and whether the three floral forms in fact represent groups each of which contains various cultivars.

In addition to 'Hon-Kirishima', Komatsu (1918) and Noma (1928) classified 'Mishō-Kirishima' and 'Inaka-Kirishima' as single-flowered, vivid scarlet cultivars in the Edo-Kirishima Group. Such characteristics as were recorded for these last two cultivars are too imprecise to allow us to identify them definitively among the living specimens that we have examined and thus to determine whether they still exist. As stated above, however, specimens of 'Hon-Kirishima' collected from Tsutsujigaoka Park and from the Noto district revealed different RAPD band patterns. It is possible that the individuals so-analyzed represent more than one of the single-flowered, vivid scarlet Edo-Kirishma cultivars mentioned by Komatsu and Noma. An alternative possibility is that 'Hon-Kirishima', although apparently a uniform entity and treated as such, is heterogeneous in reality, comprising different variants.

To clarify the characters of all these Edo-Kirishima azaleas, it will be necessary to investigate thoroughly the morphology of as many individuals as possible in Noto and other districts during their flowering seasons. Also essential to this revision is analysis by DNA marker, which will be needed to detect and compare differences between them and to trace their relationships.

The many examples of Edo-Kirishima azaleas found in the Noto district, and most abundantly towards the tip of the Peninsula, are now known as 'Noto-Kirishima-tsutsuji' in these areas, and are being used to attract tourists and to help revive the region's fortunes. Morphological examination makes it clear that these cultivars belong to, or were derived from, the Edo-Kirishima Group, which originated from wild plants collected in Kyushu's Kirishima Mountain area. Altogether less clear is the story of the development and diversification of these azaleas in cultivation, of how they were transported to the Noto district, and of how, in this remote place, they came to be grown in such numbers and conserved for so long. Addressing these questions will require the investigation of historical documents and literature, the close analysis of the Noto district's old specimens, and their comparison with plants elsewhere.

SUMMARY

In the Noto district of Ishikawa Prefecture, 286 examples of Edo-Kirishima azaleas are known to be living, each estimated to be more than 100 years old. They are found mainly in private gardens around the tip of the Noto Peninsula. Their distribution and abundance are unique: in no other part of Japan have so many Edo-Kirishima cultivars been preserved across so extensive an area. Locally, they are called 'Noto-Kirishima-tsutsuji' and used to attract tourists and hence to aid the Noto district's economy. Our morphological studies confirm that there are seven identifiable cultivars: 'Hon-Kirishima', 'Mino-Kirishima', 'Nijun-Kirishima', 'Yae-Kirishima', 'Shikizaki-Kirishima', 'Beni-Kirishima' and 'Murasaki-Kirishima'. In addition to these known cultivars, there are numerous old unidentified variants belonging to the Kera-shō category with flowers that range in form from single to incomplete hose-in-hose and fully hose-in-hose. Old textual sources indicate that the classic Edo-Kirishima cultivar 'Hon-Kirishima' was established in the Noto district before 1738, having been transported there from Edo and the Kansai region. Collected in the Noto district and in Tsutsujigaoka Park in Tateoka City, Gunma Prefecture, specimens of 'Hon-Kirishima' were analyzed by the RAPD method. Plants from the Noto district all showed the same band patterns, and these differed from the band patterns seen in specimens from Tsutsujigaoka Park. From this we conclude that the plants called 'Hon-Kirishima' in the Noto district and in Tsutsujigaoka Park are not identical clones of one cultivar.

REFERENCES

- Akabane M., Aburaya K., Funakoshi K., Kukamura H., Kunishige M., Nozawa I., Suzuki Y., and Yamazaki T., 1979, *Nihon no Engei Tsutsuji* pp.4-161, Seibundō Shinkō-sha, Tokyo.
- Hōzu County Yanagida village Bon'yū-kai, 1994, *Noto chihō no Kirishima tsutsuji Koboku no Chōsasho*, pp. 1-101, Hōzu County Yanagida village Bon'yū-kai, Yanagida village.
- Ishikawa Prefecture, 1924, *Ishikawa-ken Ten'nen-kinenbutsu Chōsa Hōkoku* No.1, pp.75-79 Kanazawa.
- Itō I. M., 1733, *Chikin-shō Furoku* (reprint edition, 1983, pp.181-182, Yasaka Shobō, Tokyo).
- Itō I. S., 1692, *Kinshū-makura*, (reprint edition, 1976, Seisei-dō Shuppan, Tokyo).
- Itō I. S., 1695, *Kadan Chikin-shō*, (reprint edition, 1983, pp.50-64, Yasaka Shobō, Tokyo).
- Kikuoka S., 1735, *Zoku Edo Sunago*, Edo.
- Kobayashi N., Handa T., Takayanagi K., and Arizumi K., 2003, 'Clarification of origin in azalea cultivars by PCR-RFLP analysis of chloroplast DNA', *Journal of Japanese Society of Agricultural Management*, 10: 143-147.
- Kobayashi, N., Horikoshi T., Katsuyama H., Handa T. and Takayanagi K., 1998, 'A simple and efficient DNA extraction method from the plants, especially from woody plants', *Plant Tiss. Cult. and Biotech.* 4: 76-80.
- Kobayashi, N., Takeuchi R., Handa T. and Takayanagi K., 1995, 'Cultivar identification of

evergreen azalea with RAPD method', *J. Japan. Soc. Hort. Sci.*, 64: 611-616.

- Komatsu S., 1918, 'Nihon-san Tsutsuji ni Tsuite (continued)', *Shokubutugaku Zasshi*, 32: 31-46.
- Kurashige Y., Kobayashi N., 2008, 'Hypothesis for tendencies of tsutsuji cultivars and their breeding in Taishō period – by examining into the discovered Tsutsuji report of Kanagawa Prefectural Agricultural Experimental Station', *J. Japan. Soc. Hort. Sci.*, 7:323-328.
- Miyazawa B., 1940, *Kaki Engei*, pp.149-181, Yōken-do, Tokyo.
- Mizuno M., 1681, *Kadan Mōmoku* (reprint edition, 1932, pp.56-60, Kyoto Horticultural Club, Kyoto).
- Nakao S., 1986, *Hana to Ki no Bunkashi*, pp.137-143, Iwanami Shoten, Tokyo.
- Noma M., 'Engei Kōza; Tsutsuji to Satsuki no Saibai (4)', *Nōkyū-en* 3(10): 105-112.
- Sakamoto T., 1804-1818, *Sangoku Meibutsu-shi*, Kanazawa.
- Author unknown, 1738, *Gunpō Sanbutsu-chō, Hakui-gun, Kashima-gun*, Kanazawa.

YUJI KURASHIGE

is the Deputy Director of Niigata Prefectural Botanic Garden. His research covers Anatomy, Botany and Taxonomy. He has expertise in evolution, taxonomy including molecular taxonomy, phylogenetic analysis, phlyogeography and Rhododendron

NOBUO KOBAYASHI

is a Professor in the Life and Environmental Science Department of Shimane University in Japan. He is a leading researcher in plant genetics with a particular interest in Tsutsuji (Japanese azaleas)

YOKO OTSUKI

is an Oxford-based specialist in the plants of her native Japan

RHODODENDRON 'HON-KIRISHIMA'   YUJI KURASHIGE

Hybridising Rhododendrons

I just can't wait to see the flower open! When you see the first bloom opening on that new seedling, you are the first person to see the very first flower from the unique combination of genes. It is truly thrilling!

It all started innocuously some 40 years ago when I sprinkled a few seeds from a rhododendron seedpod from a cross I had made in my own garden, not fully realising the consequences of my actions. Over the next 10 years or so I tried several more crosses. Rhododendron seed is very fine and in a full seedpod there are thousands of seeds

How do you make a cross then between two hybrid rhododendrons? The two main sexual organs involved are the male stamens which contain the pollen producing anthers and the female stigma to the seed-bearing ovary. The plant that carries the pollen is termed the pollen parent (father) and the receiver of the pollen is termed the seed parent (mother). Everyone has a different method of crossing flowers, mine is as follows. Having chosen the parents, I take a flower from the pollen parent on a freshly opened flower making sure that the pollen is available. The pollen ripens before the flower opens and is only available for a short time (one or two days at most). I then hold the flower base in my finger tips and remove the floret petals and the stigma. I then take the pollen bearing anthers to my chosen mother flower which has been prepared by stripping all florets off the truss except for one which will be the pollen receptor. I choose a flower that is just about to open, i.e. that is one which you know has not been visited by any pollinators. The stigma is receptive to pollen just before opening and for two or three days afterwards. The next step requires a great deal of care to avoid self-pollination. With a sharp pair of scissors, I carefully remove the floret and petals which exposes the stigma and anthers of the seed bearer and very, very carefully remove the pollen bearing anthers. It is vital that the stigma from the mother plant is not contaminated by any pollen from the plant's own anthers or the cross is lost. Once any pollen is wiped across the stigma the plant's internal mechanism prevents any further fertilisation. Once the cross is made there is no necessity to cover up the exposed stigma. The resulting cross is the product of the seed produced in the seed-bearing (mother) plant and will contain varying degrees of the attributes of both parents yet is recognizably different from each. Finally, you will need to label your cross as *Rhododendron* A × *Rhododendron* B with *Rhododendron* A being the mother or seed-bearing parent

The unique privilege you have in breeding your own plants is the excitement watching a flower open for the very first time and seeing a flower develop into a specimen which is completely new to horticulture. You are the very first person to see and admire it (or not!). These first blooms are the most exciting part since every plant and flower will be slightly different. Of course, not all seedlings develop into great plants. Some indeed are very disappointing producing poor plants with poor habit or poor flowers (see Figure 1). So, what are you looking for in breeding an outstanding rhododendron? The questions you need to ask are:

- Is it better than either parent?
- If not, is it better in different way?
- Is the foliage good?
- Is it disease free (particularly resistant to powdery mildew)?
- Has it a good habit (is it good to look at)?
- Is it hardy?
- Does it flower young?
- Is it floriferous?

It may be difficult to objectively evaluate your own "children." Are they better or sufficiently different from their parents? Are they some improvement over similar varieties? Are there faults in bloom or bush that suggest the compost pile should be their next destination? This is all part of the fun. If the seedlings meet the criteria, you may want to name, register and show them in competition. Only a very small percentage get this far, but it can be a very rewarding personal experience!

FIG. 1 THERE ARE SEVERAL REASONS TO REJECT A SEEDLING. A NONDESCRIPT PLANT WITH POOR FOLIAGE (*TOP LEFT*); A SEEDLING SHOWING A NEW SHOOT GROWING THROUGH THE FLOWER (*TOP RIGHT*); A SEEDLING WHERE SEVERAL GROWING SIDE SHOOTS HIDE THE EMERGING FLOWER (*CENTRE LEFT*); A SEEDLING WITH UNATTRACTIVE UP-CURVED LEAVES (*CENTRE RIGHT*); AN OTHERWISE GOOD SEEDLING SUSCEPTIBLE TO POWDERY MILDEW (*BOTTOM LEFT*); A STUNTED 15 YEAR-OLD PLANT DISPLAYING AN UNKNOWN GENETIC MUTATION (*BOTTOM RIGHT*)   COLIN MUGRIDGE

Out of 100 seedlings, only 4 or 5 may be worth keeping when compared against existing varieties (cultivars), perhaps 10–15 succumb to powdery mildew, probably 30–40 are nondescript and 5–10 have undesirable faults. This leaves about 30 plants that are too good to throw away and yet are not of sufficient quality to justify propagation and registration. What do you do with them? I give them away to friends and family but to be truthful I should be ruthless and bin the lot.

All good hybrids in existence today, whether you have a goal or not, were all 'chance' hybrids. Yes, you do increase your chances of producing a good hybrid with the trait you are desiring by careful selection of parents and back crossing etc, but it is the combination of genes at the

FIG. 2 RHODODENDRON FLOWERS FROM THE SAME GREX SHOWING THE HUGE VARIATION IN COLOUR AND FORM OF SEEDLINGS WHEN USING COMPLEX PROGENITORS

COLIN MUGRIDGE

moment of fertilization that is still down to chance. I would suggest that having a goal is best carried out by large professional estates and nurseries who have the staff, time and continuity to achieve a long-term objective. I am a private gardener, now retired from my profession, and my approach has been to select good quality parents but with complicated parentage. In this way the seedlings can produce very diverse forms and colours (see Figure 2). I make no apology for what appears to be my unconventional approach.

PRACTICALITIES OF RAISING HYBRID SEEDLINGS

Raising rhododendrons (or azaleas) from seed is not particularly difficult providing that light, moisture and warmth are readily available. I sow my seeds in firmed sphagnum moss or a 50% mixture of peat and sterilised garden compost. Although I cover the seeds with a glass or plastic cover it is important that light is available as they need this for germination. The most important factor is to keep the mixture moist *with high humidity* and then you can expect germination in 7 to about 21 days

From seed, I do not pinch back any of the growing shoots until the seedling forms its first flower buds. This is because a flower bud is more likely to form on a strong growing shoot rather than a weak side shoot encouraged by pinching back. Although pinching provides a more acceptable shaped plant, the flowering age can be put back a couple of years. As soon as a seedling forms a flower bud, I then nip out all other single growth buds to encourage the plant to produce as many shoots as possible. This is to ensure that if the flower is of acceptable quality then the maximum number of shoots are available to provide scions for propagation. It is important to remember that the plant you have produced is unique and it can take many years to increase the stock of your unique hybrid to enable distribution to others. Before the advent of micropropagation, it could take up to 15 years for commercial growers to have sufficient numbers for effective distribution. It is poor planning to have a fabulous flower and then find there are only 2 or 3 sideshoots available for propagation.

Once buds form I take the plants into a greenhouse to prevent frost bud damage. To cherish them for many years and then lose a developing flower bud to weather is negligent. Then to aggravate matters another year's wait is needed.

Good plants get better with age and some plants produce only a few florets on young plants only reaching their full complement after several years so don't throw them away just because the flowers are initially underwhelming!

Each spring, you will anxiously await the blossoms of old favourites as well as the first blooms of your new seedlings. It won't be long before you are giving away plants to all your friends because you have run out of room.

Should there always be a goal when hybridising? This is the main point emphasised by most hybridisers, but as an amateur just having fun I have ignored this advice. The broad aims of rhododendron breeding programs have changed little from those of the past. Improvements in flower and plant quality, plant hardiness, and disease resistance, particularly powdery mildew are actively being sought and this must start with the selection of good parents. But before we evaluate these a note on my choice of parentage. All the books I have read emphasise that you should have a goal. In other words what are you trying to achieve and how do you go about it? From seed to flowering in some plants can take two or three years but with rhododendrons it can take up to 10 years and this a very long time to wait for a result and a

RHODODENDRON 'SUNSPRAY'   **COLIN MUGRIDGE**

SEEDLING *RHODODENDRON* 'CHRIS'S CREAM' HELD BY IT'S NAMESAKE, AND CLOSE-UP OF FLOWER TRUSS OPENING
FOR THE VERY FIRST TIME
COLIN MUGRIDGE

subsequent further evaluation and then continue further to select for the trait you are looking for takes many years. I see no argument against selecting progenitors to provide a random range of seedlings. It is just as likely to throw up something special as a deliberate attempt to achieve a specific characteristic.

IS IT BETTER THAN EITHER PARENT?

One of my most useful tools for deciding which parents to use has been Homer E. Salley and Harold E. Greer's book 'Rhododendron Hybrids

RHODODENDRON 'HARWOOD DALE' ('LODER'S WHITE' x 'THOR') – ONE OF THE AUTHOR'S EARLY UNREGISTERED HYBRIDS
COLIN MUGRIDGE

– A Guide to their Origins'. This book is the standard guide to the parentage of some 4000 registered hybrid rhododendrons and is extremely valuable to rhododendron hybridisers and professional growers alike. Choosing parents is not an exact science particularly choosing ones with complex parents as it is impossible to list the many millions of genetic influences available within a genus of over a thousand species. Some will be dominant and some recessive varying from flower colour and form, leaf shape, susceptibility to disease etc. If we cross pollinate two rhododendrons without any knowledge of their genetic parenthood it is like expecting to win the National Lottery every time we purchase a ticket. So, you need to study the ancestors of a plant and have a basic understanding of plant genetics to decide. A good example is crossing a species red flower with a species yellow to produce an orange. This does not happen because the colour red is a dominant gene and you are most likely to end up with pink hybrids rather any orange flowers. Also, from this if red is a dominant gene and you don't want red flowers don't use parents that have red flowers!

HYBRIDISING IN ACTION

Some 35 years ago I was fortunate enough to visit Greer Gardens near Eugene, Oregon in the USA and met Harold Greer, who gave me a new

OFFSPRING RHODODENDRONS 'KENNETH HULME' (*BOTTOM LEFT*) AND 'BARBARA HULME' (*BOTTOM RIGHT*) FROM UNNAMED PARENT SEEDLING (*TOP*)

COLIN MUGRIDGE

seedling he introduced called 'Sunspray' (bred by WJ Swenson and registered in 1979). I have always admired this plant and one of my earliest crosses was an attempt to improve the flower. 'Sunspray' has a loose truss of 9–10 florets of deep cream, 12cm across, 6-lobed with a complicated parentage consisting mostly of *R. campylocarpum* and *R. fortunei discolor*. I

decided to backcross the flower. [Backcrossing is where a plant is crossed with one of its parents, or with a plant that is genetically similar to its parent, in order to promote a plant with genetic similarity to that of its procreator.] One of the seedlings of this cross produced a flower almost identical to its parent 'Sunspray' but instead of having 9–10 florets, it produced 19–20 florets, making for a very large truss as seen in the photographs. I named this 'Chris's Cream' (see page 53) for my son Christopher, an RAF pilot, and is one of my successful hybrids.

Another cross that produced a good set of hybrids was the use of an unnamed seedling (see opposite page, top) crossed with an old (1946) reliable Dutch red hybrid with a black blotch called 'Kluis Sensation'. Much of the ancestry of this plant is unknown. Many of the seedlings were red but some, within the grex, produced these two 'twin' hybrids which have been named 'Kenneth Hulme', for an ex-director of Ness Botanic Gardens, University of Liverpool and 'Barbara Hulme', his botanist wife. I have many unnamed seedlings but the parent I used in this case, I thought, would produce an unusual combination of form and flower colour.

I used hybrid 'Fagetter's Favourite' in one of my crosses. One of the assets of this plant is that it not only has very attractive flowers but also has good fragrance and I attempted to introduce this virtue into one group of my hybrids. This was only partially successful in that the unnamed parent seedling seen opposite is only slightly so. Many rhododendrons are very fragrant, notably the Loderi series, many species rhododendrons including the July/August flowering *R. auriculatum* and some less hardy types such as *R. fragrantissimum* and 'Lady Alice Fitzwilliam'. Although there are very many fragrant hybrid rhododendrons, this a hybridising area for future development.

IS IT DISEASE FREE?

Rhododendron powdery mildew has caused serious disease on outdoor rhododendrons in Europe since about 1980 yet its identity and origins are still uncertain. It is a fungal disease of the foliage, stems and occasionally flowers and is the main pathogen affecting rhododendron in cultivation today but fortunately some clones are resistant. Unlike the above any resistance to powdery mildew is not apparent until the plant is exposed to the pathogen. Many of my seedlings, despite choosing disease free parents, succumb to the disease and some more than others. These are obviously rejected as unworthy of propagation, but I do not cull them. I place them within the clones of selected seedlings to expose them further to the pathogen, so I can be confident

UNNAMED SEEDLING DERIVED FROM *RHODODENDRON* 'FAGETTER'S FAVOURITE'   COLIN MUGRIDGE

that those plants that remain unaffected are indeed powdery mildew resistant. *Rhododendron* 'Virginia Richards' is one of the finest American hybrids raised in the Pacific North West but has one fault of being susceptible to powdery mildew. It has awards in the USA and UK. I purchased one of these plants some 20 years ago and the plant is now 15 feet high. It has never flowered, loses most of its leaves every year and struggles to survive and with space at a premium it may only be a matter of time before it is replaced. When the clone was selected for propagation in the 1960/70's it may never have been exposed to the pathogen due to the pathogen's scarcity and then only appeared once the plant was in general cultivation. It is therefore important that we eliminate this disease by only introducing disease resistant plants and let those hybrids that are not resistant just fade away. There are many fine hybrids available, powdery mildew free, that have superseded them.

IS IT HARDY?

This is a difficult one for me. Most hardy rhododendrons will survive temperatures down to -15°C and by choosing parents that are hardy one hopes that their offspring too will indeed be cold resistant. I believe I am safe to presume that my hybrids will survive down to at least this temperature. We live in the UK with an equable climate and it is therefore almost impossible to evaluate this criterion particularly now with such mild winters.

To those who would follow my path, a caveat. Choosing parents, crossing the plants and sowing the seed is the easy part. Ten trays of 300 seedlings per tray does not occupy a large space but when this expands to 3000, ten-year-old seedlings in pots, as in my case, you need considerable space to grow these plants on. I have a large garden, but because of calciferous soil I have kept most of my plants in pots. Associated with all this is the repotting every year, the treating each spring and autumn with nematodes, to combat vine weevil and the effort of watering in dry conditions. All this takes time and dedication over many years. Having said all that, the rewards are enormous. The huge effort required is totally worthwhile.

COLIN MUGRIDGE
has won many awards for his hybrids including first prizes at Ness Gardens, Harlow Carr, and Rosemoor, 'Best in Show' at Ness. In 2017 he was awarded the prestigious Crosfield Challenge Cup at Rosemoor for 3 of his hybrids. An historic collection of his hybrids is to be established at the new RHS garden in the North West at Bridgewater near Salford, Manchester

AUTHOR HOLDING THE CROSFIELD CHALLENGE CUP AT THE MAIN RHODODENDRON COMPETITION 2017, WINNING WITH THREE UNNAMED RHODODENDRON HYBRIDS (*SEE PAGE 114*)   **COLIN MUGRIDGE**

ONE OF THE WINNING UNNAMED SEEDLINGS FROM THE CROSFIELD CHALLENGE CUP 2017
COLIN MUGRIDGE

Magnificent Magnolias at Borde Hill

BORDE HILL HOUSE WITH *MAGNOLIA GRANDIFLORA* 'GOLIATH'   JIM GARDINER

Borde Hill Garden is one of those very special gardens found in the United Kingdom which combines garden history and plant heritage with natural beauty. Located in the High Weald of Sussex, 2018 marks the 125th Anniversary of the purchase of Borde Hill by Colonel Stephenson Robert Clarke. Opening to the public for the first time in 1965, visitors could now walk through an iconic collection of specimen trees and shrubs including one of the best private collections of Champion Trees listed by the Tree Register of the British Isles (TROBI). The Garden is listed as Grade II* by English Heritage and in 2004 won the Historic Houses Association/Christie's Garden of the Year.

Colonel Stephenson Robert Clarke (SRC as he signed himself) purchased the 200 acre estate in 1893 with a vision of creating a garden rich in woody plant species from around the World. Encouraged by his friend Mr H.J. Elwes, he first started planting 'new and uncommon trees' during the early 1900s. He wanted to match their growing requirements with the variety of sites available to him. Borde Hill is situated on three ridges which run roughly east–west with variable soil types from Weald and Grinstead Clays and Tunbridge Wells Sand to rich loams and these combined with variable exposure enabled a wide range of micro-climates to evolve. As well as the 17 acre (7 hectare) formal garden which surrounds Borde Hill House, there are many plantations which make best use of their particular sites for the needs of newly introduced plants, including Warren Wood and Stephanie's Glade, Gores Wood and The Tolls.

Being a keen naturalist and avid collector, SRC was one of the sponsors of the great plant collectors of the day including Ernest Wilson, George Forrest, Reginald Farrer and Frank Kingdon Ward. He also corresponded with his friends who owned great gardens including Nymans, Leonardslee, Exbury and Caerhays Castle. Veitch, Waterer and Hillier

LIRIODENDRON CHINENSE   JIM GARDINER

looking forward patiently…to hear of its flowering. At last it has happened and I congratulate you"

As an Expedition sponsor, plant collectors including Forrest, Farrer and Kingdon Ward sent letters from China and Upper Burma about consignments of seed as well as the politics of the country. Forrest in 1922 complained that "*his cases were held up by Chinese Customs until such time as I should receive the necessary permit from the Authorities*"

SRC bought plants and seeds not only from plant nurseries at home and abroad (Japan and New Zealand) but also from garden owners including the Loders of Leonardslee, Nymans and High Beeches. On Sir Edmond Loder's death in 1920 he purchased six *Rhododendron* Loderi group plants at £20 each (equivalent to about £800 each today)!

On Stephenson Robert Clarke's death in 1948, his son Colonel Sir Ralph Stephenson Clarke along with his wife Rebecca took up the reins. Sir Ralph's main interest was to revive the fortunes of the garden which had declined during the war while one of Rebecca's interests was in *Nerine sarniensis* growing in the Victorian glasshouses of which 'Stephanie' is probably the best known Borde Hill cultivar.

It became clear to the Clarkes that the garden should open to the public, which it duly did in 1965, becoming a Charity in the same year.

Today the garden is under the enthusiastic leadership of Andrewjohn and his wife Eleni who with the help of Andy Stevens, the Head Gardener, and the Garden Council, have developed the garden into a visitor attraction open for 7 months of the year. There are 18 garden areas, many of which contain plants Borde Hill is famous for. In 1996, garden designer Robin Williams created Jay Robin's Rose Garden, (named for the Stephenson Clarke's daughter) and in 2010, his son, Robin Templar Williams designed the Italian Garden, and these gardens continue to attract visitors during the summer months. James Alexander-Sinclair re-modelled Paradise Walk, extending the season of interest into the autumn by using late flowering herbaceous plants. Most recently Sophie Walker has created a fresh contemporary design for the Round Dell (an old quarry) which will be opened during the summer of 2018. Sophie's design has sliced through the space with an arrow shaped path leading to a waterfall plunging into a small

Nurseries all sent plants to swell the burgeoning collection which was listed in a *Catalogue of Trees and Shrubs Grown at Borde Hill* in December 1932, compiled by A.B. Jackson and printed by Oxford University Press in 1935. It was Harold Hillier who described SRC as '*the greatest amateur all-rounder in the gardening world of the 20th Century*' and was recognised by the RHS in 1936 when he was awarded the Victoria Medal of Honour.

During Stephenson Robert Clarke's tenure, *Camellia* 'Salutation' and more famously *C.* × *williamsii* 'Donation' were raised. The latter is probably the best known camellia of all, and was first exhibited in 1941 at the RHS.

What makes Borde Hill so remarkable is the significant archive of letters from 1925 to 1948 between Stephenson Robert Clarke and those responsible for sending him seed and plants. Reading these accounts and then visiting them in the garden really makes the plant collection come alive! One of Borde Hill's Champions, *Liriodendron chinense* (collected in western Hubei, October 1907) illustrates this. In a letter dated 7th July 1927, when he was Keeper of the Arnold Arboretum in Boston, Massachusetts , Ernest Wilson wrote: "*I am very, very interested to learn that you have flowered the Chinese Tulip Tree. So far as my knowledge goes this is the first record under cultivation…I have been*

pool, all surrounded by bold foliage plants giving it a lush sub-tropical effect.

Also in 2018 the Stephenson Clarkes have graciously allowed me to plant a meadow next to the Garden of Allah and Warren Wood, primarily with magnolias, to be known as Magnolia Grove. As the genus is found in both the Old and New Worlds, I wanted to plant representatives of both, using *M. sprengeri* and *M. acuminata* as a starting point. Each of these species has been hybridised with *M. liliiflora and M. denudata* but giving markedly differing results. It is intended that a grass path will lead to an arc of birch, which has been closely planted and graded in stem colour from chocolate to white, while either side of the path will be magnolia circles of either *M. sprengeri* or *M. acuminata* and their hybrids. These include *M. × brooklynensis,* the United States National Arboretum hybrids, 'Galaxy' and 'Spectrum', 'Elizabeth', 'Lois', 'Asian Artistry', 'Laura Saylor', 'Apricot Brandy' and 'Peachy'. John Ravenscroft has generously donated 60 plants to initiate the planting in 2018. In addition to magnolias, other tree genera that flower at different times of the year will be added in years to come.

The Azalea Ring, the Old Rhododendron Garden and the Garden of Allah (so called because of its sheltered and tranquil nature) together with Warren Wood contain an abundance of woody plants that excite garden visitors not only for their flower power during the spring and early summer months but also by their sheer size and stature. A number of magnolias are among the Champion Trees and these include *M. fraseri, M. campbellii* and *M. obovata* the latter two notable for their girth.

Eleni Stephenson-Clarke has written that *'Borde Hill is a wonderful garden to love and care for and a lot of responsibility goes with it to enhance and protect it for the future.'*

Right from the start of planting, Stephenson Robert Clarke considered that 'Magnolias jostled with Oaks for pride of place', with 30 taxa listed in the 1932 Catalogue.

Magnolias were obtained from many sources including the French nurseryman Leon Chenault who obtained Wilson's originals *(Magnolia dawsoniana* and *M. sargentiana* var. *robusta)* via the Arnold Arboretum in Boston. Others including *Magnolia rostrata* were from George Forrest's Chinese seed sent via his friend J C Williams in

MAGNOLIA OBOVATA   JIM GARDINER

1927. Frank Kingdon Ward also sent seed of this species (KW 7628) which grew in the Long Dell and which has recently been successfully propagated. Possibly the most famous Asiatic species of the day was *Magnolia campbellii* ssp. *mollicomata* F.25655 collected in northwest Yunnan in 1924 which was being grown at Lanarth and Werrington by P.D. and J.C. Williams and at Borde Hill, with the Borde Hill plant measuring 7ft during December 1932. This did not survive beyond 1952, and scions grafted onto *M. kobus* also died. Luckily, scions had also been sent to Hilliers who were successful, and young plants are now back at Borde Hill having been planted by The Drive and in Warren Wood. Further information on specific Borde Hill magnolias is recorded in the Plant Profiles below.

Today there are over 160 *Magnolia* taxa at Borde Hill which are constantly being added to. During 2015, in celebration of the garden being open to the public for 50 years, a collection of 50 species and cultivars was planted, including the New Zealand Jury hybrids and *M. campbellii* 'Dick Banks' and 'Queen Caroline'.

It is no wonder that Andy Stevens, the Head Gardener, says, *'It's a privilege to have the opportunity to manage such a fine collection of magnolias.'*

PLANT PROFILES OF THE MORE NOTABLE BORDE HILL MAGNOLIAS

Magnolia campbellii

The 'Queen of Magnolias' is one of the giants of Borde Hill, rivalling in stature those found in Cornwall. It was one of the first Asiatic species to be introduced into this country during the middle of the 19th Century and is native to the Himalayan mountain chain. Seed of this species was sent to Borde Hill by Forrest (as *M. campbellii* ssp. *mollicomata* F.24214 and F.25655) and by Lady Phyllis Moore of Willowbrook House, Rathfarnham, Co. Dublin about 90 years ago. SRC sponsored Forrest on his 4th, 5th and 7th expeditions at an estimated £13,000 in today's money. Sumptuous pink flowers 25cm (10in) across, likened to waterlilies, are seen on leafless branches in March and April (depending on year) with *M. campbellii* in the Azalea Ring measuring 19m (62ft) in height and 3.51m (11ft 6in) in girth with ssp. *mollicomata* in the Garden of Allah slightly smaller.

MAGNOLIA CAMPBELLII SUBSP. *MOLLICOMATA*
JIM GARDINER

Magnolia dawsoniana

Wilson first saw this species in 1908 when he was collecting in western Sichuan for the Arnold Arboretum and again in 1910. Scions were sent to Leon Chenault in 1913 who distributed plants initially to Kew and latterly to Borde Hill. It was 4m (13ft) tall in 1932 and we know it flowered in April 1947 but it is unclear when it flowered for the first time. This tree fell over at some time, which resulted in the main stem being cut back. However the following spring saw strong epicormic growths appearing from dormant buds on the stem. Over time, the short stub of the main stem has decayed resulting in the crown dividing into two halves which come into flower at marginally different times.

MAGNOLIA DAWSONIANA
JIM GARDINER

MAGNOLIA SPRENGERI VAR. DIVA JIM GARDINER

Magnolia sprengeri var. *diva*

J C Williams gave a first generation seedling to Borde Hill in 1931, which was from E H Wilson's original Chinese introduction of 1908 but unfortunately, the Borde Hill plant died a few years later. In 1940, J.J. Crossfield of Embley Park in Hampshire gave Borde Hill a

MAGNOLIA X VEITCHII JIM GARDINER

layer from his plant received from Caerhays which was also a first generation seedling. This has survived, and produces rich pink flowers 15cm (6in) across during March and April on a tree which is now 11m (36ft) in height and spread. Cultivars of *M. sprengeri* var. *diva* can be variable in flower colour from a rich reddish pink to pale pink (sometimes white inside). A number of 1st and 2nd generation 'Diva' seedlings including 'Copeland Court' and 'Lanhydrock', as well as *M. sprengeri* var. *elongata* hybrids 'Joli Pompom' and 'Angel's Landing' will be planted in the Magnolia Grove. Planted alongside these well known cultivars will be plants from the Chinese–Swedish expedition to western Hubei in 1999.

Magnolia × veitchii

Peter Veitch of Exeter was the first to hybridise *M. campbellii* and *M. denudata* in 1907, producing a fast growing tall magnolia which at Caerhays has reached over 30m. (100ft) in height. Borde Hill received plants from Veitch's Nursery which flowered for the first time in 1934. The flowers open in March and April and are chalice-shaped and a pure white or soft pink splaying open to 20cm (8in) across. Two of the Borde Hill trees (one white and one pink) are over 15.5m (50ft) in height.

MAGNOLIA X SOULANGEANA 'BROZZONII'

JIM GARDINER

Magnolia × soulangeana

This is regarded as the most commonly grown magnolia throughout the UK. Raised in Paris in the 1820s it was first introduced to the London nursery of Messrs. Chandler and Sons of Vauxhall where it was seen in flower in 1834 trained against a west wall. A mature plant of *M. × soulangeana* came to Borde Hill from Croydon Lodge in 1895 and by 1932 measured 5m (16ft) high × 7.6m (25ft) across. To move this plant, SRC noted that '*it required a cart to itself*'!

There are a significant number of *M. × soulangeana* cultivars in cultivation varying in shape and colour of flower. 'Brozzonii' is a second generation seedling raised in the garden of Camillo Brozzoni of Brescia Italy in 1873, and this particular cultivar came to Borde Hill from Louis Leroy of Angers and was planted in 1908. According to Andy Stevens it fell over during the 1987 storm but has successfully regenerated after being cut back the following spring.

Magnolia grandiflora

This American species was first introduced into Europe in 1711 to Nantes in France, but it was not long before it was growing in Exmouth at the Manor House of Rill, the home of Sir John Colleton who brought plants back from South Carolina where he had recently retired as The Administrator. Plants were grown against the walls and were named 'Exmouth'.

'Goliath' a cultivar introduced by Caledonia Nursery on Guernsey in 1910 was planted by SRC against the south facing wall of Borde Hill House and by December 1932, this plant measured 4.6 m (15ft). To keep the plant of a manageable size, it is pruned back to a branch framework every five years in the Spring. *M. grandiflora* 'Kay Parris' is a recent introduction, named by Kevin Parris after his mother and it is less vigorous and has an upright habit. The flowers are quite small for a *M. grandiflora* but in the UK are produced over a long period (June to October in the south). A number of plants of *Magnolia grandiflora* have been planted at the north end of the Italian Garden and underplanted with *Myrtus communis* ssp. *tarentina* .

Magnolia 'Jim Gardiner'

On entering the Garden of Allah, just to the north of Borde Hill House, there is a small tree magnolia, about 50 years old with no information as to its origin or identity. It has been tentatively named 'Jim Gardiner'. Its soft pink flowers are seen in early April and it is thought to have *M. campbellii* in its parentage. What I consider to be distinctive is the shape and poise of the flowers having up to 20 incurved tepals surrounded by an outer ring of up to 8 broader tepals.

JIM GARDINER
WITH THE FIRST
MAGNOLIA TO
BE PLANTED IN
MAGNOLIA GROVE

DAVID MILLAIS

Magnolia obovata

The Garden of Allah contains many magnolias of great age including 3 summer flowering species: *M. obovata*, planted in the early 1930s and is a champion for its girth, *M. officinalis*, given to SRC by Col. Messel of Nymans and planted in 1933 and *M. fraseri*, planted in 1933 and flowered for the first time in 1936, all of which flower alongside the Champion *Liriodendron chinense* collected by E H Wilson in 1907.

MAGNOLIA 'JIM GARDINER'   **JIM GARDINER**

Magnolia acuminata hybrids

During the 1950's Brooklyn Botanic Garden led the way in developing yellow flowered magnolia hybrids by using *M. acuminata* and *M. acuminata* var. *subcordata*. Cultivars including 'Elizabeth' and 'Lois' have been introduced to gardens over the last 50 years.

A selection being planted in the Magnolia Grove which include, *M.* × *brooklynensis* 'Evamaria', *M.* × *brooklynensis* 'Woodsman', *M.* 'Daphne', *M.* 'Gold Star', *M.* 'Lois' and *M.* 'Yellow Lantern'.

Wayken Shaw has written about these elsewhere in this Yearbook.

Borde Hill garden continues to develop and evolve under the current generation of the Stephenson Clarke family. Its uniqueness lies in the willingness and enthusiasm of the family to continue SRC's philosophy of planting new and uncommon trees including magnolias. This has resulted in a garden where visitors can see new species and cultivars which will be of interest for many years to come.

JIM GARDINER
is Vice-President of the Royal Horticultural Society and Director of Borde Hill Garden

Selected Notes on Camellia Hunting in South-East Asia and China, 1999-2017

CAMELLIA CATTIENENSIS OREL – THE ORANGE CAMELLIA, COLLECTED ON THE DONG NAI RIVER   **G. OREL**

The first trip to Viet Nam (hereafter Vietnam, as the usual Western spelling) that I participated in took place in November and December 1999. I went there to look for rare plants, but initially, I was not looking for *Camellia*. I, and at least one of my colleagues, were hoping to locate, and if possible to collect, some unique Conifers, namely the elusive *Pinus krempfii* Lecomte. It took several trips to the jungles of the Da Lat Plateau eventually to find this morphologically unusual pine; however, it was during this initial collecting trip that I saw my first yellow flowering *Camellia*. At the end of two tough weeks in the jungle I was more than interested in the yellow flowering *Camellia* species. This was the start of *Project Camellia*.

From the very start the members of our small group were aware of rumours regarding the fabled 'purple camellia' found in the past by French botanists in the south of Vietnam. Of course, these were only just that, rumours. As far as we knew there were no living specimens in cultivation and for many decades, no one had access to wild living specimens. Photographic images of fresh flowers were not available, only some rather old herbarium samples and the original drawings of the holotype. The consensus of 'learned opinions' held at that time was that these stories referred to a now extinct plant. Three expeditions later, in 2002, our small team, against all odds, *re*-discovered *C. piquetiana* (Pierre) Sealy in the headwaters of the River Dong Nai in the South of Vietnam. This rather unexpected find provided the main impetus for further detailed and methodical research into genus *Camellia*.

The thought that - 'If this allegedly 'extinct' *Camellia* species was still extant and could actually be collected, were there any other *Camellia* species still surviving somewhere on

CAMELLIA PIQUETIANA (PIERRE) SEALY – THE FAMOUS PURPLE CAMELLIA OF VIETNAM   **G. OREL**

CAMELLIA HONGIAOENSIS OREL & CURRY – A MATURE
FLOWER   **G. OREL**

CAMELLIA OCONORIANA OREL, CURRY & LUU. THE FRESHLY
COLLECTED HOLOTYPE   **G. OREL**

the Da Lat Plateau'? The area in question was and still is recognised as a major centre of plant biodiversity. In some parts it is rugged to the extreme, steep mountains divided by deep and sometimes narrow valleys and covered in dense vegetation. During the Vietnamese war it was designated the 'R and R' area for the troops, hence damage to its ecosystems was relatively small. The moist mountains and even wetter deep and steep valleys are difficult to access. These teem with large centipedes, mosquitoes and leeches, not to mention the occasional sighting of a cobra. The vegetation is often prickly, sometimes poisonous and extremely dense so as to make access to some areas almost impossible. I give great credit to our very knowledgeable local guides who managed to keep us safe even in some extreme situations!

Over almost two decades of travelling our small group did not limit exploratory visits only to the southern parts of Vietnam; a number of expeditions to the North of the country and to 'Camellia Provinces' of southern China also took place. These were quite frequent, but the aims were always the same. We were interested in the identification, collection, documentation and preservation of known and new *Camellia* species. Where possible we sought the guidance and co-operation of the local people and the co-operation of the pertinent staff members from various scientific institutions. This made

Project Camellia a well-known international undertaking.

So, what did we actually find? Well, so far we have described and published some 35 new *Camellia* and 3 *Polyspora* species (all South-East Asian *Gordonia* are now considered to belong to genus *Polyspora* Sweet). There are another 15 to 20 new *Camellia* species in our possession which are in various stages of assessment. These are the materials, collected without any flowers or fruit during many years of travels. As these plants were, and still are, grown in Australian climatic conditions, it takes a long time to produce a sufficient crop of pertinent botanical material (mature flowers and fruit), so that detailed morphological work can be conducted. In addition, there are still a number of plants in our possession which may or may not belong to genus *Camellia*. These well looked after accessions have not produced flowers and fruit as yet, however they are under careful scrutiny.

A considerable portion of the new *Camellia* collected, so far, belong to the large leaved, tropical or sub-tropical *Camellia* species. These are usually, but not always, found in moist, heavily shaded areas, usually on the steep well drained river banks or in or near creek beds. Some of these *Camellias* are rather large shrubs, or even small trees and when not in flower most *Camellia* experts would walk past them without divining their identity.

I know that on some occasions we have done just that. It was the careful observation and examination of a plant's stature, habit, mature bark, developing leaf buds and, most importantly, the decaying detritus under the trees, that usually made us look closer. Over the years of collecting in the jungle our policy was to collect all plant materials which even superficially resembled the members of family *Theaceae*, or even remotely looked like *Camellia*.

Some of the large leaved *Camellia* accessions we collected and described possess leaves of great size. The largest mature leaves of up to 75.0 cm long and 20.0 cm wide are not unusual on some specimens of well grown *C. piquetiana* (Pierre) Sealy. There are a number of other large leaved *Camellia* species, for example *C. dongnaiensis* Orel, *C. hongiaoensis* Orel & Curry, *C. oconoriana* Orel, Curry & Luu and *C. longii* Orel & Luu. These species possess large leaves but not as large as those of *C. piquetiana* (Pierre) Sealy.

It should be mentioned that almost all of the tropical species are temperature and light sensitive and as such not suitable for an average suburban garden open to the elements. The plants in question require humid conditions and shelter from desiccating sun and winds. However, there are some of the newly discovered *Camellia* species, which, from our experience, are much hardier and will grow in shaded, frost-free gardens of

CAMELLIA LUCII. A MATURE FLOWER AND DEVELOPING FLOWER BUDS   G. OREL

Sydney. In my Blue Mountains garden *C. lucii* Orel & Curry (large leaved, with distinctively white, waxy flowers), *C minima* Orel & Curry (relatively small leaved, with small yellow flowers) and *C. concinna* Orel & Curry (small leaved, with light yellow flowers) survive and produce flowers and seed annually in some abundance at an elevation of 310 m above sea level. Grown in a relatively protected situation and given the best horticultural care, these rather rare specimens thrive, being well suited to the mild and short winters and long warm, sometimes wet Australian summers. How these plants would cope with the conditions in various parts of Great Britain or Continental Europe is anyone's guess. One could speculate that the warmer parts of Britain, under the climatic influence of the Gulf Stream, and countries in some parts of southern Europe, may be suitable for cultivation of some of these interesting *Camellia* species. However, the extreme climatic conditions recorded in Europe during the last decades of the 20th Century and indeed into the 21st Century may pose an insurmountable problem.

When looking for new *Camellia* species we soon realised that geographical areas with suitably warm sub-tropical or tropical climates, but with a relatively low annual rainfall and low average humidity, did not contain many wild, naturally occurring species of *Camellia*. A good example of such an area is the geographical region around and adjacent to Luang Prabang, a city which is an important cultural and economic centre in the Lao Peoples Democratic Republic. Depending on the strength of the monsoon the city of Luang Prabang receives on average about 1,360 mm of rain per annum, although in some years rainfall may be only half, or even less than the expected average. These fluctuations in total annual precipitation are reflected in the composition of indigenous vegetation and may have contributed to the relative paucity of *Camellia* species in the parts of Laos we visited in February 2017. In comparison, the corresponding and relatively extensive geographical regions in northern Vietnam, e.g. the Tam Dao Massif and some areas in southern Vietnam, e.g. the Da Lat

CAMELLIA LUTEOCERATA OREL. A LUCKY FIND IN THE JUNGLE   G. OREL

CAMELLIA HARLANDII OREL & CURRY. TERMINAL INFLORESCENCE   G. OREL

Plateau, where the monsoon tends to be heavier and more reliable, are extremely rich in *Camellia* species. The reasons for the exceptional abundance of *Camellia* in these regions was one of the basic questions to which, for some time, we had no satisfactory answers.

Delving into *Camellia* morphology, whilst describing the newly discovered *Camellia* species, we realised just how large the variability of parameters, i.e. of the data sets which describe the flower size, flower structure and flower colour, can be. This rather basic observation was of some import as in taxonomic terms it is mostly the flower architecture which determines whether the plant in question is, or is not, a new species, or whether it is a species at all. Unexpectedly, some of our 'new wild' accessions possessed morphological characters not encountered in the past in any of the known and described species of *Camellia*. This salient fact necessitated the widening of the existing terms of morphological reference for the genus and the adoption of a new taxonomic approach. The establishment of some seven new *Camellia* sections, and consequently of the new, updated taxonomic system of Orel & Curry, were the logical results of our extensive studies.

In order to illuminate the above statements we can present the example of one of the southern Vietnamese *Camellia* species *C. luteocerata* Orel, which eventually necessitated the establishment of the then new *Camellia* sections *Dalatia* Orel. In this case the most significant morphological trait (of course there were some others), was the spiral arrangement of the calyx and corolla parts, so far not found in any other *Camellia* species.

This was the type of morphology that is seen in some primitive plant genera still extant and in the Cretaceous fossil plant species which inhabited the North American coastal plains some 120 million years ago.

There were also a number of other newly discovered *Camellia* that possessed never before seen morphological traits or combinations thereof. Several examples can be cited. *C. harlandii* Orel & Curry possesses flowers in two morphologically distinct arrangements. The larger, white axillary flowers are mostly single, sometimes geminate, or may occur in groups of threes. The 6-petalled terminal flowers are always arranged in a spike-like inflorescence of 6 to 8 flowers. It was the observation of both types of inflorescences on one and the same plant which convinced us that these flowers do not belong to two, completely autonomous species of *Camellia*, but belong to one species only, namely *C. harlandii* Orel & Curry.

The very frail, pale-yellow-flowered *C. capitata* Orel, Curry & Luu also possesses a number of morphological characters not found in any other *Camellia* species. The most prominent of these is the flower bud arrangement. The original descriptor states:

...flower buds numerous, sessile, in clusters of 9 to12 (-14), forming a simple umbel-like structure, unevenly orbicular, usually longer than wide, bud scales prominent, terminal, initially dark red with yellow margins, later lighter reddish with areas of yellow pigmentation...

On first inspection of *C. capitata* Orel, Curry & Luu flowers we presumed, judging by the colour of the flower buds, that we were looking at another pink or possibly light red *Camellia* species. To our surprise, when we saw the mature flowers collected by our Vietnamese colleagues, the flowers were soft, pale yellow. This and the combination of other morphological traits possessed by this *Camellia* species led to the establishment of a new Camellia section *Capitatae* Orel.

Another example of a highly unusual *Camellia*, which merited its placement in a new *Camellia* section (sect. *Bidoupia* Orel, Curry & Luu), was *C. inusitata* Orel, Curry & Luu.

In the introduction to this species we noted the following:

The new species was discovered in an extremely rugged region of the southern Annamite Mountains and it seems to be confined to a specific mountainous area of rainforest. The mountain side was covered in dwarf montane, mossy forest. The shallow skeletal soil was flooded as it is the subject to periodic monsoonal inundations. The slope in question supports specialist plant species adapted to semi aquatic conditions.

C. inusitata Orel, Curry & Luu is highly unusual as it exhibits an upright, almost branchless habit, distichous leaves and few laterally compressed branchlets on the upper section of the also laterally compressed trunk. Put plainly, the plant possesses an almost branchless, long, cane-like, arching main trunk with some leaves and very few flowers at the top! This combination of morphological characters gives the new species an extreme and unique appearance. At one stage we considered this weird accession to represent a brand new genus which was to be added to family *Theaceae*. However, subsequent morphological examination of the new species' reproductive parts justified the placement in genus *Camellia*. Additional molecular work, using SSR protocols and methods, furnished data that further confirmed our conclusions. Because of the unique features of this taxon, we recognise it not only as a new species, *C. inusitata* Orel, Curry & Luu, but also as a member of a new section, *Bidoupia* Orel, Curry & Luu.

Something should also be said about this new species soft, pale yellow flowers. These are pedunculate, axillary on older stems or the trunk, or terminal, mostly solitary, seldom geminate, unevenly circular in shape and lacking scent. The senescing flowers have extremely reflexed and abaxially folded petal apices. Each plant produces only a few mature flowers and so far we were not able to collect any mature fruit.

As already mentioned, the discovery and publication of the 35 new *Camellia* species led to the creation of the updated taxonomic system which was eventually published in 2015 by Orel & Curry. The addition of some 7 new sections, of which 5, in evolutionary terms, contain a number of primitive *Camellia* species, expanded the *Camellia* taxonomic system and diversified the morphological terms of reference for the genus. The detection and confirmation of the presence of these primitive morphological traits was of immense significance. Further, it became palpably apparent that these types of primitive morphological traits, to our knowledge, were not present in *Camellia* species occurring in geographical areas lying north from the Da Lat Plateau, e.g. in northern Vietnam and southern China. Thorough research of available printed and electronic sources of information failed to find the said primitive traits in *Camellia* species located in other Asian countries with *Camellia* populations

(Laos, Kampuchea, India, Philippines, Taiwan, Japan, etc). Thus our research supplied one of the first indications which pertained to the geographical area of the origin for genus *Camellia*.

In 2006 Orel & Marchant published the paper 'Investigation into the evolutionary origins of *Theaceae* and genus *Camellia*'. This work summarised the data gained so far. But let the Introduction I wrote speak for itself:

The authors of this work would like to propose a new interpretation of known facts which pertain to the theory of the origin of the Theaceae *and in particular of the genus* Camellia. *This re-interpretation and re-evaluation of the currently accepted hypothesis is based on the very fundamentals of known data, taking into account the proposed tropical origins of green plants, some aspects of fossil evidence, the effects of Himalayan orogenic processes on the topography and climatic conditions of South East Asia and Southern China and the evolutionary processes which contributed to the creation of* Camellia *species currently extant. The evaluation of a number of* Theaceae *genera including the genus* Camellia *for their genetic traits, morphological characteristics and the evaluation of environmental conditions in which today's* Camellia *species occur forms the basis of supporting evidence which underpins the proposed hypothesis.*

The new hypothesis places the centre of the origin of the genus Camellia *geographically further south than currently suggested, perhaps within the areas that now comprise geographical units of south Vietnam, southern Laos, Cambodia, Myanmar, Malaysia, Thailand and the northern parts of the Indonesian archipelago. The theory of southern origin proposes that before the rise of Himalaya, the members of this genus, together with other Theaceae genera or possibly their precursors, formed an important floristic component in the understorey of the extensive rainforest that covered the land which was eventually to be designated as South East Asia and western Malesia. This area included the then to the*

mainland connected territory, which became separated some five million years ago and we today know as the islands of Sumatra and Borneo.

The question: 'why are there so many *Camellia* species persisting in the southern parts of Vietnam and especially on the Da Lat Plateau', may be answered in the following way. As mentioned above, our research and empirical evidence gathered over many years, indicates an unusually dense concentration of *Camellia* species in a relatively small geographical area.

It is a well-known fact that the giant South Asian phyto-geographic region is a significant biological refuge, which today acts as a preserve for the members of the family Theaceae and a centre of genetic diversity for endemic species of ancient plants. The rather loosely defined South-East Asian subdivision contains some of the oldest rainforests on Earth. Studies show, that some areas of the present day rainforest in Malaysia (Sarawak) may have existed over 100 million years ago (in the Cretaceous period) and well before the rise of Himalaya, which occurred relatively recently.

A number of scientific studies into the forests of Malesia (a biogeographical region straddling the Equator and the boundaries of the Indo-Malayan and Australasian eco-zones) indicate the area of the Da Lat Plateau and its environs to be a remnant of the pre-Himalayan, tropical rainforest which once may have extended over some parts of Malaysia, Thailand, Myanmar and Laos.

The very rapid, northward drift of the Indian tectonic plate, at some 16cm per annum, was initiated in the Upper Cretaceous period some 84 million years ago. The subsequent collision with Eurasia in the lower Eocene occurred about 48 million years ago. One of the results of this contact was the creation of the Himalayan Arc which is some 2,400km long. Its width varies from 150km to 400km. The Arc contains 14 mountain peaks which are over 8,000m in height. Some of the largest rivers of the World have their source in Himalayan glaciers, such as the Indus, Ganges, Brahmaputra, Irrawaddi, Mekong,

Salween, Huang He (the Yellow River) and the Yangtze. The importance of these rivers must not be underestimated as they sustain many millions of people and the agriculture and economy of many countries.

Thus the rise of the Himalaya and also of the much lower and smaller associated Annamite mountains, which like a spine run from the South to the North of Vietnam, occurred in a relatively short geological time. The fragmentation of the original, low-laying rainforest proceeded apace. However, different parts of the then new Annamite Mountains were uplifted at different rates. This created niche environmental conditions in different parts of the uplift. The processes of adaptive radiation, described as the rapid evolutionary diversification of a single ancestral line, which occurs when members of a single species occupy a variety of distinct niches with different environmental conditions, took place. These processes may also be termed a type of divergent evolution where a group of organisms diverges into new species.

The occurrence of a number of *Camellia* species in close proximity to each other, but completely isolated by the steepness and depth of narrow valleys, confirms these processes. Our, and other, molecular studies (published and unpublished) consistently indicate the general genetic closeness of *Camellia* species tested. Available molecular data thus indicates a relatively rapid divergence into the current *Camellia* species, which may have, in some cases, proceeded at differing rates. The retention of primitive morphological characters in some of the southern newly discovered species may be due to the absence, or the relatively slow process, of speciation.

So, what then of the future? Accelerated extinction of all plant species caused by human actions and 'natural causes' is continuing at a frightening pace. In some

CAMELLIA PYRIPARVA OREL & CURRY. CAMELLIA WITH PEAR-SHAPED FRUIT COLLECTED IN VINH PHUC PROVINCE, VIETNAM   G. OREL

parts of South-East Asia unsustainable slash and burn agricultural methods are still widely used for growing food. Large tracts of forested land are clear cut and the dead vegetation is burned to act as a fertiliser. Thus large areas of weedy fields and species poor, secondary, forests are created. As the Earth's population rises, the extinction of many living organisms is inevitable. Will the wild *Camellia* survive? Or, will it only be known from old mouldy books?

DR GEORGE OREL
of Theaceae Exploration Associates

A Lifetime of Hybridising Magnolias

As long as I have been aware of plants and trees, I have been aware of magnolias but it was not until 1981 that I really developed a passion for them during my horticultural apprenticeship at Duncan and Davies (D&D) near New Plymouth on the west coast of the North Island of New Zealand. A nurseryman friend, whose career dated back to the 1950s, took me to see the old abandoned Duncan and Davies nursery site where, in late winter, I saw the most amazing flowers on *Magnolia campbellii* ssp. *mollicomata*. Those warm pink crisp and delicate waterlily-like flowers have stuck in my mind ever since. My friend also had a *Magnolia campbellii* in his garden that could fill the blue sky with its blooms just after the shortest day of the year, offering so much hope in the dead of winter.

Through the subsequent years I worked with all aspects of growing magnolias as a nursery crop, from layering michelias to chip budding in the field. I still refer to michelias in the sense of a common name, although the accepted classification has them now under *Magnolia* Section *Michelia*.

In 1987, having joined the Research and Development department at D&D, I was encouraged to try magnolia breeding. This was about the time that *Magnolia* 'Vulcan' was making an appearance, and it was apparent that there was great opportunity to fill the gaps in the range of magnolias available. Magnolias were a major export crop at that time, so if we could breed high performance magnolias in

our mild maritime climate, we felt that they should do well anywhere in the world.

The first crosses were made mainly to see what could be achieved. Every cross teaches the breeder something, even if it is eventually discarded, and so not doing a cross can leave one wondering what might have been. It is easy to over-analyse but it is also easy to be surprised. Chromosome counts help to indicate dominance which will affect variability in the resulting hybrid. A high chromosome seed parent will give limited variation, but when used as a pollen parent, a much wider and variable set of combinations of colour and growth habit is produced. Performance of the parents is also most important. On this basis I have never used *M.* 'Vulcan' for breeding as it seems to produce off coloured flowers, especially in colder or warmer climates than in our temperate

MAGNOLIA 'MARGARET HELEN'   VANCE HOOPER

MAGNOLIA 'BRIXTON BELLE'   VANCE HOOPER

which were available at the time. Most of those crosses produce smaller growing plants, one of the key qualities I was looking for.

Between 1987 and 1992 while with D&D, I produced a good range using hybrids with *M. liliiflora* in their ancestry. From about 380 seedlings from 15 or so crosses, 10 were named and 5 or 6 reached wider circulation. Most of the named selections were smaller growing *M. × soulangeana* type hybrids. *M.* 'Billowing Cloud' was the only open-pollinated seedling named; a smaller growing white *M. cylindrica* hybrid, with good perfume. It was another 15 years before I used *M. cylindrica* again with good results.

'Amethyst Flame', 'Old Port' and 'Margaret Helen' are probably the best of the D&D range that I raised. All are small to medium sized plants with compact habit, summer flowering and a range of colours. 'Margaret Helen' was named after my mother, and is popular in the northern hemisphere as it is a very bright colour.

'Shirazz' is a very dark red, strong grower with a long flowering season, but it does have a narrow branching angle which is not ideal for windy sites.

Between 1994 and 1998 I worked for Mark Jury in his nursery where I gained further insight into magnolia breeding, as well as seeing a much wider range of magnolia species. I also got to know Felix Jury and could reflect on some of his experiences and breeding achievements.

From 2000 to 2003 I diverted from magnolias to a tropical fruit nursery where I further learned more about both nursery management and the grafting of avocados and cherimoya. This last was a great help with michelia propagation, since michelias can be thought of as tropical plants and can be treated as such.

In 2003 I came back to my horticultural roots in Taranaki and it became apparent that the magnolia breeding groundwork which I had laid

conditions. At one point it was thought there were two clones in circulation as it did not perform well in most areas of the UK.

We raised as many seedlings of every cross as we could in order to show what was possible, to give a better base to work from, and to avoid the selection of too many "new" varieties. I have come to the conclusion that while it is easy to watch your first hundred seedlings with a magnifying glass, you are better to deal with the first thousand with an axe. Once you get these large numbers, there is no time to sort them individually, but luckily they seem to sort themselves out as the eye seems naturally to be drawn to the ones you need. Early in their work, breeders tend to name a great many selections, but they become much more selective once they realise the full range of what is possible.

From the very start of my magnolia breeding, noting the trend for gardens to become smaller, my main goal has been to produce smaller plants more suited to the average garden. In 1987 I obtained a semi dwarf *M. × soulangeana* hybrid that was later named 'Sweet Simplicity', and this has been an ancestor of most of the hybrids that I have named. I crossed it with *M. liliiflora* 'Nigra' which has been the "go to" parent for breeding for many years, and I have also made a range of crosses using the best of the new and old varieties over the previous 15 years was too good to ignore. I was fortunate still to be able to access the D&D material and to continue the breeding lines. A three year sabbatical enabled me to take a fresh look at my previous work. I had made a few crosses over that time, but between 1987 and 2003 there had only been about three seasons when I did no hybridising at all.

My second phase of magnolia breeding started in 2003 with a big crossing year using 'Sweet Simplicity' hybrids in many combinations, which in turn produced about 400 seedlings. By then, I was well into second generation crosses and a few third generation ones, really establishing the smaller growing bloodline. Included in these crosses was the use of *Magnolia* 'Sir Harold Hillier', which in theory was not an obvious variety for developing smaller garden plants. This produced *M.* 'Brixton Belle' which is a small- to medium-sized *M. campbellii* tree that flowers from the first year of planting. The first seedling produced eleven flowers three years from seed

In 2006 *M.* 'Genie' was released in something of a record time, at six years from seed to market. By then, it was suggested that I was in competition with the other New Zealand breeders like Mark Jury, Ian Baldick and Peter Cave, but in reality every breeder has different goals, generating different bloodlines and ending up with entirely different results. By the third generation of seedlings one has some very individual and unique material, as evident at Magnolia Grove.

In 2006, after a trip to Europe and the UK we came back inspired by what we had seen and set about the biggest crossing year I had undertaken with over 2000 hand crossed seeds resulting in about 1500 seedlings to plant out in 2008. These crosses introduced third generations into my breeding lines with the addition of *Magnolia cylindrica* into the mix, both via the species and the use of *M.* 'Albatross'. Interestingly, however, after

seeing the original tree of 'Albatross', I am not completely convinced that we have the same clone, but the one we have has produced some interesting offspring. I had no idea how I could deal with all the seedlings that had germinated in the seedbeds in November, but as luck would have it, within a month the neighbouring property came up for sale. Purchasing it enabled us to double the garden area and in 2008 the seedlings were planted out. Two magnolia mazes and three hedges were created in the expanded field nursery. We registered the company Magnolia Grove and the breeding work took on a professional focus.

In 2003 I had obtained a small open ground seedling rootstock nursery which supported the breeding work as it developed; the hybrid raising taking place in another seedbed on the edge of the nursery. Acquiring the extra land in 2008 enabled the planting of seed orchards for *Magnolia* and *Cornus* species in the expanded field area.

The main field crops we now grow are magnolias (including michelias) and citrus. We are also developing a container nursery that supports the year round supply of mail order magnolias as well as wholesale sales of the crops we grow. The field nursery is a key part of the selection process as it enables us to test

MAGNOLIA 'SHIRAZZ'   VANCE HOOPER

MAGNOLIA 'GENIE' VANCE HOOPER

new selections to see how they perform. We look at specific characteristics like flowers in first year plants, attractive disease free foliage and a good growth habit. Once selections pass the initial test, they are planted out for further observation, and then we supply graft wood for overseas trials. All the selections we are working with now have summer flowers which are a bonus - the result of a high percentage of *M. liliiflora* in the background. Unfortunately, we cannot test for hardiness in New Zealand, and although there are tough winter climates here, magnolias would struggle to survive the summers in these areas. We have Global Network trialling in different climates and markets where the product goal is the same as ours; hardy, smaller growing, free flowering plants and a good range of colours. The tendency to summer flowering is helpful for both added seasonal interest, and slowing the development of overall tree size. I do not consider bloom size important. People love the big blousy blooms, but the trees that make these do not fit in the average garden. Over a

month period, for every bloom on say 'Albatross' or 'Felix Jury' there are ten to fifteen flowers on 'Genie'.

With a professional focus on breeding there is always the pressure for return on investment, but this has to be tempered with thorough testing of material for release.

Since 'Genie' in 2006 we have released 'Cameo' and 'Cleopatra' which are sister seedlings of 'Sweet Simplicity' × 'Black Tulip'. There were two others named from this cross but they are not in circulation. 'Brixton Belle' was released in about 2010 and has become the star on our business cards. It is named after the district we live in near New Plymouth.

We released a true miniature called 'Mighty Mouse' which is available in Europe. It was decided not to protect this variety as the perceived cost for size of plant made the royalty prohibitive. We have several local bonsai growers who have trained it, as the foliage and flowers are proportional. 'Brixton Salmon' is a 'Genie' × 'Sir Harold Hillier' hybrid we released about 4 years ago. It is the biggest tree in the

MAGNOLIA GROVE NURSERY FROM THE NORTH   VANCE HOOPER

2004 planted magnolia patch so it has a limited market. The tree size made me hesitant to start with, but the flower colour and the number of flowers produced is impressive.

We have about ten selections of various parentage on trial in Europe and North America. The American stance on plant patents makes it difficult to discuss too much about them, as it will compromise the right to protect the varieties but we have two that are very close to release. One has almost willow like foliage that has caught the eye of visitors in summer even without flowers. It is an upright small tree flowering in spring and summer. and it first flowered at three years old when it was shoulder height and had twenty blooms of bright purple pink. The other has tiered blooms reminiscent of *Camellia* 'Fircone' with a layered, inverted lantern effect. It has a rich red-purple outer tepal colour with white frosted red airbrushed interior. Both are performing well in nursery trials here and abroad.

In order to be viable, future developments in breeding on a commercial scale demand varieties that can be grown in every sort of garden. There will always be a limited place for big trees, but these will mainly be for large areas such as parks and golf courses, and will also have to be spectacular to compete with what is already available.

For the moment we have enough material to select from over the next few years, but there are still some gaps in the market for, for example, good coloured evergreen hybrids, and smaller growing, high performance evergreen varieties; a true weeper would be great. We have a 'Forrest's Pink' hybrid that weeps but so far has not flowered well. There has been a groundcover *Magnolia laevifolia* selection in circulation, but it throws upright branches occasionally, so this has not gained popularity. A future starting point for magnolia breeding would be a purple leafed seedling.

Although I consciously decided not to pursue michelia hybridising, I do have a few interesting seedlings, some from open pollinated seed lines and others that have randomly popped up in the garden.

An understanding of natural pollination has been key to obtaining seeds for rootstock production. Hand pollination could not produce the quantities needed so a solution had to be found.

Since 2004 I have been collecting seeds for rootstocks, mainly from *M.* 'Rustica Rubra'

MAGNOLIA 'CLEOPATRA'   VANCE HOOPER

20 LITRES OF FRUITS IN 2015 (*LEFT*) AND 120 LITRES OF FRUIT IN 2016 (*RIGHT*)   **VANCE HOOPER**

which produces consistent crops of seeds with resulting consistent seedlings. The benefit of these is that they appear to have a slight dwarfing influence, and produce heavier flowering plants.

Most authorities insist that magnolias are beetle pollinated but I realised that in New Zealand, honey bees do the work. I have kept bees for over 20 years so can understand the biological link with deciduous magnolias. As soon as I introduced bees to the nursery here we had an increase from 2,000 to 12,000 seeds in one year. It was important to introduce bees within our over 2 hectares (5 acres) of nursery and garden, since, although well sheltered, it is like an island in the middle of open farmland with a windy climate which is not conducive to good numbers of bees coming in from elsewhere.

When I added citrus trees to the nursery, I was aware that these needed magnesium as a trace element and so I prepared the field blocks with Dolomite Lime (Calcium Magnesium carbonate) to cater for this. Remarkably, magnolia performance improved too. Books on magnolias discourage the use of lime to condition soil, but for strong growth later in the season, particularly for michelias, we have found that calcium is beneficial, and this can be applied with foliar feeding preparations.

Over 30 years of intense observation and study of magnolias, and the development of a self-sufficient magnolia nursery from pollination to finished product, I have learned much about magnolia biology and genetic variation; I once saw a michelia seedling with a slightly toothed margin which looked rather like a holly. It can only be a matter of time and growing enough seedlings before finding what one is looking for. Hybridising speeds this up a bit, but there are also many interesting discoveries to be made along the way.

VANCE HOOPER
runs Magnolia Grove Nursery on the North Island of New Zealand; he has been working with magnolias for many years, producing some of our most popular hybrids, while also studying the role of bees in magnolia pollination

Englebert Kaempfer's place in the early Camellia Story

Recently I was browsing the shelves of a long-standing private library and my eyes noticed an extremely poorly bound old book, about 10cm wide by 20cm tall. What was remarkable was the name of the author: E. Kaempfer. This triggered a memory that he was responsible for the first botanical description of *C. japonica* to reach the West.

I took the book down from the shelf and found that it was called *Amoenitatum Exoticarum* ("Exotic Pleasures"), published in 1712. As would be expected with a book of this age, it was all in Latin! However I was able to work out that the Fifth chapter focused on Japanese Flora, with four pages devoted to what we now call Camellias, including a very good full page illustration of the plant's buds, leaves, flowers and fruit. He did not of course call it a *Camellia* as it was unknown to the West, but he used the Japanese name for *Camellia japonica*, that is *Tsubakki*.

The genus Camellia was eventually named by Carl Linnaeus after Georg Kamel, a Jesuit priest and botanist. Whilst Kamel only spent his time in the Far East in the Philippines, and was thus never able to see a *C. japonica*, it has recently been found that he did know of *Camellia sinensis* as "Tschia" and his drawing of this plant can be found in Kamel's manuscripts at Leuven in Belgium.

The species *C. japonica* was so named by Linnaeus in 1753 because of the illustration and description in *Amoenitatum Exoticarum*, which were all of plants from Japan. Linnaeus ignored the fact that this species also grew in China!

So who was Engelbert Kaempfer and how did he manage to get to Japan, when most of the West was excluded from visiting there in the 17th and 18th centuries?

He was born in Lemgo, North Rhine-Westphalia, in Germany in 1651; three years after the end of their Thirty Year's War. This last point is essential to the understanding of Kaempfer's decisions to stay away from Germany at several important cross-roads in his career.

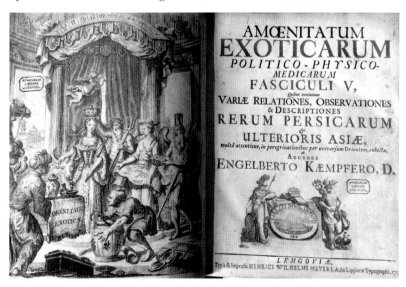

FRONTISPIECE OF
*AMOENITATUM
EXOTICARUM* BY
ENGELBERT KAEMPFER

STEPHEN LYUS

This War was fought primarily in Central Europe between 1618 and 1648. It was one of the longest and most destructive conflicts in human history with around eight million fatalities. At its start was a religious war between the northern European Protestants and the fragmenting Holy Roman Empire, but it turned into an intense rivalry between France and the Habsburg Empire for European political domination. Even after the war was over, it took a long time to persuade the mercenary troops to leave the Lemgo area. Hunger, misery and poverty was present everywhere.

Engelbert's father Johannes was a vicar who encouraged his sons to get a good education. Engelbert changed school/university about every year or two, finally ending up at Uppsala University in Sweden in 1681, aged 30. Obtaining a professional job in those days was very dependent on patronage. His knowledge and talents were sufficiently well known by then to get him a position in the Court of Charles XI, King of Sweden.

This gave him his first chance of visiting foreign parts, as he managed to be part of the Swedish legation that went to the Persian court of Shah Sulayman in 1683. The purpose of the trip was for Sweden to gain direct access to the coveted oriental raw materials, for which the Dutch then had the monopoly. The legation took a year to get to Isfahan in Persia, as they went the overland route via Moscow. He was then based in Isfahan for the next eighteen months.

DATE HARVESTING & PERSIAN FARMING BY ENGELBERT KAEMPFER   **STEPHEN LYUS**

He was clearly a very observant traveller who was prepared to view other cultures with an open mind. His extensive diaries and drawings are still extant in the British Museum. These drawings show amazing detail of the cities and palaces he visited. The first chapter of *Amoenitatum Exoticarum* documents the "Persian" period of his life.

When the legation was sent away from the Persian Court without the desired coalition, Kaempfer could have returned North with them as he had now become very familiar with the trials and hardships of travel in those days. However, news from home did not show any great improvement in the economy, so he thought it best to continue his travels East by enlisting in the Dutch East India Company (VOC). He had met a number of their influential people in Isfahan and took advantage of those contacts. In December 1684 he finally got a position as a senior surgeon within the VOC. However he had to remain in Isfahan for nearly another year, without pay, before he was allowed to travel to Bandar Abbas on the Strait of Hormuz to become the physician to the Dutch factory there. This he described as the driest, hottest, most poisonous, unhealthiest place in the World nearest to Hell! He almost died like many other Europeans, but was fortunately allowed to convalesce many hundreds of kilometres away at Bugun.

The one notable piece of botanic research he did there was on the Date Palm, "*Phoenix dactylifera*". Observations on the farming and harvesting of the Dates were documented in the 4th chapter of *Amoenitatum*. These notes remained unequalled for the next 140 years after publication!

He managed to escape to India in June 1688 and eventually arrived at the VOC's Asian Headquarters at Batavia (Jakarta) in the autumn of 1689. Here he found himself in a botanical paradise, along with several other botanists. His professional advancement was however again blocked by a Dutch superior who would not give the German a senior medical post at Batavia. Whilst there, he stayed as a guest in the house of Andreas Cleyer, another German employed by VOC. Cleyer had been to Nagasaki in 1682 and 1685

RETINUE OF THE DUTCH AMBASSADOR ON TRIP TO EDO BY ENGELBERT KAEMPFER (KAEMPFER #15, IN THE MIDDLE ON HORSEBACK) **STEPHEN LYUS**

and returned with much knowledge of Japanese flora, which he must have discussed with Kaempfer.

Kaempfer was then very fortunate that the position of physician at the VOC Nagasaki factory in Japan became vacant. He got the post because he was also qualified to collect plant specimens. The VOC regarded information on the natural conditions of each region to be essential in order to exploit those areas in the future. He departed Batavia in May 1690 and eventually arrived in the September with a stopover in Siam on the way.

The Dutch were the only Western nation allowed to trade with Japan for a period of 218 years, because of the Japanese policy of seclusion from the rest of the world. The VOC was allowed to trade at the price of absolute Japanese control over all their activities on Japanese soil. The VOC factory was established in 1641, on the artificial island of Deshima, especially created for them. They were essentially quarantined and only allowed out of their 'prison' once a year for the trip to Edo (Tokyo) to fulfil the requisite annual act of homage to the ruling shogun (Tokugawa Tsunayoshi).

As the VOC physician at Deshima, Kaempfer had the advantage of coming into direct contact with many Japanese. He was able to adapt himself to these new rules by recognising that as the Dutch were only merchants, the lowest and most despised status in Japanese culture, they had to flatter and satisfy the pride and self-interest of the Japanese. Eventually he

was able to establish a close relationship with some of them. He gave them all the information they asked for on 'medical science', astronomy and mathematics and he in turn could ask any questions he liked, providing he was alone with them!

It was the two trips to Edo that Kaempfer undertook that gave him the opportunity to botanise and collect material (highly illegal). His accounts of these trips are seen as very important documentation of those times, even now. Thunberg and Siebold also held the same post in later years and were able to take the same advantage of being out in the countryside. His first journey took 29 days, followed by 22 days of visits, audiences and the presentation of gifts in Edo. The return trip took 33 days. These trips were seen as a welcome relief from the daily monotony.

The Fifth chapter of *Amoenitatum Exoticarum* contains a list of all the plants he had been able to find on his first trip in 1691. He described 420, although he was only able to include 28 drawings in this book, a very small proportion of the magnificent drawings he had made.

ILLUSTRATION OF TSUBAKKI (*C. JAPONICA*) BY ENGELBERT KAEMPFER **STEPHEN LYUS**

He left Japan at the end of October 1692 in a convoy of 4 ships. He wrote *'I now retrieved my Japanese things, both printed and hand-written, which I had secretly hidden and distributed among the cargoes of these ships.'* showing he was well aware of the danger involved in this smuggling out to the West of Japanese materials and information.

He was now no longer employed by the VOC, so once he had obtained his 20 months salary from his time in Persia, he continued on to Amsterdam, via Cape Town, arriving October 1693.

One of the reasons he had decided to return was to complete his studies, by gaining a qualification which would enable him to secure a professional career. He eventually received his doctorate from the University of Leiden in April 1694 and then left for home.

Whilst writing up the material he had gathered in Asia, he earned a living working as a physician. Eventually he became the physician to the Count of Lippe.

He faced one difficulty after another with editing his material. He was hugely disappointed with the work of the engraver he had chosen for *Amoenitatum*, as he is on record as saying his illustrations had been ruined. His originals in the British Museum are said to be vastly superior both in clarity and detail. He also needed to refer to earlier literature, but found he could only get many of these via requests to his Dutch friends. This helps to explain why it took eighteen years to publish *Amoenitatum Exoticarum*!

His last four years were passed in ill health and he died in 1716, still with a large volume of manuscript drafts and drawings unpublished. Sir Hans Sloane got George I's personal physician (Dr Johan Steigerthal) to find where this material was stored and Steigerthal purchased it from Kaempfer's sole heir. The manuscript for his book on Japan was bought by Sloane and he got his Swiss amanuensis, Johann Scheuzer, to produce an English translation, which was published in 1727 in two volumes as the *'History of Japan'*. This became the chief source of Western knowledge about Japan throughout the 18th and up to the mid-19th century, whilst it was still closed to most foreigners.

In the Appendix of *'History of Japan'* there are twenty pages of the 'Natural History of Japanese Tea', with an accurate description of that plant, its culture, growth, preparation and uses. He quotes earlier descriptions of this plant by one of his predecessors, Dr William ten Rhyne as well as a book published by Dr Breyne ('Century of Exotic Plants'), but says he has had a much greater opportunity to observe everything to do with the plant.

His chapter on Tea (Japanese Tsjia, or Chinese The'h) is exceedingly thorough, as it starts with the growth of the plant from seed or cuttings. Once the plant is around seven years old, about the height of a man, it is cut completely back to the main stem. This results in the production of many young twigs which now have many more leaves than they would have had, if left without this drastic pruning. Great length is taken to describe which leaves and when they are taken to provide for the three chief sorts of tea. The next part of the process is the multiple roasting, rolling and cooling of the leaves to remove their 'malignant quality'. I noted that the third or coarse level of tea used by the 'Country' people often had the young leaves of plants called Sasanqua placed in their tea barrels to add a sweet scent!

Amoenitatum Exoticarum contains drawings and descriptions of the species of what are now called *C. sinensis, C. japonica* and *C. sasanqua*. There is also mention of another 23 named *japonica* varieties as well as 6 varieties of distinctive colours and flower shapes that he had seen. We will never know whether these 6 were already included in the 23 named ones.

Carl Linnaeus only cited Kaempfer for *japonica* whilst citing many others for the Tea plant (*Thea sinensis*). He did not recognise the Tea plant as being in the *Camellia* genus and created a new genus *Thea* (Tea!) for it. He also ignored the *sasanqua* description in *Amoenitatum Exoticarum*, as he probably thought it was a dwarf *japonica*?

C. sasanqua was not formally recognised as another species until the Swedish physician Carl Peter Thunberg filled Kaempfer's post in 1775/6 and published his 'Flora of Japan' in 1784.

THEA ENTRY IN 1753 *SPECIES PLANTARUM* BY CARL LINAEUS STEPHEN LYUS

Once Linnaeus had determined his binomial naming structure, his first publication ('*Genera Plantarum*') in 1737, used his new groupings according to the sexual characteristics of the flower. This shows *Thea* in the Polyandria Monogynia section (many anthers, single stigma), with the attribution to Kaempfer. However *Camellia* is to be found in the Monadelphia Polyandria section (single uterus where filaments are connected in the form of a cylinder or tube, many anthers) again attributed to Kaempfer's 'Tsubakki' on page 850 of *Amoenitatum Exoticarum*. See the scans of these entries at the end of my article.

By the time Linnaeus wrote his book on the Species ("*Species Plantarum*") in 1753, the description for *Thea sinensis* is still in the Polyandria monogynia section but he has attributions to quite a number of sources.

However there is no sign of any *Camellia* species and indeed none in his second or third editions. Further editions were published after Linnaeus' death in 1778, under the direction of Karl Ludwig Willdenow, the director of the Berlin Botanical Garden. It is not until the 1800 edition that both *C. japonica* and *C. sasanqua* finally make their appearance, with the first acknowledgement being to Thunberg this time. Thunberg was born and grew up in Sweden and went to Uppsala University where he was taught by Linnaeus. In 1775 he had filled the same post that Kaempfer had held for the VOC in Nagasaki.

I very much enjoy this kind of historic research, as I usually find it leads me up many other alleys. As an example, I spotted that a book '*Icones selectae plantarum*' (A Special Selection of Plants) was coming up when googling 'Kaempfer'. When I tracked this book down in the Linnean Society library, I found that some of Kaempfer's plant drawings that had not got into *Amoenitatum Exoticarum* had been selected and published by Sir Joseph Banks from Kaempfer's manuscript collection at the British Museum. In there also I noted these three magnolias:

They are all described as 'Tulipifera'. *Magnolia kobus* is obvious, but the other two? Mokkwuren 2 might be *M. liliiflora*? One challenge I have had all through this is translating the 17th century Latin combined with Botanic Latin using my poorly remembered Roman Latin! Is there anyone out there who can help me?

Further perusing of *Amoenitatum Exoticarum* also led me to realise that there are several pages and a picture of plants called tsutsusis. That is, Japanese evergreen azaleas in section Tsutsusi!

It would have helped if someone over the centuries had translated *Amoenitatum Exoticarum* into English. Over the last 100 years various questionable attempts have

CAMELLIA ENTRY IN 1800 *SPECIES PLANTARUM* BY WILLDENOW STEPHEN LYUS been made to translate parts of one or two chapters, into Iranian, German or English. In 2001, the year of Kaempfer's 350th birthday, there were discussions in Germany to remedy this situation. An electronic edition is now proposed with the Herzog August Library providing a home for this project by offering its 'digital library'. The German Research Foundation (DFG) supports the project with the Institute of German Studies of the Carl von Ossietzky University, Oldenburg. I have not been able to find the project timescale.

This has been a fascinating journey looking at those early days of trading with the Orient and I was pleased to see that my memory was correct!

STEPHEN LYUS
retired in 2009 and moved to the Wirral to create a garden for his ericaceous plants. He has been a committee member for many years

THEA ENTRY IN 1737 *GENERA PLANTARUM* BY CARL LINAEUS   STEPHEN LYUS

CAMELLIA ENTRY IN 1737 *GENERA PLANTARUM* BY CARL LINAEUS   STEPHEN LYUS

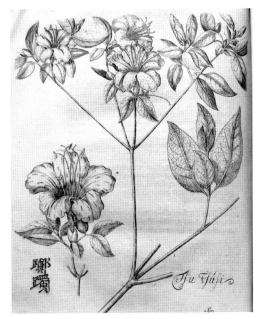

TOP LEFT: BREYNII TEA PICTURE

TOP RIGHT: AMOENITATUM TSUTSUSI PICTURE

BOTTOM: KOBUS (*LEFT*), MOKKWUREN 1 (*CENTRE*), MOKKWUREN 2 (*RIGHT*) BY KAEMPFER

STEPHEN LYUS

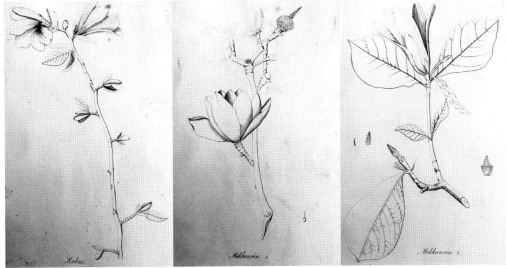

The Nagoya Protocol: the legal framework and challenges ahead

RHODODENDRON NERIIFLORUM, Salween-Mekong Divide, North-West Yunnan

RUSSELL BEESON

INTRODUCTION

In 2017 the number of countries to have ratified the Nagoya Protocol[1] reached 100, following a steady trickle since it entered into force in 2014. The Protocol is an international agreement designed to harmonise approaches to the utilisation of genetic resources and the sharing of the benefits which result. Although reaching this stage represents a significant achievement, the focus now is on the implementation and practicalities of Nagoya. How does this international agreement affect the laws of individual countries? What are its implications for governments, businesses and individuals? Perhaps most importantly, does the Protocol represent a solution to the problems it is trying to solve, or just another layer of red tape.

Addressing these questions in just a few pages is difficult, but this article aims to provide a glimpse of some of the answers – particularly in the context of plant collecting and conservation – with the caveat that in many cases they are, at least so far, not entirely clear.

BACKGROUND TO THE NAGOYA PROTOCOL

The roots of the Nagoya Protocol can be traced back to the late 1980s, when work began on creating a treaty dealing with three main concepts: the conservation of biological diversity, the sustainable use of its components and the sharing of benefits arising from such use. As a result, at the 1992 'Earth Summit' in Rio, the Convention on Biological Diversity (or CBD) was opened for signatures and entered into force at the end of 1993.

Amongst the provisions of the CBD is Art. 15, Access to Genetic Resources, recognising the sovereign rights of states over genetic resources within their territory and encouraging states to facilitate access to them, but in such a way that access is granted on mutually agreed terms and with prior informed consent, the aim being to allow 'source' countries to negotiate a fair deal with entities seeking to access and use 'their' resources. The meaning of genetic resources is set out in the CBD as "genetic material of actual or potential value"[2], with genetic material defined as "any material of plant, animal, microbial or other origin containing functional units of heredity". Emphasis is also placed on the sharing of the results of research and development and the benefits arising from the utilisation of the genetic resources. The Nagoya Protocol follows on from these provisions of the CBD, its role being to set out a structure and binding framework for implementing the CBD's third objective.

Six years after drafting work was initiated, in 2010 a final version of the Protocol was adopted in Nagoya, Japan. In July 2014, the threshold of 50 ratifying states was reached and the Protocol came into force 90 days later.

THE NAGOYA PROTOCOL – KEY PROVISIONS

The objective of Nagoya is made clear in Article 1: the fair and equitable sharing of the benefits arising from the utilisation of genetic resources[3]. Also addressed is the issue of traditional knowledge[4], following from provisions in the CBD aimed to protect knowledge, innovations and practices of indigenous and local communities relevant to the conservation and sustainable use of biological diversity and to promote the sharing of benefits arising from the utilisation of such information[5]. In this article, the focus is on Genetic Resources, but many of the issues discussed apply similarly to traditional knowledge.

The Protocol goes on to set out obligations on parties (i.e. the entities – usually countries – which have ratified the Protocol), requiring them to take steps to ensure that the Nagoya objectives are met. With this in mind, the Protocol can be seen as one of several layers of law. At the very top, there is the CBD. Then comes the Protocol, adding more clarity and detail to the general aims of the CBD. The Protocol only imposes obligations on parties to the agreement, who

then need to implement their obligations by introducing their own laws, which represent yet another, 'lower' layer of legislation.

The obligations the Protocol imposes on parties cover three main areas: access obligations (requiring parties, should they decide to regulate access to their genetic resources, to establish clear rules on what users need to do to be granted access)[6], benefit-sharing obligations (requiring parties to put in place measures to ensure that benefits arising from the utilisation of genetic resources are shared with the provider)[7] and compliance obligations (requiring parties to promote compliance with the above-mentioned access and benefit-sharing obligations by users within their jurisdiction)[8].

For those concerned about the impact of Nagoya on conservation efforts, Article 8 offers some hope, requiring that parties to the Protocol promote and encourage research which contributes to the conservation and sustainable use of biological diversity, including through simplified measures on access for non-commercial research purposes.

The Protocol also establishes an administrative structure on which the regime depends. Parties are required to designate 'national focal points' and 'competent national authorities'[9]. The purpose of national focal points is to provide information on how to obtain prior informed consent and establish mutually agreed terms. The role of the competent national authorities is, where appropriate, to grant access to resources and to issue written evidence that the relevant access requirements have been met. Information on parties' designated focal points and competent authorities is then published so that anyone wishing to access genetic resources can readily find who they should contact.

Furthermore, the Protocol brought about the existence of the Access and Benefit-Sharing Clearing-House (ABSCH) for sharing information relating to access and benefit-sharing, including details of focal points and competent authorities. The Clearing House also serves as a database of information relating to what genetic resources are accessed where; when a country grants access to its resources, the ABSCH will publish details of the permit and also publish an internationally recognised certificate of compliance, which users can then use to demonstrate their compliance.

IMPLEMENTING NAGOYA – THE EU & UK LEVEL

As mentioned above, the Protocol relies on ratifying parties implementing their own laws. In order to understand what rules are applicable to organisations and individuals in the UK, it is necessary to look at the legislation which lies one level below the Protocol.

In the case of the UK the situation is complicated by the fact that the EU, as well as the UK, is a party to the Protocol. The EU has therefore introduced two Regulations – which automatically become part of UK law – implementing the Provisions of the Protocol[10].

Just as the Protocol left a degree of freedom for parties as to how to implement their obligations, so the EU law allowed EU Member States some flexibility (e.g. as to what penalties should be imposed to enforce compliance). In the UK, these 'gaps' have been filled in by national legislation[11]. So, for entities in the UK, it is the detail of the EU Regulations, taken together with the UK Nagoya Regulations, which set out the rules by which users must abide.

For anyone contemplating using or accessing genetic resources, a key provision in the EU Regulations is Article 4 of Regulation 511/2014: Obligations of Users. This provision requires users to exercise due diligence in relation to genetic resources they utilise, verifying that they have been accessed in accordance with whatever access and benefit-sharing requirements apply and that benefits are to be shared based on mutually agreed terms. As part of this due diligence obligation, users must seek a certificate issued by the ABSCH, confirming their compliance, or, where no such certificate is available, providing detailed information on the genetic resources themselves, when, where and from/via whom they were accessed, any relevant rights relating to access and benefit-sharing, any access permits involved and any mutually agreed terms.

Further, the above due diligence information must be transferred together with the genetic resources (as well as being retained for 20 years), to ensure the information travels with the genetic resources along the 'value chain'. Wherever genetic resources are used along the chain, users are subject to the due diligence obligations set out in Article 4. Where multiple genetic resources are involved, and where each may be used in different ways and then passed on to another user, the potential administrative burden is enormous.

Importantly, the provisions of the EU law implementing Nagoya are not retrospective; they only apply to genetic resources accessed after the entry into force of the EU Regulation[12]. However, organisations wishing to rely on prior access would be advised to keep relevant material as evidence.

A question on the minds of many entities dealing with material from abroad will be 'Do my activities fall within the scope of the Protocol?' For enlightenment, one might turn to the definitions section of the EU Regulation[13], where two important definitions are set out:

'user' means a natural or legal person that utilises genetic resources or traditional knowledge associated with genetic resources; 'utilisation of genetic resources' means to conduct research and development on the genetic and / or biochemical composition of genetic resources, including through the application of biotechnology as defined in Article 2 of the Convention;

The concept of 'research and development' therefore appears key, but what counts as research and development (and are both needed or would one of the two suffice)? These terms are not defined by the Regulation, leaving significant ambiguity as to the scope of the obligations. It is at least arguable that basic research falls within the scope of Nagoya and seems relatively clear that using collected plants for breeding to create new plant varieties would also bring Nagoya into play. What about taxonomy or the mere collection of materials for conservation purposes? In both cases, there is potentially a research component; taxonomy facilitates effective classification of organisms, which brings value, and conservation ultimately preserves material which may be of use to subsequent research. At the same time, the Commission Guidance[14], which is not a binding document, indicates that just handling and storing biological material – and even describing its phenotype – will fall outside the scope of the EU Regulation. Commentators continue to wrestle with this point: a grey zone remains.

For those wishing to access genetic resources with no intention of 'use' (e.g. those wishing to collect seeds and simply sell the plants), there is less ambiguity; such activity will fall outside the scope of Nagoya – it is hard to argue there are either research or development components here. Yet if collectors want to sell-on their material to 'users', any such users will, now Nagoya is in force, need to comply with their obligations of due diligence. As such, they will have to obtain their materials either from collectors who can supply the requisite information, or else go directly to the source. Further, collectors whose work falls outside the scope of Nagoya will still have to comply with existing national rules, such as permit require-ments (e.g. covering the sale of propagated plants).

The obligations on users will depend on *where* any relevant genetic resources are sourced; the measures put in place by the relevant provider country will determine what anyone seeking to access resources under the Protocol must do. To further complicate the situation, in many cases the applicable rules have not yet been worked out. These are still early days for Nagoya and countries are still in the process of implementing provisions.

This issue is exemplified by China, one of the world's so-called 'megadiverse' countries[15] and a rich hunting ground for, amongst others, enthusiasts of Rhododendrons, Camellias and Magnolias. As of November 2017, although China has made progress on implementing Nagoya, systems to facilitate the granting of prior informed consent and agreement of mutually agreed terms had yet to be put in place. Similarly, so far there is no mechanism to allow for the issuing of compliance certificates at the ABSCH[16].

PRACTICAL GUIDANCE FOR PLANT COLLECTORS

For individuals or organisations involved in plant collecting, the new regulations on sourcing genetic materials raise practical issues which, now that the EU Regulation is in force, have to be considered. At the outset, it is important to firstly define what activities are being proposed and, secondly, to determine whether they fall within the scope of Nagoya.

Crucially, many countries have national legislation in place to control collection of their genetic resources; even in situations where activities are outside the scope of Nagoya (for example, where plants or seeds are being collected purely for personal use, and other

LAPPONICA RHODODENDRONS, Beima Shan, North-West Yunnan   RUSSELL BEESON

RHODODENDRON ADENOGYNUM, Tianbao Shan, North-West Yunnan   RUSSELL BEESON

circumstances where the 'research and development' requirement is not met), collectors must still comply with any such national legislation, obtaining consent and entering into an agreement with the relevant country as to what they can and cannot do.

In circumstances where any material collected for conservation purposes may be subsequently used in other ways – for example, for a breeding programme within a botanic garden – that subsequent use will be governed by Nagoya and, as a result, the relevant user obligations will need to be complied with. If the subsequent user is to do this, they will either need to be satisfied that the relevant genetic materials were sourced in compliance with Nagoya requirements on access and benefit sharing (either by a certificate of compliance or sufficient information on how and under what terms the materials were obtained), or they will need to contact the source country and negotiate suitable terms. Either way, they will need to be in possession of information on where and when the resources were accessed. This will inevitably have to come

from the collector. Thus, collectors will encounter difficulties transferring the genetic resources to subsequent users if they do not have detailed records for each of the relevant resources. If there is any likelihood of subsequent use (in the sense of research and/or development), it will therefore be prudent to maintain a database of collected resources and associated information.

At the other end of the spectrum, where materials are collected for purposes which clearly fall within the ambit of Nagoya, the collector will be under a direct obligation to comply with the EU Regulation.

Where collectors' activities are subject to the Nagoya Protocol, the next step will be to ascertain, from the ABSCH, whether the country from which the relevant materials are to be sourced is a party to the Protocol. If not, there are no additional obligations with which to comply but, again, the collector must have regard to whatever national permit regulations are in place. As an example, the UK has chosen not to impose collection requirements on users under Nagoya. Similarly, a country may be a party but have not yet put in place the relevant legislative provisions. To determine what regulations are in place in a given country, again, the ABSCH is the source of information. Thus, in relation to access and benefit sharing provisions for the UK, the ABSCH notes that no provisions have been put in place. If information is lacking, the relevant country's national focal point should be contacted. Where enquiries meet with no response, the Commission Guidance indicates – somewhat enigmatically – that it is up to users to decide whether or not to access or use the relevant genetic resources[17]. The implication seems to be that the due diligence requirement will have been met.

As for Mutually Agreed Terms, these are by their nature flexible; the Protocol and EU Regulation are not prescriptive and, ultimately, they can take the form which most suit the parties. They could, for example, be purely financial, or they could be based on the supply of products resulting from the genetic resources utilised. Inevitably, both parties have to agree on the relevant terms, but the requirement for Mutually Agreed Terms permits a creative and open-minded approach.

CHALLENGES AND IMPACT

Promoting awareness of Nagoya and understanding of the obligations it imposes represents a major challenge. In the case of small entities in particular, resources are limited. Apart from the administrative burden of compliance – which will likely be significant – determining whether the EU Regulation (and Nagoya) applies to any given organisation or individual requires careful consideration. Further, just knowing the position under UK law is not sufficient; users must be familiar with the requirements of provider countries.

Until the requisite access provisions have been put in place by provider countries, the full impact of Nagoya is likely to be hard to assess. A key question is whether source countries will impose measures in such a way that, as per Art. 8 of Nagoya, conservation is facilitated (for example through the imposition of simpler requirements for those conducting non-commercial research). From a UK perspective, although the scope of the EU Regulation is not entirely clear, it is arguably widely applicable. The next few years should

reveal how provider countries choose to implement Nagoya and how users cope – or struggle – with the compliance regimes.

REFERENCES

1. A convenient short-hand for the Nagoya Protocol on Access to Genetic Resources and the Fair and Equitable sharing of Benefits Arising from their Utilization to the Convention on Biological Diversity (https://www.cbd.int/abs/text/default.shtml)
2. Article 2 CBD, mirrored in Art. 3 of the EU Regulation.
3. See also Art. 3 Nagoya Protocol
4. Art. 3 Nagoya Protocol
5. Art. 8(j) CBD
6. Arts. 6 and 7 Nagoya Protocol
7. Art. 5 Nagoya Protocol
8. Arts. 15, 16, 17 and 18
9. Art. 13 Nagoya Protocol
10. Regulation 511/2014 (http://eur-lex.europa.eu/legal-content/EN/TXT/?uri=CELEX%3A32014R0511) and Commission Implementing Regulation 2015/1866 (http://eur-lex.europa.eu/legal-content/EN/TXT/?uri=CELEX%3A32015R1866)
11. The Nagoya Protocol (Compliance) Regulations 2015/821 (www.legislation.gov.uk/uksi/2015/821/pdfs/uksi_20150821_en.pdf) and The Nagoya Protocol (Compliance) (Amendment) Regulations 2015/1691 (www.legislation.gov.uk/uksi/2015/1691/pdfs/uksi_20151691_en.pdf)
12. Art. 2(1) Regulation 511/2014
13. Art. 3 Regulation 511/2014
14. This is supported by the EU Commission's Guidance document on Nagoya: 2016/C 313/01 (http://eur-lex.europa.eu/legal-content/EN/TXT/?uri=CELEX%3A52016XC0827%2801%29)
15. Conservation International
16. China's Interim National Report on the Implementation of the Nagoya Protocol (https://absch.cbd.int/countries/CN)
17. See footnote 14, above, para 3.2

CHARLES BRABIN

is a scientist by background, having studied Biological Sciences as a first degree, followed by a D.Phil. in Biochemistry/Genetics. He is now a barrister specialising in Intellectual Property, based in London, and retains an interest in the natural world outside work.
The views expressed herein are those of the author and should not be taken as legal advice.

An Update on Rhododendron Diseases

Rhododendrons have generally been considered to be fairly easy to grow and not prone to many diseases. My great uncle, J G Millais, writing in his 1917 first volume on Rhododendrons, stated that rhododendrons were almost exempt from diseases, but mentioned the problem of leaf galls on rhododendrons and azaleas, as well as rust and 'a mysterious disease causing the death of whole branches' which now sounds like a *Phytophthora*. In the 1949 yearbook, there is a report of the 1949 RHS Rhododendron Conference which had been postponed from 1940. Lord Aberconway reported disease at Bodnant was almost negligible, and that in 50 years the only treatment he had to give was to one plant with honey fungus 'which was accomplished by a bonfire on the affected ground. There was no recurrence'. However in discussion, Captain Maitland-Dougall RN, who lived near Woking, described bud blast which was first noticed in his garden in 1945, and had spread rapidly to 1948 when no less than 60,000 buds were picked off and burnt. (1020 buds were counted off one plant alone).

It seems there has been a gradual increase in the prevalence of rhododendron diseases during the last century, and perhaps we are less tolerant of blemished foliage in the same way that our supermarket fruit needs to look perfect, even at the expense of good taste. More recently, the 'open borders' policy of plant movements within Europe without official inspection, and the international trade in plant novelties and propagation material has contributed to the spread of new pests and diseases around the world. There is now a growing call for stricter movement controls such as those in place in Australasia, and 'Brexit' may enable this to be realised.

We are being challenged by new diseases, and a wave of diseases that have not been a problem until recently. But having worked with rhododendrons for more than 30 years, I continue to be amazed by nature's way of dealing with diseases, especially when given an appropriate helping hand. This article will therefore look at some of the many cultural practices to improve the health of plants, and hence avoid diseases, rather than listing a diminishing range of chemical sprays to control the problems. Over the past 10 years on the nursery, we are using more and more organic practices, and have reduced fungicide sprays from once every 3 weeks in the summer to perhaps 4 applications all year, and even those may not be necessary any longer.

POWDERY MILDEW

Powdery mildew fungi produce microscopic airborne dispersal spores which have a high water content, enabling them to infect under drier conditions. It is associated with water stress and is characterized by dark brown or black spotting on the upper and lower surfaces of the leaf. Marks are usually round, and often have a paler halo on the outside. The powdery white fungal spores can sometimes be seen on the leaf underside. Left untreated, these can spread across large areas of the leaf, weakening the plant, and causing leaf drop and plant death.

In the late 1980's and early 1990's, gardens were being decimated by Rhododendron pow-

MOUND PLANTING ON WET HILLSIDE   **DAVID MILLAIS**

dery mildew. Growers were applying copious quantities of now banned fungicides in what appeared to be a futile battle against this 'new' disease. Like roses, I could see some varieties were far more prone than others, and I found that by dropping the worst varieties from production, that the health of the remaining plants started to improve. So out went a whole series of *R. cinnabarinum* hybrids such as the lovely *R.* 'Lady Chamberlain', and also *R.* 'Virginia Richards', which was a highly sought-after new American hybrid at that time. When it comes to hardy hybrids, there are so many good trouble-free clones that it just is not worth attempting to grow a troublesome substandard variety. But a lot of people were upset with the loss of *R. cinnabarinum* and the devastation this was causing in well-known collections. But the solution was to strip out the worst offenders, and to replace with new varieties. My father, Ted Millais, had spotted that his clone of *R. cinnabarinum* ssp. *xanthocodon* was resistant to powdery mildew, and so he started a breeding programme to create powdery mildew resistant *cinnabarinum* hybrids, the most successful being *R.* 'Pink Gin' and *R.* 'Crosswater Belle', both of which continue to be clean of mildew in most situations. Powdery mildew can still be a problem today, though it is much less devastating than it was 30 years ago. There seems to be a critical time in May to June and August to September, when humidity levels increase and average temperatures are around 15°C, and this can be enough to trigger an outbreak. Some of the *R. occidentale* deciduous azalea hybrids are especially prone at the end of August and early September. Good husbandry can be very beneficial, and includes pruning overhead branches and overgrown plants to enable some gentle air movement, and correct watering to prevent moisture stress. A good weekly soak that really gets down into the roots is much better than frequent misting in dry periods which only increases humidity, and fails to make the roots search for moisture. Avoid evening watering which can leave the foliage wet all night. Mulching and correct nutrition helps to reduce plant stress and reduce mildew. SB Plant Invigorator, citrus seed oil and potassium bicarbonate are all useful in controlling powdery mildew.

PHYTOPHTHORA

There are about 100 different species of *Phytophthora*, and these are mainly root diseases, particularly affecting plants such as *Chamaecyparis lawsoniana* cultivars on damp and heavy soils. In worst case scenarios, root rots such as *P. cinnamomi* can be seen travelling down a hedge line as the spores are splashed from one plant to another. *P. cinnamomi* also affects rhododendrons and azaleas, where again, it is worse on poorly drained and stagnant soils, with high rainfall and poor root aeration.

Phytophthora species are microscopic fungus-like organisms which cause root rot and decay at the base of a plant stem. Symptoms show as wilting, poor and yellowing foliage, and shoot die-back until the whole plant collapses. In severe cases, it can be identified by a reddish brown discolouration that can be found when cutting into the stem at the base of the plant. *Phytophthora* spreads by tiny spores that swim in water and wet ground. Resting spores can remain in the ground for several years, so care should be taken when removing dead plants and their associated soil to ensure that this is all disposed of, before fresh soil is brought in. The best avoidance strategy is to improve drainage with extra drainage channels, incorporate a course fibrous material such as leaf-mould, and pine bark to aid drainage, and to plant higher in the ground so that the rootball is lifted out of damp ground. There are no chemical cures.

In 2002, the first signs of *Phytophthora ramorum* were identified, and this was followed

POCKET DIAGNOSTIC PHYTOPHTHORA TESTING KIT
DAVID MILLAIS

by *P. kernoviae* in 2003 which is more aggressive towards rhododendrons. These were new, and these were devastating, and unlike most *Phytophthora* which infect roots, *P. ramorum* and *P. kernoviae* affect leaves, shoots and stems. Known as 'Sudden Oak Death' in America, where it kills native oak and tanoak, but thankfully it has little effect on English Oak, so 'ramorum disease' is more appropriate. However, a wide range of plants including rhododendrons, camellias, viburnums, *Pieris*, *Kalmia*, larches and *Taxus* can be affected. Recognition is difficult and can be confused with other diseases, and even normal winter maturity and change of stem colour. Shoots become darkly discoloured, and the blackening extends into the leaf stalk, and through the leaf. Symptoms include the wilting and death of a branch or part of a plant.

In an attempt to control the diseases, DEFRA made them notifiable diseases requiring the destruction of all host plants within 2 metres of the outbreak. In 2009, Japanese Larch were found to be highly infectious by spreading spores from their high canopy, and this required widespread felling of forests, especially in the South-West of Britain. Rhododendrons are also highly susceptible, but as we have learnt over time, it is *R. ponticum* that has been the main problem. A programme of grubbing it out to give more space and light, with better ventilation and humidity levels has been effective, and breathed new life into overgrown gardens and plantations. Like the powdery mildew problem, the removal of the most affected plants goes a long way to halting *P. ramorum*. In this case it is Larch trees, and *R. ponticum* and those varieties closely associated with it, such as 'Blue Peter', 'Purple Splendour' and 'Cunningham's White' which are some of the main culprits.

Like other *Phytophthora*, good drainage is critical and helps to prevent infection. Zoospores are spread by splashing, so anything you can do to reduce surface water is helpful. For example, we completely rebuilt our nursery so that plants are stood on gravel which has broken the film of water that was previously around the base of the pot. Tracks have been surfaced to avoid water splash from wheels onto precious plants. Expensive, but this has made a huge difference to plant health and has contributed to avoiding *P. ramorum* and many other root diseases. In a garden situation, drainage can be improved with additional ditches, planting high in the ground to lift the plant into drier conditions, and by ensuring that water does not puddle on paths, ready to be splashed onto nearby foliage. Good plant management and hygiene goes a very long way in keeping plants clear of *P. ramorum*. Pruning out old branches, clearing the undergrowth, creating some space for the plants to breath, and growing a strong healthy plant all help. Then help your plants further with natural plant tonics, such as feeding with compost tea, seaweed, copper and sulphur tonics, citrus seed oil and garlic to strengthen your plant and build in resistance.

XYLLELA

We all need to keep a close eye on Xyllela *(Xyllela fastidiosa)* and its movement across Europe from the Mediterranean. Olives, citrus and vine crops have been devastated in Italy, Spain, southern France and Corsica since it was first identified there in 2013. There is a growing list of susceptible plants, including lavenders, acers, and red oaks. So far, rhododendrons, camellias and magnolias do not appear on the lists, but this is possibly only because they are not grown in these warm and predominantly limestone areas. The threat of Xylella is being taken seriously by DEFRA and the industry, and is subject to EU emergency measures, with movement restrictions on high-risk plants. An outbreak in the UK could lead to the destruction of all host plants within 100m, and a 5km movement ban on 'specified' plants for 5 years. This would be enough to make serious changes to the trees and plants in our landscape, and would cripple the whole horticultural industry.

HONEY FUNGUS

Honey fungus is the most destructive fungal disease in the UK. It attacks the roots of many different woody plants and is characterised by white fungal growths between the bark and wood near ground level, and clumps of 'honey coloured' toadstools in the autumn around infected plants. It spreads underground, developing brown or black rhizomorphs ('bootlaces') which spread the fungus from plant to plant at the rate of about 1 metre per year, killing the roots and decaying dead wood. To reduce the incidence of honey fungus, it is worth considering the removal of any felled or dying trees, especially on damp heavy soils. Stump grinding as much of the old root structure as possible is also recommended, but with a diseased tree, be careful not to re-use any woodchips as mulch for several years in case these are carrying spores of honey fungus.

Unfortunately there are no chemical controls, and the recommended control is to excavate the top 45cm of infected soil and dispose of it. The insertion of a vertical barrier of heavy grade polythene to the depth of 45cm can contain any further spreading.

BUD BLAST

If your rhododendron isn't flowering and you can see some dark buds, this could be either frost or bud blast. If the problem is frost, the buds will be brown or black and smooth, and whilst a little unsightly, it is the result of adverse weather conditions. Bud blast shows as small black hairy growths (like a hedgehog!) growing on the flower bud. It is a fungal disease which turns the flowering bud mouldy over winter and prevents flowering. It is spread by leaf hoppers which are a pale green insect that appears between June and September, and have been seen in greater numbers in recent summers. Some varieties are affected more than others, but this varies from garden to garden. Certainly some mauves seem worse, and those more associated with *R. ponticum*.

To control bud blast it is best to pick off and destroy as many infected buds as possible, clear out dead branches, and prune back other trees and shrubs to allow free air movement in and around the plant. Bud blast is reduced when leaf hoppers are reduced, though recent research is challenging this link. I recommend non-chemical controls such as SB Plant Invigorator which coats the foliage with a soapy solution and deters the leaf-hopper from feeding. Applications at monthly intervals may be needed to control different generations from June to September. Dual action fungicide and insecticide sprays are also effective.

A FLOWER BUD THAT HAS SUFFERED FROST DAMAGE (*TOP*); BLACK SPORES GROWING ON A FLOWER BUD (*BELOW*)
DAVID MILLAIS

LEAF SPOTS

Rhododendrons can be prone to a variety of different leaf spots, and plant collectors have noted these even in the wild. Many are cosmetic, and whilst they may be unsightly, they cause little long-term damage. Using just the naked eye, it is not possible to tell if a leaf spot has a fungal or a bacterial origin, but under magnification, tiny dot-like bodies associated with the lesions would indicate fungal spore-bearing structures. Fungal leaf spot symptoms are caused by the death of cells around the infection, and these often enlarge as the pathogen spreads.

Pycnidial leaf spot diseases include *Pestalotiopsis, Coniothyrium, Phomopsis* and *Phyllosticta*. These show symptoms on the upper leaf surface, often with irregularly shaped

PESTALOTIA ON 'LEM'S MONARCH' (*LEFT*); LEAF SPOTS ON RHODODENDRON LEAF (*RIGHT*)   DAVID MILLAIS

markings, but spreading is by spore-bearing pycnidia (asexual fruiting bodies) within the leaf. This makes control more difficult and requires translocated fungicides. Spores often spread from infected fallen leaves, which mature in spring, ready to be splashed onto tender and newly emerging leaves. Infection is spread in damp wet conditions and develops in warm humid conditions.

Good cultural growing methods which avoid plant stress do help prevent infection. This includes balanced feeding, good spacing, planting outside the drip line of trees, avoidance of late afternoon and evening watering so plants dry more quickly, and cleaning up any leaf litter and prunings which may carry disease from one season to the next. *R.* 'Lem's Monarch' and *R.* 'Markeeta's Prize' seem particularly prone to *Pestalotiopsis* when planted under dripping trees. Compost tea will increase the biological activity on the leaf surface and reduce leaf spots, and SB Plant Invigorator can act as a surface protector.

AZALEA GALL

The fungal disease *Xobasidium japonicum* disfigures the leaves of evergreen azaleas and is spread by airborne spores. Irregular shaped galls vary in size from that of a pea, to a small plum, and form mainly on leaves, but also on flowers. They are pale green at first, later becoming white which is a superficial coating of fungal spores. Spores can be spread to healthy plants by insects or by air.

Galls tend to form in early spring and picking them off before they turn white and infectious is certainly recommended to prevent spreading. If growing plants indoors, avoid high humidity to reduce spores in the air. Some varieties such as *Rhododendron* 'Rosebud', are prone to azalea gall, so often it is best to select an alternative variety.

Throughout this article, I have made regular reference to growing plants in best conditions, so that plants grow strongly, and are much more disease resistant. A plant that is stressed through being too damp, too dry, in too much shade, or cooking in full sun is far more likely to be vulnerable to disease attack. Correct site selection, mulching, feeding and watering are fundamental to growing a healthy plant. Additional resistance can be built in with a range of organic tonics such as compost tea, low dose copper sprays, liquid seaweed feeds, (eg Maxicrop with Iron) garlic and citrus seed oils and SB Plant Invigorator. For those wanting or needing chemical controls, please refer to the RHS website for up to date information, as authorised chemicals face more restrictions and are withdrawn. Statutory control measures can be seen on the DEFRA website:
• https://www.rhs.org.uk/Advice/Profile?PID=573
• https://www.gov.uk/guidance/disease-control-in-flowers-and-shrub

DAVID MILLAIS
is Chairman of the Rhododendron, Camellia and Magnolia Group, and also runs Millais Nurseries, a specialist rhododendron, camellia and magnolia nursery near Farnham, which aims to use as few chemicals as possible in the production of plants

Appreciation
Lady Cynthia Postan 1918–2017

As the fourth child of the 9th Earl of Albemarle, Cynthia was born 'the Lady Cynthia Keppel' later becoming 'Lady Postan' as the wife of the distinguished Cambridge Economist Sir Michael Postan. I believe her love of rhododendrons originated from her ownership of a cottage in the Snowdonia area and by the early 1980's she was a member of the Group's Executive Committee. In 1987 she succeeded John Sanders as Editor of the Yearbook for the Group, a position she held for 10 years.

During the Second World War, Cynthia was recruited into MI5, where she met her husband, and she wrote a definitive article on the development of the jet engine and the role played by Sir Frank Whittle. This confirmed her aptitude for research, the written word and discretion, and the Yearbook benefitted from the professional experience she brought to the task. The improvements she achieved in design and production are very evident if one looks back at the sequence of ten Yearbooks she produced – all done in the Group's pre-digital era when both editorial and production work was a good deal more laborious than it is today. She had a very strong sense of history and tradition, and was determined that, in 1996, the fiftieth anniversary of the Group's post-war resurrection as an RHS Group should be celebrated appropriately with due acknowledgement to its 1915 origins as the 'Rhododendron Society'. In place of the 1996 Yearbook she conceived the idea of a book to be called 'The Rhododendron Story' – leaving the 1997 Yearbook in due course to cover two years 1996–7. Others considered the cost of producing 'The Rhododendron Story' beyond the financial resources of the Group, but Cynthia was not to be defeated.

Single-handedly she managed to obtain a generous donation from H H Sheikh Zayed bin Sultan Al-Nahyan, the owner of the Berkshire garden Tittenhurst Park, which more than covered production costs. 'The Rhododendron Story' is surely Cynthia's memorial so far as the Group is concerned, for twenty years on it remains popular with rhododendron lovers and is a frequent reference source, made even more available now by its inclusion on the Group website.

In early 1997, following a careful but sociable vetting over lunch at Maurice and Rosemary Foster's house, Cynthia gave her approval to myself as her successor. Thereafter she continued for many years as a regular visitor to the London Shows and participant in the annual Group tours. She was always stimulating company and good fun to be with, and I am sure there are many members of the Group with their own special memories of her. My own personal favourite dates back to the 1997 Group tour to Cornwall, when I had persuaded her to write the garden reports for the Yearbook. At Lamorran, the steeply terraced garden that overlooks the town of St Mawes, Cynthia, as she walked around describing the garden, was concentrating so hard on the small dictaphone she had borrowed from me that she walked straight into an ornamental pond – if I remember correctly, up to her knees – but was typically quite unphased. Her knowledge of plants of 'our' genera was extensive, and her experience of rhododendrons, in particular, was increased in 1987 when she was invited by Ed and Ann Boscawen to join their spring expedition to Bhutan led by Keith Rushforth (Yearbook 1988/9 pp 20–26).

Whilst her Cambridge house had only a small garden she did have interesting terrace pot plants – including the only pot-grown (and flowering) *R. falconeri* I have seen. Cynthia had a long and, I believe, happy life, and the Group owes her a great debt for her service.

PHILIP EVANS
is a former Editor of the Yearbook

Notes from the International Rhododendron Registrar 2017

There is no doubt that 2017 has been the year of the evergreen azalea so far as the International Rhododendron Register and Checklist is concerned. In my last Notes I indicated that Yoko Otsuki was translating for us some of the text of the most recent editions of the Japanese Satsuki Dictionaries. This work was delivered early in the year and I am now over half way through adding the information to the nearly 1300 entries involved. The data comprises, where this information is known to the Dictionary compilers, not only parentages, but the names of raisers and the identity of individuals who have registered these names with one of the local Satsuki societies in Japan, together with the relevant dates. I have then been adding as detailed a description as I can, derived from the images published in the Dictionaries; in some cases these supplement descriptions already listed, but in many cases this is the first time we have listed such data. The 2014 Satsuki Dictionary also has a significant number of entries where we have had no previous record of the name, so the Checklist has grown significantly in this respect as well. I now learn that the 2017 edition of the Dictionary has information on several hundred new cultivars and these will need to be added to future lists of work to be done.

In addition to this Satsuki data, I have for some time been working through the text of Jozef Heursel's work *Azalea's*, published in 1999. This lists mainly the so-called Indian azaleas (actually *simsii* hybrids) and other pot plant cultivars, which have been raised, or at least have been grown commercially, in Europe in recent times. It deals with some 700 names and once again has been an invaluable source of new or revised information about these plants, as well as providing information on a number for which we have previously had no record.

All this activity, as well as the results of delving in other sources in nursery catalogues and journals has resulted in well over 500 new entries on the database, which now has well over 34,000 entries. In the year to date (this is written in November) there have been eighty-three new formal registrations in 2017, compared to a final total in 2016 of ninety-nine new registered names. For a second year there were more from Europe than from North America, but as is usual most are elepidote rhododendrons, with only one new registered vireya and 14 new azaleas. At least 21 species are directly listed in parentages, with *chamaethomsonii* ('Little Vixen') and *kesangiae* ('High Beeches Dochula') being more unusual entries in this respect. Indeed, the latter is the first

RHODODENDRON CHAMAETHOMSONII 'LITTLE VIXEN' (*LEFT*); *R.* 'KYLLIKKI' (*RIGHT*) **STEVE HOOTMAN / KRISTIAN THEQVIST**

RHODODENDRON 'PROFESSOR KONDRATOVIČS'   **GUNITA RIEKSTIŅA**

America's Distinguished Achievement Award in 1993. He was the son-in-law of Robert Gartrell and did much to document the Robin Hill cultivars raised by Gartrell, registering the names of a dozen of these evergreen azaleas himself. He wrote widely on other issues to do with azalea cultivars and was always keen to pursue nomenclatural problems and to challenge aspects of the Cultivated Plant Code. He edited the American Rhododendron Society's influential 1984 publication *A Contribution towards Standardization of Color Names in Horticulture*, still used today by the RHS in rhododendron registrations. The second commemorative cultivar recognises the achievements of Prof. Rihards Kondratovičs, who set up and ran the University of Latvia's Rhododendron Nursery Babīte. He was himself responsible for raising and naming well over 100 new rhododendron and azalea cultivars, for virtually all of which I have received impeccable registration forms over the years. His contribution to the world of Latvian rhododendrons was unequalled.

time this species has been mentioned in the Register and Checklist and represents a highly-rated selection raised at High Beeches from a seed collection made on the Dochula pass in Bhutan.

Amongst this year's novelties there is a welcome selection of nine more plants raised by Kristian Theqvist in Finland, which almost needless to say are mostly very hardy cultivars, and often dense low shrubs. Several of these (such as the purplish pink 'Stina' and the purplish pink, fading to white 'Kyllikki') have curious curved hooks at the top of the stamens, derived from growth of the connective tissue between the anthers; the filaments in 'Kyllikki' are also broadly winged, which give the flowers a distinctive appearance, and this is a characteristic the breeder is seeking to develop further in new cultivars.

Two new cultivars commemorate individuals who made notable contributions to the rhododendron world and who sadly died this year. The first of these, 'Donald H. Voss', is named for a man who was highly respected in the world of azaleas in particular and who received the Azalea Society of

RHODODENDRON 'VELZEIDE'   **GUNITA RIEKSTIŅA**

RHODODENDRON 'WINDING ROAD' (*LEFT*); *R.* 'SWEET TALK' (*RIGHT*)   JIM BARLUP

I was sad too to learn of the death of the Walter Schmalscheidt, who had been a valued correspondent for as long as I have been involved with the Register. His books on rhododendron and azalea cultivars raised in Germany have been the ultimate source for much of what is now listed about these cultivars in the Register and Checklist, to which he also contributed a great deal as one on my principal advisors in the course of preparations for the second edition in 2004. He could be a challenging correspondent (especially if one was at all dilatory or inaccurate in responding), but it kept one up to the mark and I was so pleased to have finally met him two years ago, at home in Oldenburg, where we shared tea and icecream cake!

Registrants have, as ever, been keen to name their new cultivars after many other, usually living individuals, and I noted examples this year coined for grandmothers, mothers, mothers-in-

RHODODENDRON 'HACHMANN'S LULLABY'   HOLGER HACHMANN

RHODODENDRON 'AMBER KISS' (*LEFT*); *R.* 'LUNORASK' (*RIGHT*)   HOLGER HACHMANN / SVEND ASKJAER

laws, wives, sons and daughters, granddaughters and grandsons, sisters, nieces, partners, old girl friends, other friends and even a favourite teacher. Of the plants themselves a number have stood out, although I must emphasise this is inevitably a very personal choice: 'Velzeide' ('Niobe' × 'Hexe') is a hose-in-hose evergreen azalea from the Kondratovičs stable which really packs a punch with its very wavy-edged, vivid purplish red flowers; 'Sweet Talk' (a complex hybrid involving 'Yellow Saucer', 'Anna's Riplet', 'September Song', 'Bambi', 'Grand Recital' and *proteoides*) and 'Winding Road' ('Lois Blackmore' × 'Plum Passion') are two further contributions from Jim Barlup in the USA. The former has the most lovely combination of shades of purplish pink, in very broadly funnel-shaped flowers, with rounded lobes and a prominent green stigma, whilst the latter has very neat-looking, tightly wavy-edged flowers, shading out to a strong reddish purple margin from a paler centre. There were also some striking plants amongst the broad selection registered this year from the Hachmann nursery in Germany. 'Hachmann's Lullaby' ('Fantastica' × *dichroanthum* ssp. *scyphocalyx* Herpesticum Group) has strongly bicoloured, wavy-edged flowers, strong salmon pink at the margins and with an orange-yellow centre, whilst 'Amber Kiss' ('Meteorit' × 'Goldzauber') has deeply lobed, rather narrowly funnel-shaped white flowers, with a very conspicuous blotch of red markings on the dorsal lobes. Finally, I must mention Svend Askjaer's 'Lunorask', a deciduous azalea, grown from ARS seed exchange as *prunifolium* (but perhaps crossed with *arborescens*) and raised in

Denmark: this has upward pointing, starry-faced tubular funnel-shaped flowers of a yellowish white, with a conspicuous vivid yellow blotch and even more prominent purplish red filaments. I should also mention that Svend has been generous in sharing with the Checklist the further work he has been doing in tracking down and checking information on the range of new Danish cultivars which all incorporate "Dane" in the name ('Sticky Dane', 'What a Dane', 'Woolly Dane' etc). Most of these have not been formally registered, but at least we have the data now for future reference, when one day (perhaps not too far off) the database is available for all to access.

This will be my last Notes from the Registrar, as by the time the next set is due I shall have retired from this role and indeed from work entirely. Since 1983, when I took over the position of Registrar from David Pycraft, a grand total of 7741 names has been formally registered, with the 1980s/1990s representing a peak period, with yearly totals then often over 200 and rising in one memorable year (1999) to 566! Present volumes now match the pre-1980s levels. New Checklist entries have hugely exceeded these totals, especially recently as I have pressed to improve our records of both vireya and azalea cultivars. I have been most fortunate in dealing with a wonderful range of individuals, keen to pass on their knowledge about this very varied group of plants. It has been a pleasure and a privilege to be able to share in some of that enthusiasm and to assist in ensuring that the plants are accurately recorded for posterity and future reference, and above all to ensure that their names are acceptable!

Exceptional Plants 2017
Shows

Gardening can be a solitary occupation, which is why so many gardeners like to come together for shows or to visit other people's gardens. These events enable long-term friendships to form, views to be exchanged and, let's be honest, a bit of harmless showing off as well. Not all members are able to participate in these activities, so our Yearbook is the key means of communication which every member can feel a part of, and reports of Group events are a way of vicariously taking part even if physical attendance is not possible.

Rather than being a comprehensive set of reports, these notes present a fairly random and entirely personal selection of exhibits and plants seen by the author at shows and on garden visits during 2017. Some are rare, some commonplace, but all struck me as exceptional or memorable. 2017 was a year full of riches, so the difficulty was what to leave out.

MAGNOLIA 'AURORA'   **RUSSELL BEESON**

ROSEMOOR EARLY SPRING FLOWER SHOW

The season kicked off in the South West, with the Early Spring Flower Show held at RHS Rosemoor in Devon. This show combines two RHS National competitions organised by the RHS – those for Early Camellias and Daffodils – with competitions for Rhododendrons, Magnolias and Spring Ornamentals organised by the South West branch of the Group, with grateful help from the RHS staff. Put all these plants together in one venue and, given favourable weather, a spectacular show usually emerges to delight the public, many of whom are astonished to see so many flowers in early March.

Some of the magnolias exhibited had not fully survived a warm night after being staged the evening before the show, and it was unfortunate that the extraordinary exhibits from Caerhays suffered the most in this respect. Those who had staged their exhibits early on the morning of the

RHODODENDRON INSIGNE
at Isabella Plantation, Richmond Park   **RUSSELL BEESON**

first day of the show fared better, and the Lamellen Cup was awarded to Botallick's notable spray of *Magnolia* **'Tyler James'**, with huge creamy flowers showing a slight pink tinge. There was a new award this year, the Brother Vincent SSF Cup for the best single bloom. This was won by the South West branch Chairman, Dr John Marston, with a sumptuous flower of the Blumhardt variety *Magnolia* **'Aurora'**, which originates from a cross between 'Star Wars' and *M. sargentiana* var. *robusta*. The pink cup-and-saucer-shaped flower was a worthy winner and Brother Vincent himself presented the cup.

Another unusual magnolia was a spray of the Chinese *Magnolia maudiae*, formerly included in the genus *Michelia*, shown by Trewithen. The fragrant white flowers emerging from brown furry buds were characteristic of this group of plants, which are becoming quite widely grown in the milder areas of the country and are particularly popular in New Zealand.

The Tremeer Cup for the best rhododendron in the show was awarded to Barry Starling for his fine spray of **Rhododendron luteiflorum**, a yellow-flowered species in the subsection Glauca, and closely related to the better known *R. glaucophyllum*. This early flowering species is seldom seen at its best, as it is rather vulnerable to frost damage, but this exhibitor has a remarkable record of producing floriferous specimens of some of the more difficult rhododendrons, as also exemplified by his superb spray of the deep red

RHODODENDRON LUTEIFLORUM   RUSSELL BEESON

Rhododendron vialii in the Azaleastrum subsection. This somewhat tender species is considered to be difficult to flower well except when grown under glass.

The late Edward Needham's garden at Tregye has become an outstanding exhibitor of rare and special plants over recent years, drawing on the Needham legacy as built upon by John Lanyon, who now manages this unique garden. A good

example of what it can produce was a perfect truss of an excellent form of **Rhododendron barbatum**, with large glowing red flowers.

SAVILL GARDEN, EARLY APRIL

The RHS Early Rhododendron Show has been held at Wisley for the last few years but, owing to redevelopment taking place there, a new venue was needed in 2017. Fortunately the facilities of

MAGNOLIA MAUDIAE   RUSSELL BEESON

RHODODENDRON VIALII   RUSSELL BEESON

RHODODENDRON BARBATUM   **RUSSELL BEESON**

RHODODENDRON HORAEUM   **RUSSELL BEESON**

the Savill Garden in Windsor Great Park were offered and this proved to be a perfect venue for a superb show, which also included the RHS Main Camellia and Spring Ornamental Competitions.

The Crown Estate and Exbury were among the most prolific exhibitors of rhododendrons in particular, but other famous gardens as well as several skilled amateur growers also picked up prizes. Among the wealth of outstanding rhododendrons seen, I will select just a few which caught my eye.

Firstly, a most striking rich orange flower, labelled **Rhododendron horaeum** F21850, from that fine grower of rare species, Rod White. This perhaps should more correctly be considered a variety of *R. citriniflorum*. I can find no record of this plant being used as a parent, which is surprising given its unusual colour.

The Boscawens of High Beeches have a fine record of growing the very best forms of rhododendron species and hybrids, and their exhibit of a beautiful clear pink **Rhododendron kesangiae** was a case in point, as the flowers of this quite recently introduced large-leaved species from Bhutan can often be a rather muddy purple. This exhibit deservedly won the John Hilliard Cup for the best truss in the show.

Amongst the Crown Estate's many fine exhibits was a truss of **Rhododendron glischrum** ssp. **rude** 'High Flier', with flowers of a beautiful shade of pale pink, with a dark red throat. There is some ambiguity over the exact identity of this plant. Firstly, some authorities

RHODODENDRON KESANGIAE   **RUSSELL BEESON**

regard *R. rude* as deserving specific rank and secondly, the *International Rhododendron Register* refers to 'High Flier' as a selection made at Windsor from *R. vesiculiferum* KW 10952; whatever the exact nomenclature may be, all these are very closely related forms within the Glischra subsection. This selection received an Award of Merit in 1968.

Exbury picked up one of many first prizes with an outstanding tightly-packed truss of **Rhododendron 'Colonel Rogers'**, a well-known hybrid between *R. niveum* and *R. falconeri*. This seemed to display the fine foliage one would expect from the latter and a paler form of the unusual flower colour of the former species – perhaps not everyone's favourite colour but it certainly appealed to me.

Amongst the lepidote species, High Beeches excelled again with an amazingly floriferous spray of **Rhododendron primuliflorum**, showing off the daphne-like flowers characteristic of the Pogonanthum subsection, to perfection. Such a superb specimen of this dwarf species is rarely seen.

Finally in the rhododendrons, we saw an unusually large selection of 'tender' species and hybrids, from the subsections Maddenia and Edgeworthia. An outstanding example was a spray of **Rhododendron 'Anne Teese'** exhibited by Caerhays. This is a cross of *R. ciliicalyx* with *R. formosum* – evidently a richly coloured form of the latter species, giving this fragrant hybrid an unusually deep pink shading.

RHODODENDRON GLISCHRUM SSP. RUDE 'HIGH FLIER'
RUSSELL BEESON

RHODODENDRON 'COLONEL ROGERS'   RUSSELL BEESON

RHODODENDRON PRIMULIFLORUM   RUSSELL BEESON

RHODODENDRON 'ANNE TEESE'   RUSSELL BEESON

WOLLEMIA NOBILIS   RUSSELL BEESON

The show was much enhanced by some wonderful exhibits in the Spring Ornamentals Competition. I will mention just one remarkable exhibit here, Judy Hall's magnificent vase of that most coveted conifer, **Wollemia nobilis**, quite recently discovered in Australia in exceptionally interesting circumstances, bearing a profusion of cones at the end of each shoot.

ROSEMOOR APRIL SPRING SHOW

At last, the new Garden Room at Rosemoor had been completed, and we were able to hold the late April show in this fine new building, a great improvement on the old marquee, though it proved to be too small for the staggering number of exhibits submitted for the various competitions held on this occasion, and we had to spill over into the nearby lecture theatre for additional space. The show encompassed several competitive events: the RHS Main Rhododendron Competition and the South West branch Main Magnolia, Camellia and Floral Display competitions.

As usual, Caerhays dominated the magnolia competition, and this is a marvellous showcase

for them at this time of year, though the private garden of Botallick ran them a good second in number of exhibits. Amid all the spectacular blooms, it was one of Botallick's which particularly caught my eye. The yellow flowered hybrids, based originally on *M. acuminata*, have become increasingly popular over recent years,

MAGNOLIA 'LOIS'   RUSSELL BEESON

and new hybrids appear every year, with better and deeper colours. One of the most striking of these is **Magnolia 'Lois'** and Botallick's lovely vase of this showed it at its best. In the more traditional colour ranges, Caerhays exhibited a large vase of **Magnolia 'Margaret Helen'**, a fairly recent introduction from New Zealand with large rosy-red campbellii-type flowers. This superb exhibit won 1st prize in its class.

There were many exceptional rhododendron species to be seen here and I have selected just a very few from the many which impressed me. **Rhododendron cinnabarinum** has gone through phases over recent years of being difficult to grow because most forms of the species and many of its hybrids are prone to more or less serious damage by Powdery Mildew. This disease seems to be on the wane at the moment, one result of which is that we are seeing these plants in good fettle more and more frequently on the show bench. This particular spray from Exbury was notable for its compact habit and the multitude of vivid hanging orange flowers. The judges were clearly looking for something else, because this exhibit was unplaced in its class.

Rhododendron pingianum is treated as a form of *R. argyrophyllum* by some authorities and the similarity is obvious. The *Flora of China* separates

MAGNOLIA 'MARGARET HELEN'   RUSSELL BEESON

RHODODENDRON CINNABARINUM   RUSSELL BEESON

RHODODENDRON PINGIANUM

RUSSELL BEESON

the two mainly by the number of flowers in the inflorescence, and this specimen from Exbury had well over 20 flowers in the truss, loosely spaced on long pedicels and of a beautiful clear pale pink – a very distinctive exhibit.

One often reads that **Rhododendron niveum** is an acquired taste; apparently not everyone goes for the colour of the flowers (which is inherited by several hybrids). The colour is actually quite variable and has been described in many terms: deep lilac, mauve, smoky blue, rich purple, magenta and Parma violet, to name but a few. It is certainly unusual and judges at competitions do seem to like the best forms of it. The one exhibited by Trewithen, which received 1st prize in its class, was by any standard a beautiful colour, perhaps at the paler end of the range, with a perfectly formed and tightly packed truss, and showing off the dark nectar pouches to good effect.

Finally amongst the rhododendron species, the tropical Vireyas have long been the Cinderellas of the rhododendron world. This is perhaps not very surprising, given their often delicate constitution and need for protection and warmth, so today the most important collection by far resides at RBG Edinburgh, though a few great gardens, for example Exbury, are trying to revive their collections. Still, it falls mainly to a small band of amateur growers to keep the tradition alive and to show the public what these plants are like. Pam Hayward is one of that band, and she has also played an important role in championing the Vireyas and encouraging more people to grow and propagate them. She exhibited the only Vireya species in this show, a delightful specimen of **Rhododendron jasminiflorum**, which was a good example of the exotic appearance of these plants, with its fragrant, long-tubed white flowers, with a touch of pink in the throat. One can only hope that visitors who saw this went away wondering how they can get hold of one; sadly, the answer is 'with the greatest of difficulty'.

Many fine exhibits were displayed in the classes for hybrids and the result was a spectacular demonstration of the flower-power of these plants. I will select just one of the many superb varieties on show. Exbury is of course renowned for its hybridisation

RHODODENDRON NIVEUM **RUSSELL BEESON**

RHODODENDRON JASMINIFLORUM **RUSSELL BEESON**

programmes over many decades and many of the most popular hybrids in commerce are from their stable. However, there are many more wonderful Rothschild hybrids which, for one reason or another, have never made it into the nursery trade: perhaps there are just too many of them. A good example is **Rhododendron 'Anchorage'**, a hybrid of *R. fortunei* with 'Idealist' (another Exbury hybrid involving the yellow *R. wardii*). The substantial spray showed off the result, the flowers being an unusual and restrained shade described as light yellow-green, shading to greenish white. The well-shaped and full truss made it a worthy winner of the 1st prize in its class.

RHODODENDRON 'ANCHORAGE'   **RUSSELL BEESON**

WISLEY

Although RHS Wisley was taking a break from being able to do our major shows, it did host the Centenary Cup Competition on 13th May. This is a rather small and simple show, with many fewer classes to enter, the idea being to make it less technical and therefore more accessible to the public. Judging by the number and enthusiasm of visitors, this seems to have worked well. The show has been quite fully described in the Bulletin for August 2017, including a record of the lovely unnamed yellow deciduous azalea with which Brian Long won the Cup. My purpose here is once again to present some brief notes on my personal selection of exhibits which I found particularly interesting.

To have a national show in the South of England in mid May is a rare treat for those who are able to attend, as it is an opportunity to see late flowering plants not generally available at the earlier shows. This applied to magnolias as well as to rhododendrons. In fact, as described in the Bulletin referred to above, the season was unusually advanced and many of the 'Wilson 50' evergreen azaleas were too far gone

to exhibit, though we were still able to see a comprehensive photographic and documentary exhibit on the subject, including a few of the plants themselves.

We are used to seeing the early and mid-season magnolias at our earlier shows and the rather different but still fascinating late spring and summer flowering forms were a welcome sight here. One of the most admired of these is the Japanese **Magnolia obovata**, named after the shape of its large and handsome leaves. The bloom exhibited by the Crown Estate was a perfect example, and looked almost tropical in its magnificence. The flowers are a good 20cm in

MAGNOLIA OBOVATA   **RUSSELL BEESON**

RHODODENDRON NUTTALLII   RUSSELL BEESON

RHODODENDRON 'WATERFALL'   RUSSELL BEESON

diameter, and the powerful fragrance has been likened to that of a cantaloupe melon, though I have heard some more disobliging descriptions.

Turning to rhododendrons, Robin Whiting won 1st prize for his vivid bicoloured Vireya hybrid, and this has been illustrated in the Bulletin, but I would not like to omit mention of the other **unnamed Vireya** he exhibited, as it is almost equally as striking as the winner and has that characteristic 'Vireya-look' about it which makes these plants impossible to confuse with any others.

I hesitate to include one of my own exhibits in these notes, but *Rhododendron nuttallii* is so seldom seen at our shows that I feel it may be of interest. This tree forming species has the largest flowers in the Maddenia subsection, indeed some of the largest flowers found in any rhododendron. It is not particularly difficult to grow, needing a little protection only if severe sub-zero temperatures are experienced. Patience is necessary as it does not flower until it is a sizeable shrub, though that patience is rewarded in full measure by the sumptuous, heavy-textured flowers which have a rich spicy fragrance.

Among the many excellent hybrid rhododendrons on display, one in particular attracted me. There have been many crosses made between members of the *R. cinnabarinum* clan and forms of the tender *R. maddenii*. One of the most famous is 'Royal Flush', a Williams hybrid from the 1950s, which is reputed to be particularly prone to Powdery Mildew. More recently, Bodnant has made crosses in a similar vein, and

one of the finest of these is a cross between *R. cinnabarinum* and a selected form of *R. maddenii* ssp. *crassum*. The result is **Rhododendron 'Waterfall'**, a beautiful truss of which was exhibited by Andy and Jenny Fly. The flowers have the characteristic funnel-shaped *cinnabarinum* form and are a nice shade of pale purplish pink, with other colours also present in a subtle way. The plant appears to be quite hardy and is thought to be resistant to Powdery Mildew. This is one that deserves to be much more widely grown.

UNNAMED VIREYA RHODODENDRON   RUSSELL BEESON

Garden visits

RHODODENDRON 'CHARLOTTE FOSTER'   RUSSELL BEESON

WHITE HOUSE FARM, KENT

A chance to visit Maurice Foster's extraordinary garden should never be turned down and my first visit, with members of the Wessex branch in April, was a real eye-opener. As many members will be aware, Maurice is not only a renowned authority on, and exhibitor of, magnolias and camellias, but also a grower and raiser of many trees and shrubs in a wide range of genera, including a number of fine hydrangeas in particular. His garden has been much written about, and in this brief note I will confine myself to mentioning just one very special plant with which he is associated. Walking through the glades of superb magnolias and other woody plants, my eye was attracted to a large bush of a most spectacular pink rhododendron. This proved to be **Rhododendron 'Charlotte Foster'**, a seedling selected by Maurice from a batch of seed of 'Lady Rosebery', growing cheek by

jowl with *R. yunnanense.* which is thus assumed to be the pollen parent. The hanging, funnel-shaped flowers of a delightful light purplish pink shade are presented in a most elegant fashion. It seems that this variety, an AM in 1994, has occasionally been in commerce, but not currently – a shame as I think all who saw this plant felt it would be a good addition to their own gardens.

GORWELL HOUSE, DEVON

The Group's AGM coincided with the Main Rhododendron Show at Rosemoor in late April and a spare morning presented a rare opportunity to visit the garden of Dr John Marston, chairman of the South West branch. Like Maurice Foster, John is one of those plantsmen who does not confine himself to our three genera, and his climatically favoured garden near the coast of North Devon allows him to grow a wide variety of rare trees and

RHODODENDRON EDGEWORTHII   RUSSELL BEESON

shrubs from many genera, so walking round with him is bound to be an education for any keen gardener. Once again, I am going to limit myself to just one plant out of the many fascinating, and in some cases unique, specimens to be seen in this most wonderful garden. ***Rhododendron edgeworthii*** is one of those plants which everyone loves once they have seen it, and is therefore deservedly popular among enthusiasts. It is a 'plant that has everything': highly decorative rugose leaves with a more or less thick brown indumentum on the underside, a good bushy, low-growing habit if in an open position and, above all, good-sized white flowers, often very attractively tinged with pink (as in this case), with one of the best fragrances in the genus. To cap it all, even when the flowers have fallen they leave behind a large red calyx which is attractive in its own right. This form, which was grown from seed collected some years ago in the Li Ping Valley, Yunnan, is one of the finest I have seen, and is one of the hardier forms, generally surviving unprotected in the open garden and flowering freely.

RUSSELL BEESON
is an enthusiast for our genera, and also the independent examiner of the Group's accounts

Challenge Cups 2017

ALAN HARDY CHALLENGE SALVER

Awarded at the Early Rhododendron Competition to the exhibitor attaining the most points.
Crown Estate, Windsor

THE WINNING EXHIBIT
HARVEY STEPHENS

THE LIONEL de ROTHSCHILD CHALLENGE CUP

The best exhibit of one truss of each of six species shown in Class 1 of the Main Rhododendron Competition.
Crown Estate, Windsor

THE WINNING EXHIBIT
HARVEY STEPHENS

THE McLAREN CHALLENGE CUP

The best exhibit of any species of rhododendron, one truss shown in Class 3 of the Main Rhododendron Competition.
Trewithen Gardens

Rhododendron suoilenhense

RHODODENDRON SUOILENHENSE   GARY LONG

THE ROZA STEVENSON CHALLENGE CUP

The best exhibit of any species of rhododendron, one spray or branch with one or more than one truss shown in Class 4 of the Main Rhododendron Competition.
Caerhays Castle Gardens

Rhododendron yunnanense

RHODODENDRON YUNNANENSE   CAERHAYS CASTLE

THE LODER CHALLENGE CUP

The best exhibit of any hybrid rhododendron, one truss shown in Class 34 of the Main Rhododendron Competition.
Crown Estate, Windsor

Rhododendron 'Chapeau'

RHODODENDRON 'CHAPEAU'　　　　HARVEY STEPHENS

THE CROSFIELD CHALLENGE CUP

The best exhibit of three rhododendrons, raised by or in the garden of the exhibitor, one truss of each shown in Class 36 of the Main Rhododendron Competition (see page 56).
Colin Mugridge

Three unnamed hybrids

THE WINNING EXHIBIT　　　　COLIN MUGRIDGE

THE WINNING EXHIBIT

GARY LONG

THE LEONARDSLEE BOWL
The best exhibit of twelve cultivars of camellias, one bloom of each shown in Class 10 of the Main Camellia Competition.
Trewithen Gardens

RHODODENDRON NAME UNKNOWN
VANESSA PENN

THE CENTENARY CUP'
The best exhibit in the Centenary Cup Competition, chosen from the winners of the five classes.
Brian Long

Rhododendron name unknown

Rhododendron, Camellia & Magnolia Group Trustees & Committee

Index

MAGNOLIA CAMPBELLII 'DARJEELING'
GEORGE HARGREAVES

Visit us for the centenary year of

Exbury
GARDENS

Celebrating
100 years
Exbury
GARDENS
1919 – 2019

Come and make memories
in our beautiful gardens

Over 200 acres to explore, including restaurant & café,
steam railway, and new Centenary Garden opening June 2019

www.exbury.co.uk
Tel: 023 8089 1203

Exbury Gardens, Exbury, SO45 1AZ
20 minutes from M27 junction 2 west

RHS GARDEN
Rosemoor

STUNNING GARDENS
AMAZING EVENTS

Plant Heritage Spring Plant Fair
12 & 13 May*

Rose Festival
16 June – 22 July

Rosemoor Garden Flower Show
17 – 19 August

Plant Heritage Autumn Plant Fair
23 September*

Spring Flower Competitions
9 & 10 March 2019

RHS National Rhododendron Show
20 & 21 April 2019

* Free admission for NCCPG members

RHS
Inspiring everyone to grow

Great Torrington, Devon.
Open throughout the year
except Christmas day
For tickets, events and promotions
visit **rhs.org.uk/rosemoor**

RHS Registered Charity No. 222879/SC038262

Comic Related
Collec

Survival & ...

by Sanjiv Purba & Sandy Sicilia

Published by Hobby House Press, Inc.
Grantsville, Maryland
www.hobbyhouse.com

Hobby
House
Press

Acknowledgements

We want to express our very special thanks to the following individuals who really went above and beyond the call of duty in assisting us in this initiative:

- Lee Dawson, Shawna Ervin-Gore, and Amy Huey of Dark Horse Comics, Inc.
- Carol G. Platt of Marvel Enterprises, Inc.
- Christopher Holm and Chris Cerasi of Lucasfilm Ltd.

Special thanks to Alexander, Christian, Naveen and Neil for occasional fact clarification.

Sanjiv Purba
Sandy Sicilia

Table of Contents

Introduction

Toys are a physical manifestation of human imagination, ideas, dreams and desires. They are tightly integrated with the human experience. In some form, they are one of the most basic items that infants and children cherish when they learn to play and to share. Some of the early bonds that children form with their toys end up lasting a lifetime. Other bonds evolve with the child's maturity level. The boy collecting little cars may become a teenager who collects antique die-cast cars. The girl who plays with a fashion doll may begin to collect them in their original packaging as she turns into a teenager.

In any generation, there are various types of toys being manufactured and distributed. As these become play items across a broad segment of the population, some are worn out, others are broken, and many end up being discarded. However, something interesting begins to happen over time. The people who grew up playing with specific toys remember the feelings of excitement, comfort and awe they felt when they first played with them.

Someday they might want to purchase the same type of toy that they once played with — either to save and cherish or to give to their children to encourage the same joyful experience.

To actually purchase the same type of toy they once played with requires tapping into a secondary, finite-sized marketplace that results in driving up the cost of the toys that are left over from another time or generation. These items could have once been the playthings of children who were careful to maintain them in one piece and in good overall physical condition. They could also have been toys that were purchased and stored away by a toy collector to resell to another generation. The people who maintained their toys in good condition, for any reason, are able to resell them for a profit or share them with another generation of children at a time of their choosing.

Toys inspire theme parks, television programs, books, motion pictures and vice versa. It is big, big business based on the human need to play, imagine, identify, and belong. There

4

Copyright: Marvel
10in (25cm) Deluxe Cyclops *X-Men* action figure.

are many different types of toys, so for this price guide we have focused on those that are based on comic book characters. These have sold for as long as the comic books themselves. In many cases, the toy actually costs more than the comic book once did. Although some people collect both items, there are many people who may never read a comic book, but who still want to collect the toys based on them.

We cover several different types of comic book-related toys in this price guide, namely the following:

(1) Action Figures
(2) Statues
(3) PVCs
(4) HeroClix
(5) Premiums
(6) Oddities/Other

Copyright: Marvel
Extra Large HeroClix.

Intended Audience

This book is written for anyone interested in buying, collecting, or trading toys based on comic book characters. It provides you with information to help you enjoy your collection, invest wisely, and to get a fair market price for individual toy items. It is written for collectors, speculators and general hobbyists. This book also helps people understand that sometimes the best value a toy can serve is to let a child play with it until it wears out.

Chapter 1

Editorial Comments

Who buys toys? Clearly lots of people do, as this is one of the largest and most repeatable industries in the world. Many specific events such as birthdays and holidays drive the ongoing success of this market. Non-specific events like the release of a blockbuster movie or advertising also drive sales. There are three groups of toy purchasers that are central to the theme of this book. These are children, collectors and speculators.

In simplified terms, children are driven by the need to play with toys, collectors are driven into the hobby for sentimental or emotional reasons, and speculators are driven by financial objectives. The characteristics exhibited by members in each of these groups drive a vibrant global toy marketplace. People can, of course, move from one group to another or belong to more than one group at a time. In this case, they will exhibit some combination of characteristics from each of the groups. It can, of course, get confusing and interesting when objectives begin to get confused. The teenager that wants to play with

a HeroClix may end up buying several copies of the same piece – one to play with, one to save, and one to eventually sell.

The first group of buyers are adults who buy toys for children, which creates a large pool of toys that are actively played with. Many toys end up being worn, torn, discarded, lost, and broken. So from the large set of toys that are sold for use by children, only a small subset are actually maintained in a condition that makes them desirable as a "hobby collectible."

Toy purchases for children are highly dependent on price points and the coolness factor. Although someone else usually purchases the item for a child, be it a parent or a family friend, the motivation behind the purchase is the child's interest to have the toy. This is where the "coolness factor" comes into play. Anything that makes a toy "hot" at a specific point in time will get a lot of media and word-of-mouth attention. Purchasers are therefore on the lookout for these items to present as gifts for a special occasion. This is where the price point comes into play, especially in the case of family friends being the purchasers. There is willingness to only spend up to a certain amount for a toy that will be presented to someone else's child as a gift. This is heavily influenced by the family's social circle. The price point may be $20, $50, $100, or even $200+. There is also usually a minimum price point as well. The acceptable range for the high and low monetary values usually fits into a narrow price range, say 20%-30% from a certain price point (say $50).

A second group of toy purchasers are collectors. Collectors purchase toys and maintain them in good condition as a hobby. The primary drive for collectors is sentiment and emotion. They have several common objectives that include appreciation of the genre, rekindling memories, an affinity for the type of toy being collected and perhaps, a desire for wealth creation if their toy collectibles appreciate in value.

Finally, speculators may appreciate the toys they are purchasing, but their primary motivation is to generate a strong financial return on their investment. They purchase toys for the purpose of reselling them at a higher price in the future. Their selection is usually made after various research activities are completed and they feel they have found future winners. Sentiment and emo-

tion are rarely part of their business plan.

Acceptable price points for collectors and speculators tend to be much higher than they are for gifts to children. Quality, value, and appreciation potential are more important considerations for the long-term than the temporary "coolness factor" or trends – which wax and wane from year to year anyway. This group of buyers is also willing to be a regular purchaser of these items for their collections.

Here is a summary of some of the main reasons that toys are purchased and collected all over the world:

Enjoyment

Toys are fun! People from all age groups and demographics like to play with toys. This often leads to personal attachments and sentimental relationships that can outlast the toys themselves. These feelings are usually shared with children, creating cross-generational demand for certain types of toys.

Wealth Creation

Well-kept toys can offer the potential of strong value appreciation. There is a significant market that focuses on the resale of toy collectibles. Cross-promotion of toys with other popular genres, such as motion pictures, television programs, and the Internet will continue to promote these collectibles in the future.

Decor

Toys are often used as decoration pieces in homes, cars, and office areas. People who may never actually play with a toy, or have not done so since childhood, can be seen displaying an action figure or a PVC in their place of work or play.

Art form

Some toys, especially sculptures produced in limited editions, are wonderful and sought after works of art. The limited runs provide a degree of exclusivity and rarity that attracts art collectors. It is not unusual to have some sort of hand craftsmanship put the final touches on a high-end toy such as the final painting or gloss.

Memories

Toys, like pleasant fragrances, remind people of cherished

Copyright: Marvel
The Vision from *The Avengers* action figure series by Toy Biz.

1966 *Justice League of America* Robin PVC play piece.

childhood memories or other sentimental events. Toys offer a window into the past. They let people remember important feelings and past events. This is true of both men and women who use toys to re-live childhood through their children.

Gaming

Stand-alone toy pieces, like the pieces of a chess set, are increasingly being used in adventure, role-playing games. These are often well-crafted, expensive, and purchased independently.

Market Watch

Toys have remained popular throughout the last decade; even while comic book collecting took a major hit. Many comic book specialty stores suffered

Above:
Copyright: Marvel
Limited edition
porcelain statues of
the *Fantastic Four*.
The Thing and
Invisible Woman
are visible in the
foreground.

Copyright: Marvel
HeroClix game
piece of the Thing
wearing fancy
clothing.

sharp declines in the sale of comic books, but continued to grow overall due to dramatic increases in toy sales. Toy sales have shown strong resilience in several areas:

* *Price Points*: The price point for toy purchases has significantly more tolerance than other collectibles.
* *Sources*: The best selling toys appear to be tied to strong advertising and tie-ins to other media. Television shows and motion pictures continue to have the strongest influence. A successful commercial movie like *Star Wars*, *Shrek*, *Toy Story*, *The Lion King*, *Lord of the Rings*, *Harry Potter* and *Spider-Man* has a dramatic impact on the number of related toys that are sold especially during the holiday season.
* *Resilience*: This hobby enjoys popularity across all age groups and demographics. Toys fit in nicely with just about any lifestyle. Furthermore, changes in the economy do not damage the viability of this market as heavily as other collectibles.
* *Franchises and Licensing*: We continue to see the existence of strong toy franchises like *Lord of the Rings*, *Harry Potter* and *Spider-Man* continue to sell a lot of product. Looking at the future motion picture and television pipeline suggests that this trend will continue.

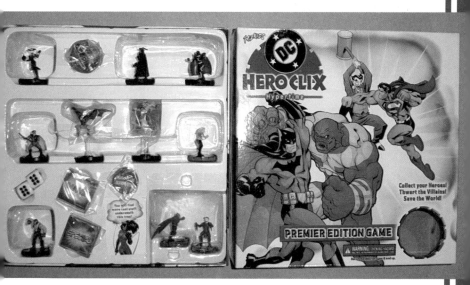

Copyright: DC
Starter HeroClix Premier Edition Game Set.

13

- *Games*: Miniature games have fuelled a strong demand in toys like HeroClix by WizKids. This is a toy and a game at the same time.
- *Video Games*: Toys continue to enjoy cross-product popularity. Strong video game sales promote strong toy sales and vice versa.
- *Retailers*: There has been a strong growth in the number of retailers that only sell toys and are able to increase their year over year sales.
- *Anime/Manga*: Toys based on Japanese animation continue to be very strong sellers.

Copyright: Marvel
Spider-Man action figure from the 1970s (foreign edition).

Above:
Copyright:
Hanna Barbara
PVCs going from
left to right: Dino,
Wilma Flinstone,
Fred Flintstone,
Barney Rubble,
and Betty Rubble
– still popular
almost half a
century after their
first appearance.

Copyright: Marvel
Porcelain statue
of Electra, now
the star of the big
screen starring
Jennifer Garner.

15

Above:
Copyright: McDonalds
Fully assembled Inspector
Gadget premium surround-
ed by the individual packs
that were given out by
McDonalds Restaurants.
In our opinion, this is one
of the best-assembled toys
given out by a restaurant.

Copyright: DC
This is considered to be
an oddity – a plastic bread
wrapper imprinted with
Batman and Robin dating
back to the 1960s.

Chapter 2

What Fans Collect

There are many different types of toys. There are certainly too many to list and price in a single edition of a book. We decided to shorten the scope by segmenting on comic-related toys. There were still too many toy categories to list and price in a single book. We then further segmented the scope of this book to focus on the toy categories that are very hot and are likely to remain hot in the future from a collectibles perspective. Sales in these toy categories are heavily influenced by popular culture. This will continue to drive interest and attention towards these toys regardless of the state of the economy.

There is enough variety in the types of toys available to support an ongoing periodical in this area. Some of the really hot collectible toys in the market are action figures, statues, PVCs, HeroClix, Premiums, and Oddities/Other.

Action Figures

Action figures are among the most popular toys around the world. They are an evolu-tion of dolls with an action-oriented twist. Action figures, as we think of them today, origi-nated in the 1960s with G.I.JOE in 1964 and then with Captain Action in 1966. As one of our colleague's explains, "It wasn't welcomed with open arms as I remember buying my first G.I.JOE in 1964 and being teased by older kids for playing with dolls. This wasn't a cool thing for a boy to do in the 1960s." Time has changed this perception. Action figures are the best selling toys in many age groups. They are used in action play and collected in their origi-nal packaging. People often buy duplicates so they can be stored away in Mint condition until a future date.

Because action figures expe-rience a lot of active play by energetic children, they have to be more durable than items in the other toy categories. These items are designed with move-able limbs, body parts, and torsos. There is a substantial secondary market that includes accessories like guns, swords, and shields for the action figures. With all the active play these toys endure, many of these parts are lost or broken. Children bend, throw and drop action figures so their condition deteriorates very quickly. This happens almost from the time they are purchased and removed from their packaging. It's very scary to see what two small boys can do to the *Incredible Hulk* within an hour.

An irony to consider is that the packaging that is thrown away by excited kids or their tired parents has the potential of being worth 5 times the value of the toy by itself somewhere down the road. The further you go back in time, the more difficult it becomes to find a toy's packaging.

Statues

Statues epitomize the artistic merits of the toy-collecting hobby. They are usually intricately designed and crafted in porcelain with exquisite colors and detail. Collectors often like to display their statue collectibles on mantle pieces, bookcases and desks. Due to limited production runs and the relatively expensive production costs, porcelain statues have shown strong appreciation potential in the past. Because of the increased popularity in this space, we believe there is significant room for future price appreciation. Consider that the average production run for a statue is in the neighborhood of 2000 (plus or minus 500) which

is not very high when considering the potential number of people wanting to purchase it.

PVCs

The PVC is an unbendable plastic figure, which has been around a lot longer than action figures and was better accepted as a play item for boys. They usually had male-based, action-oriented themes such as army men, knights and their horses, cowboys and other super hero characters. In fact, any characters that could fight one another have been the topic of a PVC.

HeroClix

Is it a toy? Is it a game? HeroClix, from WizKids, is really both and has become an ultra-hot collectible. The concept is absolutely brilliant. Based on the popularity of miniatures and role/action playing games, HeroClix figures, built around popular comic book characters, are selling rapidly as collectors buy up their favorite pieces.

HeroClix figures are exactly that-super heroes on a stand that also acts as a clicker. Players manipulate the clicker to gain points, move, attack, defend, and register the extent of damage endured by the piece. This is the key innovation in this piece.

Typically, there are three versions of characters. Each version is recognized by the style of ring that encircles the outer part of the base on which the super hero stands – not by the color of the clicker. This product comes in a starter set that has 10 HeroClixs, maps, rules, dice and everything that you need to play this desktop game. You can then purchase packs that each contain 4 HeroClix toys. The unique versions of the characters are the most valuable ones.

Limited Edition (LE) HeroClixs can only be acquired at conventions or won at tournaments. These are among the rarest of these items and offer the best investment potential.

Players can collect the HeroClix toys separately and keep them as decoration items, or they can opt to use them to participate in game play with others.

Premiums

Premiums, namely fast food premiums, are toys that are given away with some sort of children's meal. Due to the large usage of fast food restaurants, especially in North America, many people have managed

Copyright: Marvel Invisible Woman action figure from the *Marvel Superheroes* Toy Biz series. This item had low distribution and is considered to be a rare item.

to accumulate fast food toy premiums over the years. Not surprisingly, the more rare ones, and the ones corresponding to popular characters are highly sought after collectible items.

Fast food chains typically compete for the rights to hot properties that are usually Disney, Super-Hero, or Anime/Manga based.

Oddities/Other

Many manufactured toys do not fit neatly into one of the other categories. Pricing information is not generally available for these items. We are going to be cataloging as many of these items as possible and allocating prices based on Internet research and store surveys on an ongoing basis.

Copyright: DC
Porcelain statue of Wonder Woman with
exquisite detail in the shields, spears and hair.

Copyright: Marvel
X-Men character PVCs going from left to right:
Rogue, Storm, Marvel Girl, Havoc, Wolverine and Cyclops.

Copyright: DC
DC Deluxe action figure set containing Aquaman, Aqualad and accessories.

Copyright:
Marvel
Three different
HeroClix
versions of
the Invisible
Woman. This
is the only
example of
a character
with three
different
HeroClix
versions at
the time of
publication.

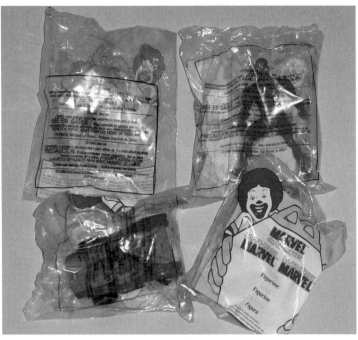

Copyright: Marvel
Superhero toys given away with
children's value meals at McDonalds Restaurants.

Copyright: DC
This is a Batman and Robin stamp set. The left piece is the top cover. This item is considered to be an oddity.

Copyright: Marvel
Limited edition pin set signed by the artist, John Romita, Sr.
This is number 57 out of a set of 1,500 units.

Chapter 3

Ten Basic Survival Rules

There are basic survival rules in all hobbies. These are general guidelines that are designed to help you enjoy the hobby without being taken for a ride or losing money. Here are some basic survival rules, based on many decades of collecting and selling toy collectibles, to help you to maximize your enjoyment, minimize regrets, and make some money along the way in this vibrant hobby:

1. **Enjoy your collection**
2. **Know the intent of a toy purchase**
3. **Never sell when you need money**
4. **Never sell when you lose interest in the hobby**
5. **To create wealth, speculate on "blue chip" items that nobody wants today, but may want tomorrow**
6. **Avoid fad purchases**
7. **Educate yourself on grading toys**
8. **Find a trustworthy dealer**
9. **Protect your collection**
10. **Keep the original packaging intact**

1. Enjoy your collection

This is the first survival rule of any hobby. Enjoying what you do provides immediate and long-term validation that makes other advantages icing on the cake.

2. Know the intent of a toy purchase

If a toy is purchased as a child's plaything, just go ahead and accept this fact and relax. The toy is going to get scratched, broken or damaged in some way. That's okay as long as the toy is allowing a child to have fun. However, if your intent is to generate long-term value, separate the concept of a toy intended for play from the one intended for someone's toy collection. The same toy cannot serve both purposes. Buy more than one of the same toy if you want to do both.

3. Never sell when you need money

No matter what you collect, avoid selling parts of your collection when you need money. Since toys are generally not as liquid as say gold, precious stones, stocks or bonds, and since the prices are certainly not as standardized, your urgency to sell will be inversely proportional to the price you will likely get for your toys. In other words, when you're desperate to sell, you will likely be paid a lower price.

4. Never sell when you lose interest in the hobby

Being human, our interests evolve over periods of time. There will be times when you lose interest in a hobby and may feel that you've outgrown it. Avoid selling your collection during these times. Due to your perceived lack of interest, you may undersell your collection, only to find your interest reawakened in the future. Then you'll have to restock your collection at future, probably higher, prices. We have seen this happen many, many times to many collectors.

5. To create wealth, speculate on "blue chip" items that nobody wants today, but may want tomorrow

There are properties like *Lord of the Rings*, *Spider-Man*, *Batman*, *Superman*, *Bugs Bunny*, *Mickey Mouse* and the *Simpson's* that are likely to remain part of the global popular culture well into the future. Good quality toys based on these properties are likely to remain in demand as well. As more and more people get interested in the property, older toys (with limited availability in good condition) experience a strong growth in demand and

price. Try and find *Bugs Bunny* toys from the 1960s at their original prices. It will be very difficult, if not impossible.

6. Avoid fad purchases

There are always hot items that get a lot of public and media attention and which demand premium prices. Understand the reason why you are buying one of these items. Satisfying a child's interest to own a hot toy may be acceptable. However, as an investment, there may be better places to put your money. Does anyone remember the Pet Rock, Mood Ring, *Rubik's Cube*™, *Cabbage Patch Dolls*™ and *Pokemon*® cards? All of these were ultra-hot collectibles that have since cooled.

7. Educate yourself on grading toys

Grading is a common process in many collectibles-based hobbies. This involves physically inspecting the condition of a toy and assigning it a grade based on its condition. Toys are more difficult to grade than collectibles such as coins, stamps, and comic books as they require the packaging to be graded as well. However, a similar grading legend can be defined in terms of Mint, Near Mint, Fine, Good, Fair and Poor conditions to describe their physical appearance.

8. Find a trustworthy dealer

The best contact you can have in any collecting hobby is a trustworthy, honest, fair dealer.

Let the dealer make a fair profit, but demand fair pricing, accurate grading, access to excellent collectibles and great overall service in return.

9. Protect your collection

Some toys can break, shatter, scratch, tarnish or experience other physical problems that reduce its condition and attractiveness. This reduces its value. If your intent is to assemble a valuable collection, take the time to protect it from being damaged by the elements, repeated handling and curious pets.

10. Keep the original packaging intact

If you are assembling a toy collection, try to keep a purchase in its original packaging. If you want to remove it, be careful to preserve the packaging and store it in a safe place. Packaging is an important part of the future potential value of a collectible. It will be worth more in its original packaging or if sold alongside it.

Copyright: DC
PVC characters from the 1960s *Justice League of America* set.
Pictured are Flash, Aquaman, Superman and Wonder Woman.

Above:
Copyright: Marvel
PVCs of two of
the strongest
super heroes in
the Marvel
universe-Thor
and the Hulk.

Copyright: DC
DC Direct Green
Lantern and Green
Lantern Corps
action figures.

27

Chapter 4

Where to Buy and Sell Toys

Toys are available from various sources. The table below identifies some of the channels that carry toys and suggests the type of advantage that a particular channel offers to a buyer or collector. A legend explaining the various symbols used in the columns follows the table.

The following are terms for the many attributes that determine the value of your overall experience in the hobby. Specialty stores that cater to specific hobbies (like comic book stores or toy stores) appear to offer a consistent advantage over the other channels. The remaining channels offer specific advantages that might be appropriate for you at any particular point in time.

	Quality Advantage	Price Advantage	Convenience & Availability	Selection Depth & Breadth	Trust/ Reliability	Returnable/ Exchanges
Department Stores	◆	◆	●	◆	●	●
Specialty Stores	●	●	●	●	●	●
Toy Conventions	○	●	○	●	◆	○
Online Auctions	○	●	○	●	○	○
Online Sources	○	◆	◆	◆	◆	○
Mail Order	○	○	◆	◆	○	◆
Flea Markets	○	●	◆	○	○	◆
Garage Sale	○	●	○	○	○	○
Newspaper Ads	○	◆	○	○	○	◆

Legend:

○ – offers no major advantage   ◆ – offers a slight advantage over other channels
● – offers a significant advantage over other channels

Following is a brief description of the channels that sell toy products from the leftmost column of the preceding table:

Quality Advantage:
Refers to the overall quality and integrity of the product. The toy should be free of scratches, damage, and stress marks right out of the box. Are you safe to have the expectation that the product packaging is in mint condition as well?

Price Advantage:
Ability to purchase the product at a steep discount off the retail price or at less than the current market value of the item.

Convenience and Availability:
Availability of the channel to meet customer needs. Are products available at different times of the day or on the weekends? How easy is it to find sellers in this channel (e.g. department store)? Are sellers located in convenient locations?

Selection Depth and Breadth:
Refers to the variety of product category that is available through the channel. Are you given the opportunity to buy a wide range of items produced in this product category or is the selection limited?

Trust/Reliability:
What level of trust do you have in what you are buying? Can you depend on the seller to be honest about what you're buying?

Returnable/Exchanges:
Will the channel accept returns or at least offer an exchange in the event that you are dissatisfied with your purchase for any reason?

Department Stores
These are general retail stores that sell a variety of products. Toys are one of the products that are sold. Department stores generally stock current products only.

Specialty Stores
These are stores that focus on selling toys especially those dealing with comic book characters. These stores offer a diverse variety of toys that can date back many, many decades.

Toy Conventions
Toy conventions are organized in major cities across the world by toy fans and related organizations every year. These offer a good opportunity to meet with toy distributors, other fans and possibly locate many hard-to-find items.

Online Auctions
There are Internet sites such as eBay® that allow sellers and buyers from around the world to meet in a common bazaar. The anonymity of this channel creates some unique challenges that buyers and

sellers must keep in mind when transacting business (e.g. don't send cash through the mail).

Online Sources

There are many websites managed by retailers that offer a diverse group of toy products for sale or trade. Again, specific precautions should be taken to ensure quality and delivery of product when dealing over the Internet, especially with someone that is new to you.

Mail Order

Mail order is a traditional sales channel that is usually found through print advertisements in trade magazines. Specific precautions, such as not sending cash through the mail, should be taken when transacting business through this channel.

Flea Markets

There are flea markets in cities and towns all over the world that offer a chance to buy toys at various prices. Frequenting a few flea markets opens up the possibility of finding some rare items at a good price. Many different collectors and buyers pass through flea markets each week so the transaction volumes are quite large opening up the possibility of finding some really fine collectibles.

Garage Sales

Garage sales are a good place to find toys that may have more intrinsic value than what you're being asked to pay. However, the results are unpredictable. Auctions are similar to garage sales in terms of potentially being able to secure a great bargain. Again, there are no guarantees. You could end up spending a lot of unproductive time in this pursuit. However, if you enjoy the hobby, you may be able to justify the time spent on these activities. We do know examples of collectors who have enjoyed 1000:1 returns in both of these cases.

Newspaper Ads

Good deals or rare products can show up in newspaper advertisements. Dealers or other private collectors that may want to sell items place these ads. You may be able to negotiate a good price depending on the response the seller is getting to the advertisement and their need to sell. Note that some collectors also advertise to purchase collections, thus giving you a potential sell opportunity. You can also place an ad to sell your own collections possibly giving you an opportunity to sell your product at a higher margin than if you sold to a toy dealer who must pay overhead to stay in business.

Be careful NOT to meet with strangers in places that can compromise your safety. Take reasonable precautions to protect your person when making an appointment to view someone's private collection.

Copyright: DC
DC *Super Powers* videos which are difficult to find in any condition.

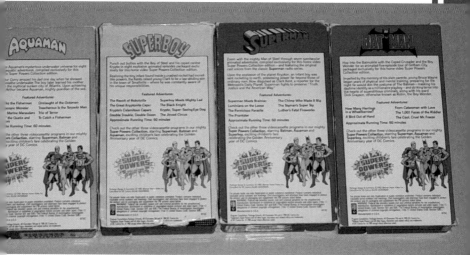

Copyright: DC
DC *Super Powers* video flip sides.

Where to Buy Toys

You can buy toys from a variety of different sources. Some provide a potential quality advantage, others offer price advantages, and still others offer convenience. The following table cross-references various toy categories from this book to the channels that can best source them.

	Action Figures	PVCs	HeroClix	Statues	Premiums	Oddities/ Other
Department Stores	●	●	○	○	○	●
Specialty Stores	●	●	●	●	●	●
Toy Conventions	●	●	●	●	●	●
Online Auctions	●	●	●	●	●	●
Online Sources	●	●	●	●	●	●
Mail Order	●	●	○	○	○	●
Flea Markets	●	●	○	○	○	●
Garage Sale	●	○	○	○	○	●
Newspaper Ads	●	○	○	○	○	●

Legend:
● – generally considered to be a good source to buy these types of items
○ – generally not considered to be a good source for this type of item

Where to Sell Toys

For a variety of reasons, the channels that sell toys to you are not always in a position to buy them back at a later point. Department stores, for example, are geared up to sell you a reasonable selection of toys at predictable prices. However, they cannot buy toys back at a higher value. For this, you need to access the reseller markets. The following table identifies the channels that are available to you to resell toys at a potentially higher value than you paid to acquire them.

There are many reasons people sell items from their

Copyright: DC Interesting items can be found for sale on the Internet like this Batman window prop.

Copyright: DC
Garage sales offer a good venue for finding interesting items like this Batman and Robin board game. Unfortunately, items can be soiled, damaged, and have missing pieces.

collections – hopefully a profit. Before you start selling your collection, revisit the 10 survival rules mentioned earlier in the book to ensure that you are doing this for the right reasons and positioning yourself to get the best prices possible.

	Action Figures	PVCs	HeroClix	Statues	Premiums	Oddities/ Other
Department Stores	O	O	O	O	O	O
Specialty Stores	●	●	●	●	●	●
Toy Conventions	♦	♦	♦	♦	♦	♦
Online Auctions	●	●	●	●	●	●
Online Sources	♦	♦	♦	♦	♦	♦
Mail Order	O	O	O	O	O	O
Flea Markets	♦	♦	♦	♦	♦	♦
Garage Sale	O	O	O	O	O	O
Newspaper Ads	♦	♦	♦	♦	♦	♦

Legend:
O – generally not considered to be a good source to sell items from your toy collection
♦ – this market is worth exploring
● – generally considered to be a good market to try and sell your toy collection

Grading Toys

Grading toys is fundamentally different and more complicated than grading items in other collectibles-related hobbies like comic books, stamps and coins. Toys, by their very nature, are very different from each other in material, shapes and sizes. You also need to include the condition of the original packaging in the overall grade. The age of the toy is very important. The physical condition of the packaging on older toys is more important than the condition of the toy.

It is necessary to broaden the definitions of standard terms like Mint, Near Mint, Fine, and Good to have a broad-

Grading Table: Physical Imperfections	Mint	Near Mint	Fine	Good	Fair	Poor
Any physical characteristic that detracts from the original appearance of the toy		●	●	●	●	●
Small imperfections		●	●	●	●	●
Small rips along the surface of the toy			●	●	●	●
Color loss on the toy surface or its pieces			●	●	●	●
Wear and tear on the surface			●	●	●	●
Stress lines on the surface of the toy			●	●	●	●
Soiling of the fabric or materials				●	●	●
Noticeable impact on the surface of the toy					●	●
Extensive damage to the toy, missing parts, missing accessories						●

The condition or existence of the original packaging impacts the combined grade based on the age of the item. The exact ratios are shown in the pricing section of this guide.

er scope as shown in the following table. Notice that a toy in Mint condition cannot exhibit any of the imperfections shown in the first column of the table.

Using the Grading Table:

Use this table as you physically inspect a toy that you are grading. Start at the bottom of the list of imperfections (the leftmost column in the table). If that imperfection is visible in the toy being inspected, move your eye or finger horizontally to the right in the row until you reach the filled in circle. Move your eye to the column heading to get the grade for the toy being inspected.

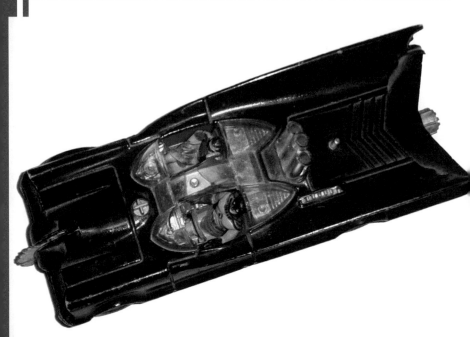

Top view of a die-cast Batmobile from the 1960s. The overall quality of this item looks high, but cannot be determined until the other sides are examined.

A side view shows that all the wheel decals are in place and the wire cutter at the front is fully extendable. The wheels still rotate smoothly.

A red knob is missing on the rocket launcher meaning that this item cannot be considered to be in mint condition.

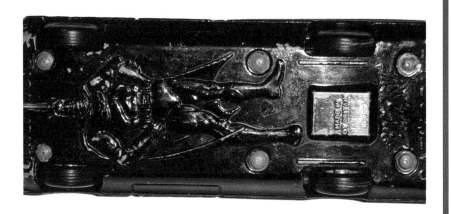

A bottom view of the Batmobile shows that the Batman figure is still visible, but with some paint starting to chip. Overall grade for this item considering the different views of the Batmobile is Fine (F).

Chapter 5

Protecting Your Collection

Many hobbies consist of collecting and reselling fragile items. For example, comic books, silverware, leather books, stamps, ceramics, and paintings can all get damaged quite easily. Comic books can get ripped with a simple flip of the finger, silverware gets tarnished without any human contact, and ceramics can break when someone is trying to move the object. For the most part, however, most of these objects are designed to be used a few times or not all and can be stored away in a safe, dry environment for long periods of time.

Toys, on the other hand, are generally sold with the knowledge that they are going to be used in active play by one or more children until the toy is either broken or outdated. This means that there is going to be a lot of physical handling and touching of the toys. It is unrealistic to expect toys that are played with to remain in Mint condition. This introduces some unique challenges that have to be considered if you view your collection as a potential investment that will appreciate in value over time. This section provides some considerations for toy collectors to safeguard their toy collections.

Common Dangers

There are general hazards that can hurt the quality and value of a toy, as shown in the following table.

Activity	Hazard
Buying	Bending, ripping, folding
Playing	Breaking, tearing, scratching, losing
Storing	Bending or breaking
Displaying	Getting too dusty, being knocked down
General Hazards	Light, moisture, heat

Copyright: Marvel
Normal handling easily damages paper items such as these TV guides and other forms of packaging.

Copyright: Marvel
Statues with extensive workmanship are nice to look at, but extensions like the pole in this porcelain bisque are delicate and easily broken by even small amounts of force or movement.

Copyright: Marvel
Dust on a statue, like the one shown of Iron Man, can generally be dusted off; however, the statue can be damaged while being handled and swiped with a cloth. The dust can also begin to merge with the paint on the base of the statue. The fingertips on this item can break very easily.

Exposures by Toy Category

In addition to general hazards shown in the previous table, each toy category has an affinity for certain types of problems as shown in the following table.

Toy Category	Hazards
Action Toys	Getting bent out of shape. Loss of limbs. Loss of accessories and other pieces. Getting chewed up by a pet or a child. Joints become very loose.
PVCs	Getting chewed up by a pet or a child.
HeroClix	Fragile bases that are exposed by repeated play. Fragile pieces.
Statues	Often made from fragile and breakable materials like porcelain or glass. Should not be played with, but stored in a safe place.
Premiums	Generally given away at places like restaurants, so they often get soiled by food or get lost on the way home.
Oddities/Other	These are often one-off items that are neglected or misplaced. Since they do not always fit nicely into a collectible box or area, they can be difficult to store safely.

This is the proper way to store toys. Individual items are in their original packaging and stacked in a cupboard without the risk of tipping over or falling.

Highly breakable Burger King premium drinking glasses with characters from *Star Wars Episode V.* "The Empire Strikes Back" stamped on the side.

Copyright: Marvel
The craftsmanship on this statue of Phoenix (A.K.A. Jean Gray)
is beautiful, but the edges can snap off quite easily.

Copyright:
An army of unprotected HeroClix-an accident waiting to happen.

42

Protecting Toys

Protecting a toy collection involves several different activities that are discussed in this section:

Safe Handling

If you want to keep the toy as a part of a high quality collection, learn to handle it properly as you would a child – no jerky movements, no moisture on your hands, no food nearby.

Proper and Safe Storage

Safe and proper storage of a toy means the following activities:

* Keep the toy in its original packaging if possible.
* Wrap the toy in additional acid free sleeves, folders, or containers if more protection is required.

* Store in a safe, dry, cool place. Keep a regular check on the collection to ensure its safety.
* Seal away from animals, insects, little children or other things that can damage the collection.

Toy Insurance

Insurance against common hazards should be considered. It tends to be expensive when you're talking about a lot of different toys, but if you have a couple of key, expensive items, it might be worth looking into. Some toys will be covered under a portion of your homeowner's policy.

Copyright: DC
Action figures and accessories protected in their original packaging.

Copyright: Marvel HeroClix protected in its original packaging, but can still be damaged if something heavy is placed on top of it.

Below: Not a recommended way to store a toy collection. There is no protection for the toys from rough handling, loose pets and rambunctious children.

Chapter 6

Price Guide

This section contains prices for individual toys in the following six categories, as discussed earlier in this book:

A. Action Figures
B. HeroClix
C. PVCs
D. Statues (Porcelain)
E. Fast Food Premiums
F. Oddities

Our prices are based on information obtained from the Internet, retail stores, and distributors at the time of publication.

Prices are quoted for toys in Near Mint condition with similar original packaging. Apply the following factors to the price shown if the toy has the corresponding physical grade:

Grade	Multiplication Factor
Mint	1.25
Near Mint	1.0
Fine	0.6
Good	0.3
Fair	0.15
Poor	0.05

The condition or existence of the original packaging impacts the combined grade based on the age of the item, as shown in the following table:

	Pre 1980	1980-1987	1987-present
No packaging available	Value drops 50%	Value drops 65%	Value drops 80%
Packaging is damaged	Degree of damage to package impacts the price	Degree of damage to package impacts the price	Degree of damage to package impacts the price

A. Category: Action Figures

This section contains pricing information on action figures and related accessories:

Copyright: DC
Assorted Superhero action figures from the *Super Powers* collection.

Below:
Copyright: Marvel
Two different versions of Wolverine from the *X-Men* Toy Biz series.

Alpha Flight (Marvel)
Toy Biz 1999

Northstar and Aurora	$12
Sasquatch and Vindicator	$12
Snowbird and Puck	$12

Avengers: Earth's Mightiest Heroes (Marvel)
Toy Biz 1997

Iron Man	$10
Loki	$10
Scarlet Witch	$10
The Mighty Thor	$28

Avengers: United They Stand (Marvel)
Toy Biz 1999

Ant-Man	$7.50
Captain America	$15
Falcon	$7.50
Hawkeye	$7.50
Kang	$5
Tigra	$5
Ultron	$5
Vision	$7.50
Wasp	$7.50
Wonder Man	$7.50

Avengers: United They Stand–Shape Shifters (Marvel)
Toy Biz 1999

Ant-Man	$9
Captain America	$10
Hawkeye	$9
Thor	$10

Avengers: United They Stand (Marvel)
Accessories
Toy Biz 1999

Air Glider	$15
Sky Cycle	$15

Batman: The Adventures of Batman and Robin (DC)
Kenner 1996

Bane	$9
Batman, Hover Jet	$25
Batman, Paraglide	$28
Batman, Rocketpack	$25
Joker, Pogo Stick	$10
Ra's Al Ghul	$9
Robin, Bola Trap	$18

Batman: The Adventures of Batman and Robin (DC)
Kenner 1997

Harley Quinn	$22
Joker (Machine Gun)	$25
Accessories 1996	
Nightsphere (figure included)	
	$72

Batman: The Adventures of Batman and Robin – Crime Squad (DC)
Kenner 1996

Batman, Bomb Control	$35
Batman, Disaster Control	$32
Batman, Fast Pursuit	$20
Batman, Skycorter Deluxe	$50
Batman, Supersonic	$22
Batman, Tri-wing Deluxe	$35

Batman: The Adventures of Batman and Robin–Duo Force (DC)
Kenner

Batgirl, Wind Blitz	$20
Batman, Cycle Thruster	$9
Batman, Turbo Surge	$18
Batman, Vector Wing	$18
Mr. Freeze	$12
Riddler, Roto Chopper	$12
Robin, Air Strike	$18
Robin, Hydro Storm	$9

Copyright: Marvel
The Wasp action figure
from *The Avengers* Toy
Biz series.

Copyright: Marvel
The Mighty Thor is a
founding member of
The Avengers.

Opposite page:
Copyright: DC
Batman action figure
with standard costume.

Copyright: DC
Batman action figure
wearing a non-stan-
dard uniform.

Copyright: DC
Poison Ivy and Frostbite action figures.

49

Batman: The Animated Series (DC)
Kenner 1992

Batman, Combat Belt	$60
Batman, Turbojet	$30
Penguin	$95
Robin	$30
Two Face	$35
Accessories	
Aerobat	$30
B.A.T.V. Vehicle	$30
Bat Signal Jet	$30
Batcycle	$28
Batmobile	$45
Crime Stalker	$25
Hoverbat Vehicle	$28
Robin Dragster	$395
Turbo Batplane	$95

Batman: The Animated Series (DC)
Kenner 1993

Batman, Infrared	$22
Batman, Sky Dive	$22
Bruce Wayne	$22
Catwoman	$30
Joker	$30
Manbat	$22
Ninja Robin	$22
Scarecrow	$28
Accessories	
Batcave	$175
Street Jet (figure included)	$75

Batman: The Animated Series (DC)
Kenner 1994

Batman, Anti Freeze	$18
Batman, Ground Assault Deluxe	$28
Batman, High Wire Deluxe	$40
Batman, Knight Star	$18
Batman, Lightning Strike	$18
Batman, Mech Wing Deluxe	$28

Batman, Ninja and Robin (2 Pack)	$25
Batman, Power Vision Deluxe	$28
Batman, Rapid Attack	$25
Batman, Tornado	$25
Clay Face	$18
Dick Grayson	$18
Killer Croc	$18
Mr. Freeze	$25
Poison Ivy	$30
Accessories	
Batman (16in [41cm])	$65
Ice Hammer	$18

Batman: The Animated Series (DC)
Kenner 1995

Bane	$20
Batman, Cyber Gear	$32
Batman, Radar Scope	$32
Robin, Glider	$22

Batman: The Animated Series–Crime Squad (DC)
Kenner 1995

Batman, Air Assault	$20
Batman, Land Strike	$20
Batman, Piranha Blade	$32
Batman, Sea Claw	$30
Batman, Stealthwing	$30
Batman, Torpedo	$20
Robin, Ski Blast	$25
Accessories	
Batcycle	$25
Triple Attack Jet	$35

Batman: Batman and Robin (DC)
Kenner 1997

Bane	$8
Batgirl	$10
Batgirl, Icestrike Cycle Deluxe	$35

Batman, Blast Wing
Deluxe $16
Batman, Heat Scan $8
Batman, Hover Attack $8
Batman, Rooftop Pursuit
Deluxe $16
Bruce Wayne, Battle Gear $9
Mr. Freeze, Ice Blast $8
Mr. Freeze, Ice Terror
Deluxe $16
Poison Ivy, Jungle Venom $9
Robin, Blast Wing $16
Robin, Glacier Battle $16
Robin, Iceboard $8
Robin, Razor Skate $8
Robin, Redbird Cycle $30

Batman: Batman and Robin (DC)
Kenner 1998

Batman, Ambush Attack $12
Batman, Ice Blade $12
Batman, Neon Armor $12
Batman, Snowtracker $15
Batman, Wing Blast $12
Frostbite $18
Mr. Freeze, Sonic Blast $22
Robin, Blade Blast $15
Robin, Talon $12
Robin, Triple Strike $12

Batman: Batman and Robin – with Batman Ring (DC)
Kenner 1998

Batman, Battle Board $14
Batman, Ice Bade $18
Batman, Laser Cape $14
Batman, Neon Armor $15
Batman, Rotor Blade $14
Batman, Sky Assault $18
Batman, Thermal Shield $14
Batman, Wingblast $14
Mr. Freeze, Jet Wing $22
Mr. Freeze, Ultimate Armor $22

Robin, Attack Wing $14
Robin, Talon Strike $18
Robin, Triple Strike $20
Accessories
Batcave Wayne Manor $65
Batgirl 12in (31cm) $45
Batman 12in (31cm) $38
Batman VS Poison Ivy
12in (31cm) $48
Batman, Ultimate $42
Batmobile $28
Cryo Freeze Chamber $18
Ice Fortress $18
Ice Hammer $20
Jet Blades $22
Mr. Freeze 12in (31cm) $38
Nightsphere $28
Robin 12in (31cm) $38
Robin, Ultimate $42
Sonic Batmobile $28

Batman: Batman Beyond (DC)
Kenner 1999+

Batman, Ballistic Blade $10
Batman, Bat-Hang $10
Batman, Covert $10
Batman, Energy Strike $10
Batman, Future Armor $10
Batman, Future Knight $12
Batman, Hydro Force $10
Batman, Justice Flight
(200th) $18
Batman, Laser $12
Batman, Lightning Storm $10
Batman, Manta Racer $10
Batman, Neon-Como
Deluxe $15
Batman, Power Armor $10
Batman, Shatterblast $10
Batman, Sonar Strike $12
Batman, Strato Defense
Deluxe $15

Batman, Strikecycle Deluxe $15
Batman, Surface to Air
   Deluxe $15
Batman, Thunderwhip $12
Batman, Tomorrow Armor
   Deluxe $15
Blight $20
J's Gang Power Throw $15
The Joker $22
Accessories
Batmobile $25

Batman: Batman Beyond –
Batlink (DC)
Kenner 2000
Batman, Circuitry $7
Batman, Codebuster $7
Batman, Energy Surge
   (CD ROM) $7
Batman, Mainframe Attack $7
Batman, Particle Burst $7
Batman, Power Grid $7
Batman, Search Engine $7
Joker, Virtual $10
Robin, Firewall $10

Batman: Batman Beyond –
Return of the Joker (DC)
Kenner 2001
Batman, Golden Armor
   Deluxe $9
Batman, Gotham Defender $7
Batman, Gotham Night $7
Bruce Wayne, Rapid Switch $8
Joker, Arkham Assault $7
Accessories
Batman 13in (33cm) $15
Batman Retractable Batrope
   9in (23cm) $18
Batman, Afterburner
   11in (28cm) $12
Net Escape Playset $12
Net Runner Batmobile $18
Virtual Bat $12

Batman: Batman Returns
(DC)
Kenner 1992
Batman, Air Attack $32
Batman, Arctic $32
Batman, Bola Strike (Tru) $38
Batman, Claw Climber (Tru) $38
Batman, Crime Attack $32
Batman, Deep Dive $32
Batman, Laser $32
Batman, Polar Blast (Tru) $38
Batman, Power Wing $32
Batman, Shadow Wing $32
Batman, Sky-Winch $32
Batman, Thunderwhip $32
Bruce Wayne $35
Catwoman $32
Penguin $35
Penguin Commandos $20
Robin $30
Accessories
All-Terrain Batskiboat $60
Bat Cave Command Center $95
Batmobile $325
Bruce Wayne Custom Coupe $45
Jetfoil Robin $35
Laser Blade Cycle $40
Penguin Umbrella Jet $45
Sky Drop Airship $50
Skyblade $85
Turbo Jet Batwing $120

Batman: Batman Returns
(DC)
Kenner 1993
Batman, Aero Strike $25
Batman, Fire Bolt Deluxe $60
Batman, Rocket Blast Deluxe
   $60

Batman: Batman Returns
(DC)
Kenner 1994
Batman 16in (41cm) $45

Batman, Hydro Charge	$18		

Batman, Hydro Charge $18
Batman, Jungle Tracker $20
Batman, Night Climber $18
Batman, Toxic Guard $18
Accessories
Camo Attack Batmobile $125

Batman: Dark Knight (DC)
Kenner 1990
Batman, Crime Attack $22
Batman, Iron Winch $22
Batman, Tech-Shield $25
Batman, Wall Scaler $22
Bruce Wayne $22
Joker, Sky Escape $30
Accessories
Batcycle $30
Batcopter $75
Batjet $65
Batmobile $250
Batwing $125
Joker Cycle $30

Batman: Dark Knight (DC)
Kenner 1991
Batman, Blast Shield
   Deluxe $40
Batman, Claw Climber
   Deluxe $40
Batman, Night Glider
   Deluxe $45
Batman, Power Wing $32
Batman, Thunder Whip $32
Joker, Knock-out $52
Accessories
Armor Set $38
Batarang Blaster $48
Bola Bullet $22
Crime Control Set $38
Sky Blade $60
Sonic Neutralizer $20
Strike-Wing $25

Batman: Forever 1 (DC)
Kenner 1995
Batman, Blast Cape $18
Batman, Fireguard $18
Batman, Manta Ray $18
Batman, Night Hunter $18
Batman, Sonar Sensor $18
Bruce Wayne $25
Dick Grayson (eyes/no eyes) $20
Riddler $15
Robin, Hydro Claw $15
Robin, Street Biker $15
Two Face $15

Batman: Forever 2 (DC)
Kenner
Batman, Attack Wing
   Deluxe $15
Batman, Batarang $12
Batman, Iceblade $12
Batman, Laser Discs
   Deluxe $15
Batman, Light Wing
   Deluxe $15
Batman, Neon Armor $12
Batman, Night Flight $12
Batman, Power Beacon $12
Batman, Recon Hunter $12
Batman, Solar Shield $12
Batman, Street Racer $12
Batman, Wind Blast $12
Riddler (black/green highlights)
   $14
Robin, Martial Arts Deluxe $15
Robin, Skyboard $10
Robin, Talking Deluxe $17
Robin, Triple Strike $10
Accessories
Batboat $28
Batcave $75
Batmobile $50
Batwing $38
Power Center, Batman $15
Power Center, Riddler $15

Robin Cycle	$16	*Batman: Legends of*	
Triple Action Vehicle	$50	*Batman* (DC)	
Wayne Manor	$75	Kenner 1996	

Batman: Knight Force Ninja (DC)
Kenner 1998

Batman VS Catwoman			
12in (31cm)			$38
Batman, Buccaneer			$10
Azrael	$13	Batman, Egyptian VS	
Batman and Joker	$20	Egyptian Catwoman	$22
Batman, Arsenal	$12	Batman, Energy Surge	
Batman, Fist Fury	$12	Deluxe	$85
Batman, Knight Blade	$12	Batman, Gladiator	$10
Batman, Knight Warrior	$12	Batman, Knight Quest	
Batman, Street Warrior	$12	14in (36cm)	$38
Batman, Thunder Kick	$12	Batman, Pirate VS Pirate	
Killer Croc	$15	Two Face	$22
Riddler	$15	Batman, Ultra Armor	$18
Robin, Hyper Crush	$14	Joker, Laughing Man	$12
Robin, Martial Arts	$13	Robin, First Mate	$12
Accessories		**Accessories**	
Batmobile	$25	Batcycle (figure included)	$35
Wal-Mart Batmobile		Batmobile (no flames)	$30
(figure included)	$40	Batmobile (with flames)	$60
		Skybat	$35

Batman: Legends of
Batman (DC)
Kenner 1994

Batman: Legends of
Batman (DC)
Warner Brothers Exclusive 1

Batcycle (figure included)	$25	Batman, Crusader	$20
Batman, Crusader	$22	Batman, Cyborg	$20
Batman, Cyborg	$18	Batman, Future	$20
Batman, Dark Rider	$18	Batman, Knight Quest	$20
Batman, Future	$18	Batman, Power Guardian	$20
Batman, Knightquest	$24	Nightwing	$22
Batman, Power Guardian	$18		
Catwoman	$18	*Batman: Legends of*	
Joker	$18	*Batman* (DC)	
Nightwing	$18	Warner Brothers Exclusive 2	

Batman: Legends of
Batman (DC)
Kenner 1995

Batman, Knightsend			$20
Batman, Long Bow			$20
Batman, Samurai			$20
Batman, Viking			$20
Batman, Dark Warrior	$18	Riddler	$22
Batman, Long Bow	$18	Robin, Crusader	$22
Robin, Crusader	$18		

Batman: Legends of Batman (DC)
Warner Brothers Exclusive 3

Batman, Buccaneer	$12
Batman, Dark Warrior	$12
Batman, Gladiator	$12
Catwoman	$14
Joker	$12
Robin, First Mate	$14

Batman: Legends of the Dark Knight (DC)
Kenner

Bane, Lethal Impact	$30
Batman, Assault Gauntlet	$28
Batman, Neural Claw	$28
Batman, Spline Cape	$28
Robin, Dive Claw brown or black hair	$32
Scarecrow	$30
Accessories	
Skywing Street Bike	$40

Batman: Legends of the Dark Knight (DC)
Kenner 1997

Batman, Bat Attack	$22
Batman, Glacier Shield	$22
Catwoman	$25
Joker, Laughing Gas	$25

Batman: Legends of the Dark Knight (DC)
Kenner 1998

Batgirl	$42
Batman, Dark Knight	$50
Batman, Lava Fury	$22
Batman, Under Water Assault	$18
Manbat	$22
Penguin	$22
Robin, Jungle Rage	$22

Batman: Mask of the Phantasm—The Animated Movie (DC)
Kenner 1994

Batman, Decoy	$22
Batman, Rapid Attack	$22
Batman, Retro	$35
Batman, Tornado	$22
Batman, Total Armor	$25
Joker, Jet Pack (face green)	$25
Joker, Jet Pack (face white)	$30
Phantasm	$35

Batman: Spectrum of the Bat (DC)
Hasbro 2001

Batgirl, Sonic Stun	$10
Batman, Gama Blast	$6
Batman, Infrared Armor	$6
Batman, Ultra Frequency	$6
Batman, Ultra Violet Ambush	$6
Jervis Tetch, Technocast	$6
Joker, Terrocast	$8
Robin, Sub-Pulse Detonator	$15
Robin, X-Ray Assailant	$10

Batman: The New Batman Adventures (DC)
Kenner 1997

Batman, Detective	$48
Mad Hatter	$28
Night Wing, Crime Solver	$30
Robin, Crime Fighter	$28

Batman: The New Batman Adventures (DC)
Kenner 1998

Batman, Knight Glider	$15
Batman, Steel Strike	$9
Bruce Wayne	$9
Joker, Wild Card	$15
Night Wing, Force Shield	$12
The Creeper	$9

Batman: The New Batman Adventures 12in (31cm) (DC)
Kenner
Batgirl	$25
Batman	$60
Harley Quinn	$22
Joker	$50
Nightwing	$22
Robin	$22

Accessories
Batmobile	$45
Joker's Toxic Lab	$18
Knightstriker (Batmobile)	$32
Team Bat Cycle	$18

Batman: The New Batman Adventures–Mission Masters 1 (DC)
Hasbro 1997+
Batman, Anti Blaze	$15
Batman, Cave Climber	$15
Batman, Desert Attack	$15
Batman, Glider Strike	$16
Batman, Jungle Tracker	$16
Batman, Silver Defender Deluxe	$20
Batman, Slalom	$15
Batman, Speedboat	$16
Mr. Freeze, Insect Body	$17
Nightwing, Hydrojet	$22
Riddler, Rumble Ready	$16
Robin, Arctic Blast	$20

Mission Masters 2 (DC)
Hasbro
Batman, Infrared	$10
Batman, Knight Strike	$10
Batman, Land Strike	$10
Batman, Radar Deluxe	$15
Batman, Sea Claw	$10
Batman, Skychopper Deluxe	$15
Joker, Hydro Assault	$12
Robin, Arctic Ambush	$12

Mission Masters 3 (DC)
Hasbro
Batman, Anti Virus (Bruce Wayne) Deluxe	$14
Batman, Capture Cape	$10
Batman, Firewing Deluxe	$14
Batman, Freestyle Deluxe	$14
Batman, Gotham Crusader	$10
Batman, Ground Pursuit	$10
Batman, Highwire Zip-Line	$10
Batman, Inferno Extinction	$10
Batman, Knight Assault	$10
Batman, Mountain Pursuit	$10
Batman, Quick Attack	$10
Batman, Sky Attack	$10
Batman, Virus Delete	$10
Mr. Freeze, Virus Attack	$12

Mission Masters 4 (DC)
Hasbro
Batman, Lunar Attack	$6
Batman, Midnight Hunter	$6
Batman, Midnight Pursuit Deluxe	$10
Batman, Night Shadow	$6
Batman, Shadow Blast Deluxe	$10
Batman, Shadow Chopper Deluxe	$10
Mr. Freeze, Rocket Blast	$7
Nightwing, Turbo Force Deluxe	$10
Robin, Night Fury	$7

Accessories
B.A.T.V.	$12
Hoverbat	$10
Night Fury-Night Shadow Multi Pack	$15

Batman (DC)
Shadowcast Batcave	$60
Shadowcast Batmobile	$25
Shadowcast Batplane	$25
Team Batcycle	$20

Copyright: DC
Nightwing, formerly
known as Robin the
Boy Wonder.

Below:
Copyright: DC
Assorted Batman
action figures.

57

Copyright: DC
The Joker Cycle

Copyright: DC
Two different Robin action figures.

Captain Action
Ideal 1966

	Mint No Box	Mint Box
Aquaman	$425	$950
Batman	$495	$1250
Buck Rogers	$495	$1800
Captain Action	$295	$850
Captain America	$495	$1200
Dr. Evil	$295	$750
Flash Gordon	$295	$895
Green Hornet	$1500	$4995
Lone Ranger (blue shirts)	$500	$1800
Lone Ranger (red shirt)	$295	$950
Phantom	$295	$895
Sgt. Fury	$295	$825
Spider-Man	$1500	$8500
Steve Canyon	$295	$825
Superman	$495	$1250
Tonto	$395	$1250

DC Direct Action Figures (DC)
1999 Release

Alfred E. Neuman	$20
Death	$15
Plastic Man	$15
Plastic Man Variant (with hammer and wrench)	$20
Preacher	$15
Sandman	$18
Sandman with Mask	$45
Spider Jerusalem	$15
Spy VS Spy Black Spy	$15
Spy VS Spy White Spy	$15
Starman	$18
Wonder Woman	$30
Wonder Woman with axe	$46

DC Direct
2000 Release

Black Canary (Hard-Traveling Heroes)	$15
Demon	$15
Golden Age JSA Flash	$25
Golden Age JSA Green Lantern	$22
Golden Age JSA Starman	$22
Golden Age JSA Wonder Woman	$30
Green Arrow (Hard-Traveling Heroes)	$15
Green Lantern-Hal Jordan (Hard-Traveling Heroes)	$15
Hellblazer (Mages, Mystics & Magicians)	$15
Impulse	$15
JLA Amazo (Amazing Androids)	$15
JLA Hourman (Amazing Androids)	$17
JLA Tomorrow Woman (Amazing Androids)	$15
JSA Dr. Fate (Mages, Mystics & Magicians)	$25
JSA Spectre (Mages, Mystics & Magicians)	$18
Kid Flash (New Teen Titans)	$15

Copyright: DC
Star Sapphire DC
Direct action figure.
She is a villain for
those who don't
know.

Copyright: DC
DC Direct action figure
of Power Girl. Some
say she is as strong as
Superman or at least
Superboy.

Copyright: DC
Golden Age Sandman
action figure from the
Justice Society.

Copyright: DC
Saturn Girl action
figure from the
*Legion of
Superheroes*.

61

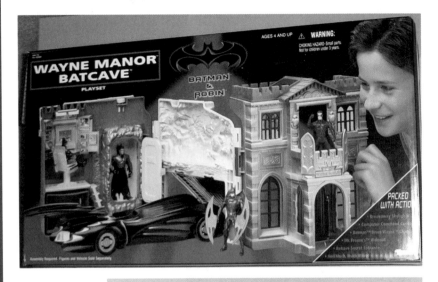

Above:
Copyright:
DC
The Batcave
to be used
with action
figures from
DC Direct
and the
Batman and
Robin series.

Copyright:
DC
Action figure
of a future
Batman

Max Mercury	$15
Starfire (New Teen Titans)	$20
Swamp Thing	$40
Zatanna (Mages, Mystics & Magicians)	$15

DC Direct
2001 Release

Alfred E. Neuman as Batman	$20
Alfred E. Neuman as Superman	$20
Ares (Wonder Woman Amazons and Adversaries)	$15
Artemis (Wonder Woman Amazons and Adversaries)	$15
Captain Cold (Flash Rogues Gallery)	$15
Cheetah (Wonder Woman Amazons and Adversaries)	$15
Cosmic Boy (Legion of Superheroes)	$15
Cyborg (New Teen Titans)	$15
Deadman (Other Worlds)	$15
Demon (Other Worlds)	$15
Dr. Mid-Night, Golden Age JSA	$45
Eclipso	$15
Gorilla Grodd	$15
Hal Jordan Spectre (Other Worlds)	$18
Hourman, Golden Age JSA	$26
Lightning Lad (Legion of Superheroes)	$18
Martian Manhunter	$20
Mirror Master (Flash Rogues Gallery)	$15
Raven (New Teen Titans)	$20
Red Tornado	$16
Sandman, Golden Age JSA	$35
Saturn Girl (Legion of Superheroes)	$18
Sinestro (Green Lantern)	$15

Star Sapphire (Green Lantern)	$18

DC Direct
2002 Release

Blue Beetle (Classic Heroes)	$15
Brainiac 5 (Legion of Superheroes)	$16
Green Lantern Corps John Stewart	$18
Green Lantern Corps Tomar Re	$18
Green Lantern Fatality	$15
Green Lantern Kyle Rayner	$18
JSA Power Girl	$15
JSA Solomon Grundy	$16
JSA Wildcat	$15
Mon-El (Legion of Superheroes)	$15
Phantom Lady (Classic Heroes)	$15
Sgt. Rock	$15
Shazam Black Adam	$22
Shazam with Mr. Mind	$20
The Question (Classic Heroes)	$15
The Shade (JSA Villains)	$15
Uncle Sam (Classic Heroes)	$15
Vandal Savage (JSA Villains)	$15

DC Direct Deluxe Action Figure Sets

2000 Hawkman and Hawkgirl	$90
2000 Mister Miracle and Big Barda	$35
2000 Shazam	$35
2001 Aquaman and Aqualad	$40
2001 Flash and Kid Flash (Silver Age)	$40
2001 Orion and Darkseid	$35

Copyright: DC
Four overlaid
packages of Green
Lantern figures.

Below:
Copyright: DC
Shazam and Black
Adam action
figures from DC
Direct.

Above:
Copyright: DC
Hawkman and
Hawkgirl deluxe action
figure set with assorted
accessories.

Copyright: DC
Phantom Lady action
figure from the *Classic
Heroes* set.

2001 Wonder Woman and
Wonder Girl $40
2002 Lobo and Cycle $30
2002 Green Arrow and Speedy
$40
2002 Superman and Lois Lane
(Silver Age) $40

DC Direct PVC Box Sets
1999 Legion of Superheroes
(clubhouse 7 piece) $35
1999 JSA series 1 (7 piece) $38
2000 JSA series 2 (7 piece) $38
2000 Green Lantern (7 piece)
$35
2001 Silver Age JLA Villains
(7 piece) $30
2002 JSA series 3 (7 piece) $35
Smallville (7 piece) $28
New Teen Titans (7 pieces) $28
Direct Danger Girl (7 pieces) $25
Metal Men (7 pieces) $28

DC Heroes
Toy Biz 1990
Aquaman $25
Batman $25
Bob the Goon $20
Flash $18
Green Lantern $25
Hawkman $25
Joker (face hair) $28
Joker (no face hair) $18
Lex Luthor $18
Mr. Freeze $18
Penguin (long missiles) $35
Penguin (no tails) $20
Penguin (short missiles) $40
Penguin (with tails) $18
Riddler $18
Superman $32
Two Face $18
Wonder Woman $28

Fantastic Four (Marvel)
Toy Biz 1995
Annihilus $8
Attuma $10
Black Bolt $15
Blastaar $8
Dr. Doom $8
Dragon Man $8
Firelord $10
Gorgon $8
Human Torch (flames on) $15
Human Torch
(glow-in-the-dark) $10
Invisible Woman (clear) $10
Invisible Woman (painted) $15
Mole Man $8
Mr. Fantastic $10
Namor $15
Silver Surfer $10
Super Skrull $10
Terrax $8
Thanos $8
The Thing $10
The Thing II $10
Triton $12

Fantastic Four (Marvel)
Toy Biz 1996
Human Torch, Firestorm
Action $8
Medusa $10
Psycho Man $6
The Thing, Breaking Action $6
Wizard $6
Accessories
Dr. Doom
10in (25cm) Deluxe $10
Fantasticar $32
Galactus $15
Human Torch
10in (25cm) Deluxe $10
Johnny Storm
10in (25cm) Deluxe $10
Mr. Fantastic's Sky Shuttle $12

Complete package of the *Justice League of America* PVC Set Series 3.

Complete package of the *Justice League of America* villains PVC set.

Superman action figure with cape

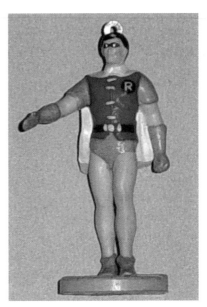

Robin PVC that can also be used
as a hanging ornament

Above:
Copyright: Marvel
Johnny Storm, Doctor
Doom, Black Bolt action
figures from the *Fantastic
Four* Toy Biz series

Copyright: Marvel
Close-up of the Johnny
Storm action figure

68

Silver Surfer
10in (25cm) Deluxe — $10
The Thing
10in (25cm) Deluxe — $10
The Thing Projectors — $2
The Thing's Sky Cycle — $12

Ghost Rider (Marvel)
Toy Biz 1995
**(Comic included with 5in [13cm]
figures)**
Blackout — $5
Blaze — $5
Blaze 10in (25cm) Deluxe — $10
Blaze, Spirits of Vengeance — $10
Blaze's Dark Cycle — $8
Ghost Rider — $5
Ghost Rider
10in (25cm) Deluxe — $10
Ghost Rider 12in (31cm) — $12
Ghost Rider Ghost Fire Cycle
— $8
Ghost Rider II — $5
Ghost Rider, Spirits of
Vengeance — $10
Skinner — $5
Vengeance — $5
Vengeance
10in (25cm) Deluxe — $10
Vengeance, Spirits of Vengeance
— $10
Vengeance's Steel Skeleton
Cycle — $8

Ghost Rider (Marvel)
Toy Biz 1996
**(Comic included with 5in [13cm]
figures)**
Blaze, Armor — $5
Ghost Rider, Exploding — $5
Ghost Rider, Original — $5
Outcast — $5
Zanathos — $5

Iron Man (Marvel)
Toy Biz 1995
Backlash — $6
Blizzard — $6
Century — $6
Dreadknight — $6
Grey Gargoyle — $6
Iron Man, Arctic Armor — $8
Iron Man, Hologram — $8
Iron Man, Hulkbuster — $8
Iron Man, Hydro Armor — $8
Iron Man, Plasma Gun — $8
Iron Man, Space Armor — $8
Iron Man, Stealth Armor — $8
Mandarin — $6
Modok — $6
Spider Woman — $10
Titanium Man — $6
Tony Stark — $8
War Machine — $6
Whirlwind — $6

Iron Man (Marvel)
Toy Biz 1996
Crimson Dynamo — $5
Iron Man, Inferno — $5
Iron Man, Samurai — $5
Iron Man, Subterranean — $5
War Machine II — $5

The Incredible Hulk (Marvel)
Toy Biz 1996
Abomination — $8
Hulk, Grey — $10
Hulk, Rampaging — $10
Hulk, Savage — $10
Leader — $8
She Hulk — $10

*The Incredible Hulk – Smash
and Crash* (Marvel)
Toy Biz 1997
Doc Samson — $8
Hulk — $8

Copyright: Marvel
Grey Gargoyle and the Mandarin,
both villains from the *Iron Man* collection.

Hulk, Battle Damage	$8	**Accessories**	
Leader	$6	Hulk, Raging (figure included)	
Zzzax	$6		$12
		Bump and Go Motorcycle	
The Incredible Hulk –		(figure included)	$8
Transformations (Marvel)		Rage Cage (figure included)	$12
Toy Biz 1996			
Absorbing Man	$8	***Marvel Super Heroes***	
Hulk 2009	$8	**(Marvel)**	
Hulk, Smart	$8	**Toy Biz 1990**	
Maestro	$8	Amazing Spider-Man	$24
		Captain America	$15
The Incredible Hulk-		Daredevil	$60
Outcasts (Marvel)		Dr. Doom	$10
Toy Biz 1996		Dr. Octopus	$10
Chain saw	$6	Incredible Hulk	$15
Hulk, Battle	$9	Punisher	$12
Hulk, Leader	$8	Silver Surfer	$25
Two-Head	$8		
Wendigo	$25		

Copyright: Marvel
Punisher action figure
from the *Marvel Super
Heroes* collection.

Copyright: Marvel
Iron Man action figure
with the removable
mask from the *Marvel
Super Heroes* collection.

Copyright: Marvel
Silver Surfer action
figure from the
Marvel Super Heroes
collection

Below:
Copyright: Marvel
Talking Spider-Man
action figure and a
Spider-Man shooter
action figure

Marvel Super Heroes
(Marvel)
Toy Biz 1991

Green Goblin	$18
Green Goblin (with lever)	$35
Iron Man	$18
Punisher	$18
Spider-Man, Web Climbing	$28
Spider-Man, Web Shooting	$24
Thor	$20
Thor (with lever)	$32
Venom	$18

Marvel Super Heroes
(Marvel)
Toy Biz 1991
Accessories

Captain America Turbo Coupe	$40
Marvel Super Heroes Training Center	$42
Punisher Van	$110
Spider-Man Dragster	$32
The Hulk Rage Cage	$28

Marvel Super Heroes
(Marvel)
Toy Biz 1992

Annihilus	$10
Deathlock	$10
Human Torch	$15
Invisible Woman (vanishing color action/low distribution)	$80
Mr. Fantastic	$15
Silver Surfer (chrome)	$15
Spider-Man (with spider tracer)	$15
Spider-Man II (with multi-movable joints)	$15
The Thing	$15
Venom	$15

Marvel Super Heroes
(Marvel)
Toy Biz 1993

Captain America (reissue)	$4
Dr. Doom (reissue)	$3
Dr. Octopus (reissue)	$3
Hulk (reissue)	$4
Punisher, Cap Firing	$7
Venom, Water Squirting	$10

Marvel Super Heroes
(Marvel)
Toy Biz 1991
Talking

Cyclops	$18
Hulk	$18
Magneto	$18
Punisher	$15
Spider-Man	$25
Venom	$18
Wolverine	$18

Marvel Universe (Marvel)
Toy Biz 1997+

Apocalypse	$3
Beast	$5
Bishop	$4
Cable, Cyborg	$4
Cable, Deep Space	$4
Carnage	$3
Colossus	$5
Cyclops	$5
Dark Phoenix	$5
Dead Pool II	$3
Dr. Doom	$4
Dragon Man	$3
Genesis	$3
Ghost Rider	$4
Green Goblin	$4
Halloween Jack	$3
Hobgoblin	$3
Human Torch	$5
Iceman	$5

Copyright: Marvel
Two Spider-Man action figures, one with the classic uniform.

Copyright: Marvel
Two Spider-Man action figures wearing non-classic costumes.

74

Copyright: Marvel
Another variation on the Spider-Man costume. Not for those with Arachnophobia.

Iron Man	$5
Iron Man Stealth Armor	$5
Iron Man, Arctic Armor	$5
Iron Man, Hologram Armor	$5
Iron Man, Hulk Buster	$5
Iron Man, Hydro Armor	$5
Iron Man, Inferno Armor	$5
Iron Man, Samurai Armor	$5
Iron Man, Space Armor	$5
Junkpile	$3
Kingpin	$4
Mandarin	$3
Man-Spider	$4
Morbius	$4
Mysterio	$4
Outcast	$3
Peter Parker	$5
Psycho Man	$3
Rogue	$5
Sabretooth	$4
Scorpion	$4
Silver Surfer	$5
Skinner	$3
Spider-Man, Battle Ravaged	$9
Spider-Man, Launching Web Action	$9
Spider-Man, Super-Poseable	$12
Spider-Man, Wall Crawling Action	$9
Spider-Man, Web Glider	$9
Spider-Man, Web Swinging	$9
The Protector	$3
The Thing	$5
The Thing II	$4
Tony Stark	$5
Venom	$4
War Machine	$3
Wizard	$3
Wolverine	$6
Wolverine, Battle Ravaged	$5
Wolverine, Space Armor	$5
Wolverine, Spy	$5
Wolverine, Weapon-X	$5

Copyright:
Marvel
A close-up of
the Talking
Spider-Man
action figure.

Copyright: Marvel
Spider-Man villain
Venom from the
Marvel Super Heroes
collection.

Marvel Universe 10in (25cm)
(Marvel)
Toy Biz 1997+

Apocalypse, Meteor Might	$5
Beast	$6
Bishop	$5
Blade	$5
Cable	$6
Captain America	$8
Captain Marvel	$7
Cyclops	$8
Cyclops, Cyber Armor	$6
Daredevil (red and yellow)	$8
Daredevil (red)	$6
Dead Pool	$5
Forge	$5
Green Goblin	$5
Iceman	$8
Iron Man, Deep Space	$6
Jean Grey	$8
Moon Night	$7
Nick Fury	$6
Peter Parker	$6
Polaris	$5
Professor-X	$6
Rogue, Ninja	$8
Scarlet Spider	$8
She Hulk	$8
Sinister, Asteroid Assault	$5
Spider-Man	$8
Spider-Man (black and white)	$8
Spider-Man (removable mask)	$6
Spider-Man 2099	$5
Spider-Man, Cosmic	$6
Spider-Man, Night Shadow	$5
Spider-Man, Symbiote	$5
Spider-Man, War Armor	$5
Storm	$8
The Spot	$5
Union Jack	$5
Venom	$5
Vision	$5
Wolverine	$8
Wolverine (yellow and blue)	$8
Wolverine (yellow, blue shorts, black stripes)	$6
Wolverine, Cosmic	$5
Wolverine, Ninja	$6
Wolverine, Star Blast	$6

Marvel Universe – Civilian Heroes (Marvel)
Toy Biz

Ben Grimm\The Thing	$6
Logan\Wolverine	$6
Peter Parker\Spider-Man	$6

Marvel Universe – Flying Heroes (Marvel)
Toy Biz

Demogoblin	$5
Spider-Man	$6
Wolverine	$5

Marvel Universe – Heroes United (Marvel)
Toy Biz

Captain America	$6
Spider-Man, Scarlet	$5
Wolverine	$5

Marvel Universe – Heroes Unmasked (Marvel)
Toy Biz

Spider-Man\Peter Parker	$6
Venom\Eddie Brock	$5
Wolverine\Logan	$5

Marvel Universe – Heroes and Legends (Marvel)
Toy Biz

Ghost Rider	$5
Iron Man	$6
Spider-Man	$6

Copyright: Marvel
10in (25cm) Sabretooth
deluxe action figure.

Copyright: Marvel
10in (25cm) Wolverine
deluxe action figure.

78

Marvel Universe – Marvel Knights (Marvel)
Toy Biz
Black Panther	$6
Daredevil	$8
Punisher	$6

Marvel Universe – Marvel Mutations (Marvel)
Toy Biz
Man-Spider	$5
Spider-Lizard	$5
Venom the Vampire	$5

Marvel Universe – Marvel Team-Ups (Marvel)
Toy Biz
Gambit	$7
Silver Surfer	$7
Spider-Man	$7

Marvel Universe-Marvels (Marvel)
Toy Biz 1997
Green Goblin	$5
Human Torch	$7
Spider-Man	$6

Marvel Universe – Metal Warriors (Marvel)
Toy Biz
Dr. Doom	$5
Iron Man, Steel Tech	$5
Spider-Man, Cyber	$5

Marvel Universe – Savage Force (Marvel)
Toy Biz
Kraven, Jungle Hunter	$5
Savage Angel	$5
Wolverine, Feral	$6

Marvel Universe – Spider Wars (Marvel)
Toy Biz
Carnage	$5
Mysterio	$6
Spider-Man	$6

Silver Surfer (Marvel)
Toy Biz 1997
Beta Ray Bill	$5
Meegan Alien	$5
Nova	$7
Silver Surfer	$7

Silver Surfer – Alien Fighters (Marvel)
Toy Biz
Galactus and Silver Surfer	$8
Ivau and Ant Warrior	$6
Silver Surfer, Cosmic and Pip the Troll	$6
Silver Surfer, Solar and Draconian Warrior	$6

Silver Surfer – Blasters (Marvel)
Toy Biz
Drax the Destroyer	$5
Raze	$5
Silver Surfer	$6
Thanos, Star Surfer	$5

Silver Surfer – Space Rangers (Marvel)
Toy Biz
Adam Warlock	$5
Ronan the Accuser	$5
Silver Surfer, Molten Lava	$6
Silver Surfer, Sun Powered	$6
Super Nova	$15

Copyright: Marvel
Dr. Strange action figure
with mystical accessory
from the Spider-Man
collection.

Copyright: Marvel
Kingpin action figure
from the *Spider-Man*
collection.

Copyright: Marvel Die-cast Spider-Man from the *Web of Steel* collection.

Silver Surfer (Marvel)		Hobgoblin	$14
Toy Biz		Smythe	$10
Accessories		Spider-Man, Web-Racer	$16
Galactus 14in (36cm)	$18	Spider-Man, Web-Shooter	$16
Silver Surfer 10in (25cm)	$12	Venom	$12
Silver Surfer (electronic talking)	$15	***Spider-Man – The Animated Series 2*** (Marvel)	
The Command Ship (attack playsets)	$20	**Toy Biz**	
The Star Cruiser (attack playsets)	$20	Alien Spider Slayer	$14
		Kingpin	$14
		Kraven	$14
Spider-Man – The Animated Series 1 (Marvel)		Peter Parker	$14
Toy Biz 1994+		Spider-Man, Web Parachute	$16
Carnage	$14	The Lizard	$16
Dr. Octopus	$14	Vulture	$14

Spider-Man – The Animated Series 3 (Marvel)
Toy Biz

Green Goblin	$14
Rhino	$30
Scorpion	$14
Shocker	$14
Spider-Man, Spider Armor	$16
Spider-Man, Super Poseable	$16

Spider-Man – The Animated Series 4 (Marvel)
Toy Biz

Chameleon	$10
Mysterio (dark green)	$10
Mysterio (light green)	$15
Spider-Man, Black Costume	$15
Spider-Man, Night Shadow	$16
Spider-Man, Web Glider	$15
The Prowler	$10
Venom II	$10

Spider-Man – The Animated Series 5 (Marvel)
Toy Biz

Morbius	$10
Nick Fury	$15
Spider Sense	$14
Spider-Man, 6-Armed	$14
Spider-Man, Battle Ravaged	$14
Spider-Man, Web Lair KB Toys	$32
Spider-Man, Web Trap KB Toys	$32
The Punisher	$10

Spider-Man – The Animated Series 6 (Marvel)
Toy Biz

Carnage II	$10
Man-Spider	$10
Spider-Man, Octo	$12
Spider-Man, Web Cannon n	$14
Tombstone	$10

Spider-Man – The Animated Series 7 (Marvel)
Toy Biz

Rhino, Total Armor	$8
Spider-Man, Venom 2099	$12
Spider-Man, White Axe 2099	$12
Spider-Man, Yellow Axe 2099	$12
Spider-Woman	$12
Venom, Stealth Black	$8
Venom, Stealth Clear	$8

Spider-Man 10in (25cm)–The Animated Series 1-6 (Marvel)
Toy Biz

Carnage	$15
Dr. Octopus	$12
Hobgoblin	$18
Kraven	$10
Mysterio	$14
Punisher	$14
Spider-Man	$22
Spider-Man, Armor	$18
Spider-Man, Sensational	$18
Spider-Man, Silver Webing	$18
Spider-Man, Spider Armor	$18
Spider-Man, Spider Sense	$20
Spider-Man, Super Pose	$25
Spider-Man, Wall Hanging	$20
The Lizard	$18
The Vulture	$15
Venom (black)	$20
Venom (blue)	$10

Spider-Man – The Animated Series (Marvel)
Toy Biz
Accessories

Big Time Action Hero	$25
Daily Bugle	$55
Hobgoblin, Wing Bomber	$30
Kingpins Crime Central	$15
Scorpion Spider Slayer	$32

Copyright:
Paramount
Action figure
holder and
Troi from the
*Star Trek:
The Next
Generation*
series.

Copyright: Paramount
Worf from the *Star Trek: The Next Generation* series and
a list of the available characters from the back of the package.

Smythe Attack Vehicle	$25	Mr. Spock	$35
Wacky Wall Crawler (red or blue)	$6	Scotty	$35

Star Trek–Mego 1974

		Star Trek–Mego 1980	
Captain Kirk	$125	Acturian	$150
Dr. McCoy	$150	Betelgeusian	$195
Klingon	$100	Klingon	$150
Mr. Spock	$125	Megarite	$185
Scotty	$150	Rigillian	$150
Uhura	$110	Zaranite	$150

Star Trek–Mego 1975

Star Trek–Mego Accessories

Captain Kirk	$60	Astrotank (Remko)	$175
Cheron	$225	Command Bridge	$95
Dr. McCoy	$110	Command Console	$150
Gorn	$250	Communicators	$195
Keeper	$250	Enterprise Bridge	$150
Klingon	$50	Mission VI	$495
Mr. Spock	$60	Phaser Battle Game	$150
Neptunian	$325	Phaser Guns	$35
Scotty	$110	Trekulator	$150
		Tricorder	$150

Star Trek–Mego 1976

		Wrist Communicator	$150
Androrian	$795		
Mugato	$650	**Star Trek–Ertl 1984**	
Romulan	$1250	Kirk	$35
Talos	$525	Klingon	$38
		Scotty	$35
		Spock	$35

Star Trek–Mego 1979 (12')

Star Trek V–Galoob 1989

Acturian	$100	Dr. McCoy	$32
Captain Kirk	$75	James Kirk	$32
Decker	$195	Klaa	$40
Klingon	$95	Mr. Spock	$32
Lila	$95	Sybok	$38
Mr. Spock	$75		

Star Trek–(3¾in [10cm]) Mego 1979

Star Trek: The Next Generation Galoob 1988

Captain Kirk	$35	Captain Picard	$16
Decker	$40	Commander Riker	$16
Dr. McCoy	$35	Data (blue face)	$95
Lila	$40		

Data (dark face)	$35	Benzite	$12
Data (flesh)	$22	Borg	$10
Data (spotted)	$20	Captain Picard	$10
Lt. LaForge	$16	Captain Scott	$10
Lt. Worf	$16	Commander Riker	$10
Yar	$22	Commander Selay	$10
		Counselor Troi (red uniform)	$10

Star Trek: The Next Generation
Galoob 1989

		Dr. Crusher	$10
		Guinan	$10
Antican	$65	K'Ehlyr	$12
Enterprise-Die Cast	$75	Locutus	$12
Ferengi	$50	Lore	$10
Ferengi Fighter	$75	Lt. Commander Data	$14
Galileo Shuttle	$80	Lt. Commander LaForge	
Phaser	$30	(dress uniform)	$14
Q	$50	Lt. Commander LaForge	$12
Selay	$50	Lt. Worf (Klingon warrior)	$12
		Q	$12
		Vargon	$12

Star Trek: The Next Generation
Playmates 1992

		Wesley	$10
		Accessories	
Borg (reverse negative)	$30	Bridge	$85
Borg	$18	Classic Set	$50
Captain Picard	$18	Communicators	$18
Commander Riker	$18	Enterprise D	$28
Counselor Troi	$18	Klingon Cruiser	$38
Ferengi (black on boots)	$22	Phaser	$12
Ferengi (no black)	$28	Shuttle	$18
Gowron (gold trim)	$18	Transporter	$28
Gowron	$25	Tricorder	$28
Lt. Commander Data	$18		
Lt. LaForge (removable visor)		**Star Trek: The Next**	
	$35	**Generation**	
Lt. LaForge	$25	**Playmates 1994\Package**	
Lt. Worf	$18	**Contains Pog**	
Romulan	$18	Ambassador Spock	$12
		Benzite	$22

Star Trek: The Next Generation
Playmates 1993\Trading Card Included

		Borg	$35
		Captain Picard	$22
		Commander Riker	$22
		Commander Selay	$12
		Counselor Troi (red uniform)	$22
Admiral McCoy	$10	Dathon	$395
Ambassador Spock	$10	Dr. Crusher	$14

Guinan	$15	Enterprise (glider)	$25
K'Ehlyr	$15	Enterprise	$60
Locutus	$22	Klingon Bird of Prey	$35
Lore	$12	Phaser	$15
Lt. Commander LaForge			
(dress uniform)	$20		

Star Wars — Episode 1
Kenner 1999\Commtech Chip Included\NO Variations listed at this time

Lt. Data	$25	Adi Gallia	$8
Lt. Worf (as warrior)	$28	Anakin Skywalker, Naboo	$6
Lt. Worf	$22	Anakin Skywalker, Pilot	$10
Q	$12	Anakin Skywalker, Tatooine	$6
Vorgon	$75	Battle Droid	$8
Wesley (cadet)	$22	Boss Nass	$7
		C-3PO	$8

Star Trek: The Next Generation
Playmate1994 (7th Season)

		Captain Panaka	$9
Ambassador Lwaxana (pog [Canadian only])	$135	Captain Tarpals	$9
		Chancellor Valorum	$9
Ambassador Serek (no pog [Canadian only] 1993)	$125	Darth Maul, Jedi Duel	$10
		Darth Maul, Sith Lord	$12
Captain Picard (Dixon Hill)	$12	Darth Maul, Tatooine	$9
Captain Picard (Romulan)	$12	Darth Sidious	$9
Captain Picard	$12	Darth Sidious, Hologram	$15
Commander Riker (Malcorian)		Destroyer Droid	$7
	$12	Destroyer Droid, Damaged	$12
Commander Riker (Thomas Riker)	$95	Gasgano and Pit Droid	$7
		Jar Jar Binks (swimming)	$18
Counselor Troi	$12	Jar Jar Binks	$8
Dr. Soong (pog)	$14	Ki-Ad-Mundi	$6
Esoqq	$75	Mace Windu (hooded)	$6
Gowron	$45	Naboo Royal Guard	$15
Hugh Borg	$12	Naboo Security	$6
Lt. Barclay	$12	Nute Gunray	$6
Lt. Commander LaForge	$12	Obi-Wan Kenobi, Jedi	$12
Lt. Data (Redemption)	$295	Obi-Wan Kenobi, Naboo	$8
Lt. Data (Romulan)	$12	Obi-Wan, Jedi Duel	$8
Lt. Data	$12	Ody Mantrell and Pit Droid	$6
Lt. Worf	$12	OOM-9	$6
Q	$15	Padme Naberrie	$6
Ro Laren	$15	Pit Droids	$12
Wesley	$15	Queen Amidala, Battle	$16
Accessories		Queen Amidala, Coruscant	$12
Borg Cube	$50	Queen Amidala, Naboo	$8
Communicator	$22		

Copyright: Paramount
An honorable rendition
of Worf from *Star Trek:
The Next Generation*.

Below:
Copyright: Paramount
A Klingon from the
original series. No
official explanation for
the missing crab on the
head has ever been
given; however, it could
have been a practical
joke by the character
"Q".

Above:
Copyright: LucasFilm
Action figures from
Star Wars—Darth
Maul and Princess
Amidala.

Copyright: LucasFilm
R2-D2 action figure.

Qui-Gon Jinn, Jedi Duel $8
Qui-Gon Jinn, Jedi Master $12
Qui-Gon Jinn, Naboo $8
R2-B1 $12
R2-D2 $6
Ric Olie $6
Rune Haako $6
Senator Palpatine $7
Sio Bibble $25
TC-14 $18
Watto $8
Yoda $8

Accessories
Commtech Reader $15
Flash Speeder $10
Hyperdrive Repair Kit $10
Naboo Accessory Set $12
Naboo Fighter $18
Pod Racer Refuel Station $10
Podracer includes Anakin $16
Podracer includes Sebulba $18
Rappel Line Kit $8
Sith Accessory Set $12
Sith Speeder (includes Darth
  Maul) $16
Stamp and Battle Droid $10
Tatooine Disguise Kit $9
Trade Federation Droid Fighters
  $12
Underwater Set $10

Superfriends: Super Powers Collection (DC)
Kenner 1984
Aquaman $60
Batman large card $95
Batman small card $60
Brainiac $35
Flash $30
Green Lantern large card $95
Green Lantern small card $60
Hawkman $75
Joker $28
Lex Luthor $28

Penguin $40
Robin large card $50
Robin small card $30
Superman large card $60
Superman small card $30
Wonder Woman large cards $42
Wonder Woman small card $28

Super Power (DC)
1984
Accessories
Batmobile $295
Hall of Justice $175
Lex-soar 7 $28
Super Powers Carrying Case $18
Supermobile $42

Super Powers (DC)
1985
Darkseid $32
Desaad $24
Dr. Fate $95
Firestorm large card $42
Firestorm small card $26
Green Arrow $65
Kalibak $22
Mantis $42
Martian Manhunter large card
  $45
Martian Manhunter small cards
  $30
Parademon $42
Red Tornado large card $95
Red Tornado small card $60
Steppenwolf (with comic) $80
Steppenwolf (without comic)
  $50

Super Powers
1985
Accessories (DC)
Boulder Bomber $25
Darkseid Destroyer $42
Delta Probe One $35

Above left:
Copyright: LucasFilm
Princess Amidala
action figure.

Above right:
Copyright: LucasFilm
Yoda action figure.

Left:
Copyright: LucasFilm
Yoda PVC.

90

Copyright: DC
Wonder Woman action figures from two different toy collections.

Copyright: DC
A Batmobile from the *Super Powers* collection.

Copyright: DC
Large and small packaging of the Red Tornado from
the *Super Powers* collections.

Copyright: DC
Assorted *Justice League of America* characters from
the *Super Powers* collection.

92

Super Powers (DC)
1986 (distribution not as large as other two series)

Clark Kent (mail in not on card)	$75
Cyborg	$395
Cyclotron	$95
Golgen Pharaoh	$195
Mr. Freeze	$75
Mr. Miracle	$150
Orion	$75
Plastic Man	$165
Riddler (Super Amigos)	$95
Samurai	$125
Shazam	$25
Tyr	$95

(Other Super Amigos are 60% of regular issue)

Super Powers
1986
Accessories (DC)

Batcopter	$195
Justice Jogger	$65

X-Men 5in (13cm) Figures
(Marvel)
Toy Biz 1991

Apocalypse	$8
Archangel	$8
Colossus	$8
Cyclops	$10
Juggernaut	$8
Magneto	$9
Night Crawler	$12
Storm	$15
Wolverine I	$12

Vehicles and Danger Rooms
(Marvel)
Toy Biz

Combat Cave	$15
Light Force Arena	$15

Magneto Magnetron	$18
Wolverine Mutant Cycle	$15

All action figures in 1991 were re-released in 1992 except for

Storm	$5

X-Men (Marvel)
Toy Biz 1992

Banshee	$8
Forge (brown holster)	$35
Forge (yellow holster)	$22
Gambit	$10
Icemam	$28
Magneto II	$8
Mr. Sinister	$8
Sabretooth	$8
Sauron	$8
Weapon X	$10
Wolverine II	$18
Wolverine III	$28

X-Men (Marvel)
Toy Biz 1993

Archangel (gray wings)	$8
Colossus (no yellow)	$8
Cyclops (red belt)	$8
Iceman (bluish)	$8
Juggernaut	$8
Magneto	$8
Mr. Sinister	$8
Night Crawler	$8
Sauron	$8
Storm	$10
Weapon X (Wolverine IV)	$25

X-Men – Series 2 (Marvel)
Toy Biz 1993

Apocalypse	$7
Bishop	$8
Omega Red	$8
Strong Guy	$7
Tusk	$7
Wolverine V	$18

Above:
Copyright: DC
Justice League of America Hall of Justice from the *Super Powers* collection.

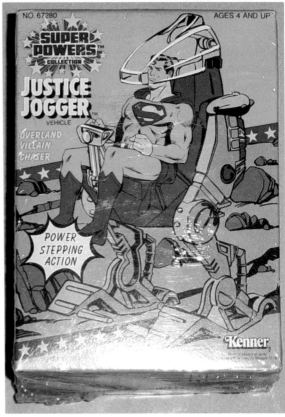

Copyright: DC
Super Powers
Justice Jogger.

94

Copyright: Marvel
Weapon X and Wolverine.

Copyright: Marvel
X-Men Danger Room.

Above:
Copyright: Marvel
Dr. Doom and Magneto
action figures.

Copyright: Marvel
Iceman action figure
from the *X-Men*
collection.

X-Men Series 3 (Marvel)
Toy Biz 1993

Ahab	$6
Brood	$6
Cyclops	$6
Longshot	$6
Professor X	$6
Sabretooth	$6

X-Men (Marvel)
Toy Biz 1994

Beast	$10
Morph	$8
Random	$8
Robot Wolverine VI	$12
Silver Samurai	$8
Trevor Fitzroy	$8

Above:
Copyright: Marvel
A Wolverine action figure based on the hit movie with Hugh Jackson playing the role.

Copyright: Marvel
Alpha Flight action figure.

Copyright: Marvel
A Wolverine action
figure with snap-out
claws.

Copyright: Marvel
Rogue action figure.

B. Category: HeroClix

The colors and meaning of the codes in the tables that follow are:
R = Rookie -Yellow
E = Experienced -Blue
V = Veteran-Red
U = Unique-Silver
LE = Limited Edition

The more experienced the character, the more points and power he or she has. Here is a listing and pricing of the Marvel and DC HeroClix at time of this publication.

Marvel HeroClix
Infinity Challenge (All Are Marvel™)

CHARACTER	LEVEL	POINT	SCARCITY	PRICE
#001 S.H.I.E.L.D Agent	R	10	1	$1
#002 S.H.I.E.L.D Agent	E	12	2	$1.50
#003 S.H.I.E.L.D Agent	V	14	3	$2
#004 S.H.I.E.L.D Medic	R	12	1	$1
#005 S.H.I.E.L.D Medic	E	15	2	$1.50
#006 S.H.I.E.L.D Medic	V	16	3	$2
#007 Hydra Operative	R	9	1	$1
#008 Hydra Operative	E	11	2	$1.50
#009 Hydra Operative	V	13	3	$2
#010 Hydra Medic	R	12	1	$1
#011 Hydra Medic	E	15	2	$1.50
#012 Hydra Medic	V	16	3	$2
#013 Thug	R	6	1	$1
#014 Thug	E	8	2	$1.50
#015 Thug	V	10	3	$2
#016 Henchman	R	11	1	$1
#017 Henchman	E	12	2	$1.50
#018 Henchman	V	13	3	$2
#019 Skrull Agent	R	11	1	$1
#020 Skrull Agent	E	13	2	$1.50
#021 Skrull Agent	V	16	3	$2
#022 Skrull Warrior	R	14	1	$1
#023 Skrull Warrior	E	16	2	$1.50

CHARACTER	LEVEL	POINT	SCARCITY	PRICE
#024 Skrull Warrior	V	17	3	$2
#025 Blade	R	26	1	$1
#026 Blade	E	28	2	$1.50
#027 Blade	V	33	3	$2
#028 Wolfsbane	R	28	1	$1
#029 Wolfsbane	E	32	2	$1.50
#030 Wolfsbane	V	39	3	$2
#031 Electra	R	18	2	$2
#032 Electra	E	22	3	$3
#033 Electra	V	34	4	$4.50
#034 Wasp	R	24	2	$2
#035 Wasp	E	33	3	$3
#036 Wasp	V	37	4	$4.50
#037 Constrictor	R	37	2	$1.50
#038 Constrictor	E	45	3	$2.50
#039 Constrictor	V	55	4	$4
#040 Boomerang	R	24	2	$1.50
#041 Boomerang	E	34	3	$2.50
#042 Boomerang	V	44	4	$4
#043 Kingpin	R	24	2	$2
#044 Kingpin	E	29	3	$3
#045 Kingpin	V	43	4	$4.50
#046 Vulture	R	15	2	$2
#047 Vulture	E	20	3	$3
#048 Vulture	V	24	4	$4.50
#049 Jean Grey	R	31	2	$2
#050 Jean Grey	E	39	3	$3
#051 Jean Grey	V	50	4	$4.50
#052 Hobgoblin	R	34	2	$2
#053 Hobgoblin	E	53	3	$3
#054 Hobgoblin	V	62	4	$4.50
#055 Sabretooth	R	38	2	$2
#056 Sabretooth	E	51	3	$3
#057 Sabretooth	V	69	4	$4.50
#058 Hulk	R	103	2	$2.50
#059 Hulk	E	117	3	$3.50

CHARACTER	LEVEL	POINT	SCARCITY	PRICE
#060 Hulk	V	147	4	$5
#061 Puppet Master	R	25	2	$2
#062 Puppet Master	E	35	3	$3
#063 Puppet Master	V	42	4	$4.50
#064 Annihilus	R	83	2	$1.50
#065 Annihilus	E	103	3	$2.50
#066 Annihilus	V	129	4	$4
#067 Captain America	R	41	3	$3.50
#068 Captain America	E	47	4	$5
#069 Captain America	V	62	5	$9
#070 Spider-Man	R	61	3	$3.50
#071 Spider-Man	E	82	4	$5
#072 Spider-Man	V	110	5	$9
#073 Wolverine	R	44	3	$3.50
#074 Wolverine	E	61	4	$5
#075 Wolverine	V	75	5	$9
#076 Professor Xavier	R	59	3	$3.50
#077 Professor Xavier	E	67	4	$4.50
#078 Professor Xavier	V	83	5	$9
#079 Juggernaut	R	97	3	$3.50
#080 Juggernaut	E	125	4	$4.50
#081 Juggernaut	V	146	5	$9
#082 Cyclops	R	55	3	$3.50
#083 Cyclops	E	68	4	$4.50
#084 Cyclops	V	78	5	$9
#085 Black Panther	R	27	3	$3.50
#086 Black Panther	E	36	4	$4.50
#087 Black Panther	V	46	5	$9
#088 Blizzard	R	35	3	$3
#089 Blizzard	E	46	4	$4
#090 Blizzard	V	53	5	$7
#091 Pyro	R	27	3	$3
#092 Pyro	E	35	4	$4
#093 Pyro	V	42	5	$7
#094 Whirlwind	R	20	3	$3
#095 Whirlwind	E	32	4	$4

CHARACTER	LEVEL	POINT	SCARCITY	PRICE
#096 Whirlwind	V	41	5	$7
#097 Daredevil	R	30	3	$3.50
#098 Daredevil	E	42	4	$5
#099 Daredevil	V	50	5	$9
#100 Bullseye	R	26	3	$3
#101 Bullseye	E	31	4	$4
#102 Bullseye	V	43	5	$7
#103 Scarlet Witch	R	29	3	$3.50
#104 Scarlet Witch	E	36	4	$4.50
#105 Scarlet Witch	V	40	5	$9
#106 Quicksilver	R	18	3	$3.50
#107 Quicksilver	E	24	4	$4.50
#108 Quicksilver	V	28	5	$9
#109 Mr. Hyde	R	37	3	$3
#110 Mr. Hyde	E	50	4	$4
#111 Mr. Hyde	V	62	5	$7
#112 Klaw	R	60	3	$3
#113 Klaw	E	74	4	$4
#114 Klaw	V	90	5	$7
#115 Controller	R	31	3	$3
#116 Controller	E	50	4	$4
#117 Controller	V	69	5	$7
#118 Hercules	R	54	3	$3.50
#119 Hercules	E	67	4	$4.50
#120 Hercules	V	83	5	$8
#121 Rogue	R	38	3	$3.50
#122 Rogue	E	77	4	$5
#123 Rogue	V	88	5	$9
#124 Dr. Strange	R	64	3	$3.50
#125 Dr. Strange	E	71	4	$5
#126 Dr. Strange	V	87	5	$9
#127 Magneto	R	80	3	$3.50
#128 Magneto	E	89	4	$5
#129 Magneto	V	103	5	$9
#130 Kang	R	133	3	$3
#131 Kang	E	178	4	$4.50

CHARACTER	LEVEL	POINT	SCARCITY	PRICE
#132 Kang	V	190	5	$7.50
#133 Ultron	R	111	3	$3
#134 Ultron	E	139	4	$4.50
#135 Ultron	V	188	5	$7.50
#136 Firelord	R	66	3	$3
#137 Firelord	E	81	4	$4
#138 Firelord	V	97	5	$7
#139 Vision	U	112	6	$20
#140 Quasar	U	122	6	$15
#141 Thanos	U	185	6	$25
#142 Nightmare	U	163	6	$20
#143 Wasp	U	44	6	$15
#144 Electra	U	36	6	$15
#145 Professor Xavier	U	92	6	$15
#146 Juggernaut	U	111	6	$15
#147 Cyclops	U	39	6	$15
#148 Captain America	U	35	6	$20
#149 Wolverine	U	64	6	$20
#150 Spider-Man	U	116	6	$20
#151 Gabriel Jones	U	17	LE3	$15
#152 Tia Senyaka	U	18	LE4	$15
#153 Operative	U	16	LE3	$12
#154 Medic #519	U	17	LE4	$12
#155 Knuckles	U	10	LE3	$12
#156 Joey the Snake	U	14	LE3	$12
#157 Nenora	U	17	LE3	$12
#158 Raksor	U	19	LE4	$12
#159 Blade	U	37	LE3	$12
#160 Rahne Sinclair	U	42	LE3	$12
#161 Frank Schlichting	U	63	LE3	$15
#162 Fred Myers	U	48	LE4	$15
#163 Wilson Fisk	U	47	LE4	$20
#164 Adrian Toomes	U	30	LE4	$18
#165 Jean Grey	U	59	LE4	$35
#166 Ned Leeds	U	73	LE4	$40
#167 Victor Creed	U	75	LE5	$85

CHARACTER	LEVEL	POINT	SCARCITY	PRICE
#168 Bruce Banner	U	151	LE5	$110
#169 Philip Masters	U	56	LE5	$45
#170 Annihilus	U	146	LE5	$45
#171 Wolverine (Exclusive-*Inquest Magazine*)	U	70	LE	$60
#172 Yellowjacket (Exclusive 2002 Convention)	U	39	LE	$50
#173 Ant-Man (Exclusive 2002 Convention)	U	45	LE	$65

Copyright: Marvel
Infinity Challenge HeroClix in original packaging.

Copyright: Marvel
Fantastic Four HeroClix items showing founding members
Mr. Fantastic and the Thing.

Copyright: Marvel
X-Men HeroClix characters.

Copyright: Marvel
Spider-Man HeroClix examples – one with multiple arms,
the other with a black suite.

Clobberin' Time (Marvel™)

CHARACTER	LEVEL	POINT	SCARCITY	PRICE
#001 Shield Trooper	R	11	1	$1
#002 Shield Trooper	E	14	2	$1.50
#003 Shield Trooper	V	17	3	$2
#004 Shield Sniper	R	11	1	$1
#005 Shield Sniper	E	14	2	$1.50
#006 Shield Sniper	V	18	3	$2
#007 Mandroid Armor	R	28	1	$1
#008 Mandroid Armor	E	32	2	$1.50
#009 Mandroid Armor	V	36	3	$2
#010 AIM Agent	R	13	1	$1
#011 AIM Agent	E	14	2	$1.50
#012 AIM Agent	V	15	3	$2
#013 AIM Medic	R	14	1	$1
#014 AIM Medic	E	16	2	$1.50
#015 AIM Medic	V	17	3	$2
#016 Skrull Commando	R	11	1	$1
#017 Skrull Commando	E	14	2	$1.50
#018 Skrull Commando	V	18	3	$2
#019 Vampire Lackey	R	12	1	$1
#020 Vampire Lackey	E	17	2	$1.50
#021 Vampire Lackey	V	20	3	$2
#022 Black Cat	R	16	1	$1.50
#023 Black Cat	E	32	2	$2.25
#024 Black Cat	V	36	3	$3
#025 Yellow Jacket	R	22	1	$1.50
#026 Yellow Jacket	E	32	2	$2.25
#027 Yellow Jacket	V	37	3	$3
#028 Doombot	R	27	1	$1.50
#029 Doombot	E	33	2	$2.25
#030 Doombot	V	38	3	$3
#031 Avalanche	R	19	2	$1.50
#032 Avalanche	E	26	3	$2.50
#033 Avalanche	V	32	4	$4
#034 Blob	R	31	2	$1.50
#035 Blob	E	42	3	$2.50

CHARACTER	LEVEL	POINT	SCARCITY	PRICE
#036 Blob	V	51	4	$4
#037 Toad	R	23	2	$1.50
#038 Toad	E	30	3	$2.50
#039 Toad	V	37	4	$4
#040 Glaive Electra	R	18	2	$2
#041 Glaive Electra	E	22	3	$3
#042 Glaive Electra	V	26	4	$4.50
#043 Invisible Girl	R	37	2	$3
#044 Invisible Girl	E	57	3	$4
#045 Invisible Woman	V	80	4	$6
#046 Thing	R	75	2	$2.50
#047 Thing	E	110	3	$3.50
#048 Thing	V	134	4	$5
#049 Human Torch	R	40	2	$2.50
#050 Human Torch	E	59	3	$3.50
#051 Human Torch	V	73	4	$5
#052 Hawkeye	R	29	2	$2.50
#053 Hawkeye	E	43	3	$3.50
#054 Hawkeye	V	64	4	$5
#055 Black Widow	R	30	2	$2.50
#056 Black Widow	E	41	3	$3.50
#057 Black Widow	V	50	4	$5
#058 Blastaar	R	98	2	$2.50
#059 Blastaar	E	117	3	$3.50
#060 Blastaar	V	138	4	$5
#061 Thor	R	109	3	$3.50
#062 Thor	E	144	4	$5
#063 Thor	V	187	5	$9
#064 Sandman	R	61	3	$3
#065 Sandman	E	79	4	$4
#066 Sandman	V	106	5	$7
#067 Logan	R	40	3	$3
#068 Logan	E	49	4	$4
#069 Logan	V	60	5	$7
#070 Mr. Fantastic	R	48	3	$3.50
#071 Mr. Fantastic	E	74	4	$5

CHARACTER	LEVEL	POINT	SCARCITY	PRICE
#072 Mr. Fantastic	V	113	5	$9
#073 Dr. Doom	R	121	3	$3.50
#074 Dr. Doom	E	163	4	$5
#075 Dr. Doom	V	198	5	$12
#076 Dr. Octopus	R	22	3	$3.50
#077 Dr. Octopus	E	44	4	$5
#078 Dr. Octopus	V	66	5	$9
#079 White Queen	R	61	3	$3.50
#080 White Queen	E	80	4	$5
#081 White Queen	V	94	5	$9
#082 She Hulk	R	59	3	$3.50
#083 She Hulk	E	110	4	$5
#084 She Hulk	V	120	5	$9

Copyright: Marvel
Clobberin' Time HeroClix in original packaging.

CHARACTER	LEVEL	POINT	SCARCITY	PRICE
#085 Night Crawler	U	83	6	$30
#086 Nick Fury	U	62	6	$25
#087 Moon Dragon	U	71	6	$20
#088 Spider-Man	U	67	6	$25
#089 Mojo	U	100	6	$20
#090 Super Skrull	U	127	6	$25
#091 Red Skull	U	47	6	$20
#092 Spiral	U	56	6	$20
#093 Titania	U	85	6	$20
#094 Mr. Fixit	U	104	6	$25
#095 Medusa	U	57	6	$20
#096 Enchantress	U	91	6	$20

Copyright: Marvel
Sandman HeroClix—part of the villain's gallery.

Copyright:
Marvel
Doctor
Octopus—part
of the villain's
gallery.

Copyright: Marvel
White Queen—part
of the villain's
gallery.

DC HeroClix
Hypertime (All are DC™)

CHARACTER	LEVEL	POINT	SCARCITY	PRICE
#001 Gotham Policeman	R	11	1	$1
#002 Gotham Policeman	E	13	2	$1.50
#003 Gotham Policeman	V	15	3	$2
#004 Metropolis SCU	R	16	1	$1
#005 Metropolis SCU	E	18	2	$1.50
#006 Metropolis SCU	V	21	3	$2
#007 Checkmate Agent	R	11	1	$1
#008 Checkmate Agent	E	14	2	$1.50
#009 Checkmate Agent	V	16	3	$2
#010 Checkmate Medic	R	13	1	$1
#011 Checkmate Medic	E	17	2	$1.50
#012 Checkmate Medic	V	19	3	$2
#013 Intergang Agent	R	18	1	$1
#014 Intergang Agent	E	23	2	$1.50
#015 Intergang Agent	V	25	3	$2
#016 Intergang Medic	R	20	1	$1
#017 Intergang Medic	V	26	2	$1.50
#018 Intergang Medic	R	29	3	$2
#019 Lackey	R	7	1	$1
#020 Lackey	E	9	2	$1.50
#021 Lackey	V	11	3	$2
#022 Criminal	R	10	1	$1
#023 Criminal	E	12	2	$1.50
#024 Criminal	V	14	3	$2
#025 Huntress	R	18	1	$1.50
#026 Huntress	E	23	2	$2.25
#027 Huntress	V	35	3	$3
#028 Robin	R	17	1	$1.50
#029 Robin	E	20	2	$2.25
#030 Robin	V	22	3	$3
#031 Hawkman	R	32	2	$2.50
#032 Hawkman	E	43	3	$3.50
#033 Hawkman	V	48	4	$5
#034 Harley Quinn	R	27	2	$1.50

CHARACTER	LEVEL	POINT	SCARCITY	PRICE
#035 Harley Quinn	E	36	3	$2.50
#036 Harley Quinn	V	42	4	$4
#037 Catwoman	R	48	2	$2
#038 Catwoman	E	59	3	$3
#039 Catwoman	V	68	4	$4.50
#040 Man-Bat	R	23	2	$1.50
#041 Man-Bat	E	27	3	$2.50
#042 Man-Bat	V	31	4	$4
#043 Riddler	R	34	2	$2
#044 Riddler	E	39	3	$3
#045 Riddler	V	47	4	$4.50
#046 Mad Hatter	R	26	2	$1.50
#047 Mad Hatter	E	33	3	$2.50
#048 Mad Hatter	V	41	4	$4
#049 T.O. Morrow	R	21	2	$1.50
#050 T.O. Morrow	E	26	3	$2.50
#051 T.O. Morrow	V	28	4	$4
#052 Aquaman	R	27	2	$2.50
#053 Aquaman	E	36	3	$3.50
#054 Aquaman	V	41	4	$5
#055 Blue Beetle	R	26	2	$2.50
#056 Blue Beetle	E	35	3	$3.50
#057 Blue Beetle	V	43	4	$5
#058 Booster Gold	R	28	2	$2.50
#059 Booster Gold	E	38	3	$3.50
#060 Booster Gold	V	47	4	$5
#061 Nightwing	R	42	3	$3.50
#062 Nightwing	E	53	4	$5
#063 Nightwing	V	72	5	$9
#064 Changling	R	31	3	$3
#065 Changling	E	43	4	$4.50
#066 Changling	V	53	5	$7
#067 Steele	R	66	3	$3
#068 Steele	E	70	4	$4.50
#069 Steele	V	74	5	$8
#070 Gorilla Grodd	R	54	3	$3

CHARACTER	LEVEL	POINT	SCARCITY	PRICE
#071 Gorilla Grodd	E	76	4	$4.50
#072 Gorilla Grodd	V	86	5	$8
#073 Solomon Grundy	R	48	3	$3
#074 Solomon Grundy	E	69	4	$4.50
#075 Solomon Grundy	V	75	5	$8
#076 Black Manta	R	24	3	$3
#077 Black Manta	E	34	4	$4
#078 Black Manta	V	38	5	$7
#079 Weather Wizard	R	31	3	$3
#080 Weather Wizard	E	42	4	$4
#081 Weather Wizard	V	50	5	$7
#082 Clayface III	R	36	3	$3
#083 Clayface III	E	43	4	$4
#084 Clayface III	V	50	5	$7
#085 Hawk	R	45	3	$3
#086 Hawk	E	55	4	$4.50
#087 Hawk	V	69	5	$8
#088 Dove	R	46	3	$3
#089 Dove	E	51	4	$4.50
#090 Dove	V	69	5	$8
#091 Bane	R	61	3	$3
#092 Bane	E	76	4	$4.50
#093 Bane	V	85	5	$8
#094 Doomsday	R	137	3	$3.50
#095 Doomsday	E	159	4	$5
#096 Doomsday	V	174	5	$9
#097 Joker	R	49	3	$3
#098 Joker	E	69	4	$4.50
#099 Joker	V	91	5	$8
#100 Plastic Man	R	40	3	$3
#101 Plastic Man	E	43	4	$4.50
#102 Plastic Man	V	58	5	$8
#103 Flash	R	68	3	$3.50
#104 Flash	E	82	4	$5
#105 Flash	V	98	5	$12
#106 Batman	R	85	3	$3.50

CHARACTER	LEVEL	POINT	SCARCITY	PRICE
#107 Batman	E	92	4	$5
#108 Batman	V	116	5	$12
#109 Superman	R	155	3	$3.50
#110 Superman	E	173	4	$5
#111 Superman	V	219	5	$18
#112 Arcane	R	74	3	$3
#113 Arcane	E	83	4	$4
#114 Arcane	V	96	5	$7
#115 Swamp Thing	R	73	3	$3.50
#116 Swamp Thing	E	84	4	$5
#117 Swamp Thing	V	93	5	$8
#118 Brainiac 13	R	101	3	$3.50

Copyright: DC
Hypertime HeroClix booster packs in original packaging.

114

CHARACTER	LEVEL	POINT	SCARCITY	PRICE
#119 Brainiac 13	E	122	4	$5
#120 Brainiac 13	V	133	5	$7
#121 Parasite	U	107	6	$15
#122 Desaad	U	47	6	$15
#123 Darkseid	U	151	6	$15
#124 Commissioner Gordon	U	44	6	$20
#125 The Key	U	89	6	$15
#126 Joker	U	95	6	$20
#127 Catwoman	U	85	6	$20
#128 Flash	U	101	6	$25
#129 Batman	U	103	6	$25
#130 Superman	U	125	6	$25

Copyright: DC
Golden Age Flash and Batman HeroClix.

Copyright: DC
The Changling
HeroClix.

Below:
Copyright: DC
Joker and
Catwoman
HeroClix – more
villains from the
gallery. The silver
rings make these
items rare.

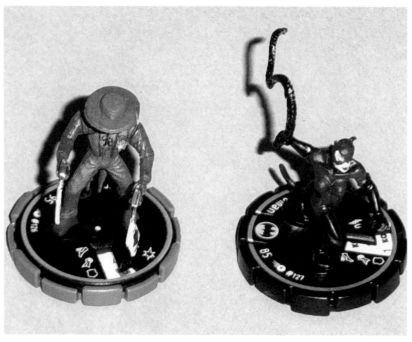

Above:
Copyright: DC
Joker and Riddler
HeroClix.

Copyright: DC
Aquaman HeroClix.

117

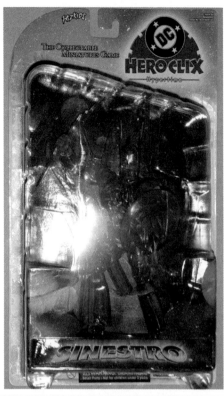

Copyright: DC
Super large Sinestro (a
Green Lantern villain)
HeroClix.

Below:
Copyright: Marvel
Launch of a new
HeroClix series at time
of writing—*Xplosion
Expansion Booster
Pack*.

118

C. Category: PVCs

Here is a sampling of PVCs from some popular genres.

Star Trek (Paramount Pictures) Produced in 1991 by Hamilton. They are approximately 4in (10cm) in height and were made in China. Name list on Bottom of PVC

Andorian	$8
Captain Kirk	$8
Dr. McCoy	$8
Gorn	$10
Lt. Scott	$8
Lt. Sulu	$8
Mr. Spock	$8
Mugato	$15
Talosian	$12
Tellanite	$12
Uhura	$8

Star Trek Generations (Paramount Pictures) Produced in 1994 by Applause. They are approximately 3in (8cm) in height and were made in China. No name list on bottom of PVC.

B'tor	$8
Captain Picard	$6
Commander Ricker	$6
Dr. Soran	$8
Guinan	$7

Kirk	$6
Lt. Data	$6
Lt. LaForge	$6
Lt. Worf	$6
Lursa	
	$8

Flintstones (Hanna-Barbera) Produced in 1990 by Applause. They range in height from 1½-2¼in (4-6cm) and were made in China.

Bam Bam	$8.50
Barney	$7.50
Betty	$7.50
Dino	$9
Fred	$7.50
Pebbles	$8.50
Wilma	$7.50

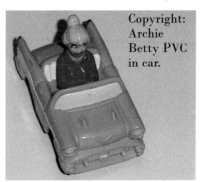

Copyright:
Archie
Betty PVC
in car.

Copyright: Nintendo
PVC evolution of Pokemon
characters flame.

Copyright: Nintendo
PVC evolution of second set of Pokemon characters.

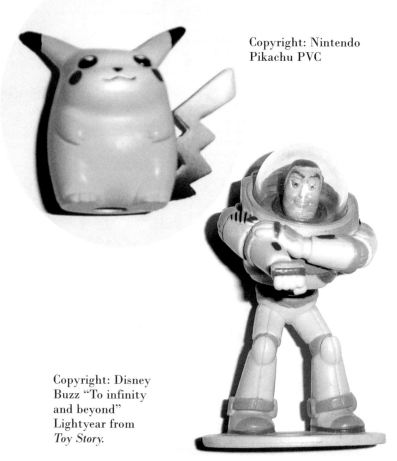

Copyright: Nintendo
Pikachu PVC

Copyright: Disney
Buzz "To infinity
and beyond"
Lightyear from
Toy Story.

Copyright: Disney
Assorted Disney characters.

Marvel PVCs
All have date stamped on them and are made in China. They vary in size, but most are about 3½ in (9cm). Most of the following PVC's sell for $6-$10 each.
Black Panther 1990
Captain America (Applause) 1990
Colossus 1990
Cyclops 1990
Daredevil 1990
Dr Doom 1990
Hobgoblin 1990
Hulk (Applause –green/purple pants) 1990

Hulk (gray with blue pants) 1990
Mr. Fantastic 1990
Night Crawler 1990
Scarlet Witch 1990
Silver Surfer 1990
Spider-Man (Applause) 1990

Storm 1990 (arms down, black outfit)
Thing 1990
Thor 1990
Wolverine 1990
Archangel 1991
Bullseye 1991
Cable 1991

Dr. Octopus 1991
Dr. Strange 1991
Rogue 1991
Sabretooth 1991
Storm (arms up black outfit) 1991
The Lizard 1991
Ghost Rider 1992

Punisher 1992
Iron Man 1993
Gambit 1995
Spider-Man (holding up gray unit) 1995
Spider-Man 1995
Storm (white outfit with yellow trim) 1995

Copyright:
Marvel
Spider-Man
PVC in car.

Copyright: Marvel
X-Men PVCs.

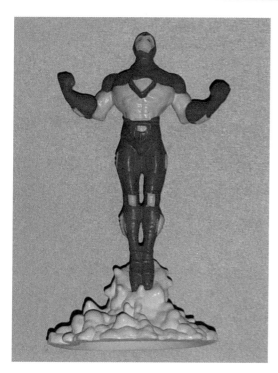

123

D. Category: Statues (Porcelain)

Statues, especially those made from porcelain, are popular decoration pieces and show strong appreciation in value over time:

Austin Powers Shag-A-Delic (Dark Horse)	$30
Barb Wire (Dark Horse)	$185
Batgirl (DC)	$125
Batman (DC)	$1250
Black Widow (Bowen Designs-Marvel)	$115
Captain America-Golden Age (Bowen Designs-Marvel)	$215
Captain America-Silver Age (Bowen Designs-Marvel)	$295
Catwoman (DC)	$150
Cyclops (Bowen Designs-Marvel)	$165
Daredevil-red (Bowen Designs-Marvel)	$335
Daredevil-yellow (Bowen Designs-Marvel)	$315
Darkseid (DC)	$125
Dawn (Bowen Designs-Marvel)	$115
Dr. Doom (Bowen Designs-Marvel)	$195
Electra (Bowen Designs-Marvel)	$135
Electra -red (Creative License-Marvel)	$95
Electra -white (Creative License-Marvel)	$135
Flash-Golden age (DC)	$115
Flash-Silver Age (DC)	$215
Flash of Two Worlds (DC)	$175
Gambit (Creative License-Marvel)	$215
Green Arrow (DC)	$165
Green Goblin (Bowen Designs-Marvel)	$165
Green Lantern-Alan Scott (DC)	$175
Green Lantern-Hal Jordon (DC)	$145
Green Lantern-Kyle Rayner (DC)	$135
Green Lantern, Justice League (DC)	$115
Green Lantern, Power Battery A. S. (DC) (Not Porcelain)	$225
Green Lantern, Power Battery H. J. (DC) (Not Porcelain)	$295
Harley Quinn (DC)	$125
Hawkgirl, Justice League (DC)	$125
Hawkman (DC)	$165
Hellblazer (DC)	$95
Hellboy (Bowen Designs-Marvel)	$375
Hulk-gray (Bowen Designs-Marvel)	$395
Hulk-green (Bowen Designs-Marvel)	$395
Human Torch (Bowen Designs-Marvel)	$195
Impulse, young justice (DC)	$95
Invisible Woman-clear (Bowen Designs-Marvel)	$165
Invisible Woman-painted (Bowen Designs-Marvel)	$195
Iron Man-classic (Bowen Designs-Marvel)	$175
Iron Man-gold (Bowen Designs-Marvel)	$135
Iron Man-gray (Bowen Designs-Marvel)	$135
Iron Man-retro (Bowen Designs-Marvel)	$135
Iron Man (Creative License-Marvel)	$175

Above:
Copyright: DC
Interlocking Green
Lanterns porcelain
statues.

Copyright: Marvel
Thor porcelain
statue.

Joker (DC)	$185	Robin (DC)	$135
Lady Death (Moore Creations)		Robin, young justice (DC)	$105
	$225	Rogue (Creative License-	
Lobo (DC)	$315	Marvel)	$135
Martian Manhunter, Justice		Sandman (DC)	$750
League (DC)	$115	Shi (Moore Creations)	$145
Mr. Fantastic (Bowen Designs-		Silver Surfer (Creative License-	
Marvel)	$195	Marvel)	$225
Nexus (Dark Horse)	$60	Spider-Man-on tower (Bowen	
Phoenix -fire base (Bowen		Designs-Marvel)	$150
Designs -Marvel)	$150	Storm (Bowen Designs-Marvel)	
Phoenix -water base (Bowen			$135
Designs -Marvel)	$150	Superboy, young justice (DC)	
Punisher (Bowen Designs-			$115
Marvel)	$165	Supergirl (DC)	$275

Copyright: Marvel
Classic battle between good versus evil-Spider-Man
versus the Green Goblin porcelain statues.

Superman-Golden Age
(Hallmark) $65
Superman-Silver age
(Hallmark) $50
Superman (DC) $550
Superman, Justice League (DC)
$115
Swamp Thing (DC) $115
The Thing (Bowen Designs-
Marvel) $185
Thor (Bowen Designs -Marvel)
$425
Vampirella (Bowen Designs-
Marvel) $95
Vampirella (Moore Creations)
$155

Witchblade (Moore Creations)
$165
Wolverine-brown (Bowen
Designs-Marvel) $135
Wolverine-yellow (Bowen
Designs-Marvel) $145
Wolverine (Creative License-
Marvel) $205
Wonder Woman-Golden Age
(Hallmark-DC) $95
Wonder Woman-Silver age
(Hallmark-DC) $105
Wonder Woman (DC) $195
Wonder Woman, Justice
League (DC) $105

Copyright: DC
Superman porcelain
statue seen in the
background on
Seinfeld episodes.

Copyright: DC
Supergirl, cousin to
Superman, porcelain
statue.

Below:
Copyright: DC
Batgirl porcelain
statue.

128

Copyright: Marvel
Cyclops from the
X-Men porcelain
statue.

Copyright: Moore
Witchblade porcelain
statue.

Above:
Copyright: Marvel
Rogue porcelain statue
(the white streak in the
hair gives her away).

Copyright: Warren
Vampirella Porcelain
figure.

E. Category: Fast Food Premiums

McDonalds and Burger King are two of the biggest contributors to the fast-food collectibles market. They are joined by many other restaurants, such as Wendy's, Dairy Queen, Denny's, KFC, Arby's, Hardee's, and Jack In The Box. These stores have contributed collectibles that range from action figures to cars, trucks, dolls, and probably every other type of toy imaginable. Here are a few examples of the toys that have been put out throughout the years.

We have provided a short list of some of the fast food items to give you a taste of some of the toys that were released and an estimate of their value based on Internet and retail back sales:

Superman PVC and Cup, 1988-Burger king	each $8
Dino-motion Dinosaurs, 1993-McDonalds (6)	each $1.50 set $10
Batman, The Animated Series, 1993-McDonalds (8)	each $3 set $20
Flintstones Happy Meal, 1994-McDonalds (5)	each $2 set $8
Spider-Man 1995-McDonalds (8)	each $2.50 set $18
Marvel Super Hero's, 1996-McDonalds (8)	$2.50 each set $18
Superman, 1997-Burger King (5)	each $2 set $12
Disney Video Favorites, 1998-McDonalds (6)	each $1.50 set $10
Inspector Gadget, 1999-McDonalds (8)	each $2 set $15 watch $4
Tarzan, 1999-McDonalds (8)	each $1 set $6
Spy Kids 2, 2000-McDonalds (6)	each $2 set $10
Tarzan, 2000-McDonalds (8 Plush Toys)	each $1.50 set $10
X-Men Evolution (includes Mini CD) 2001-Burger King (8)	$2 each set $15
Lord of the Rings, 2002-Burger King (19)	each $1.50 set $35
Marvel City of Heroes, 2002-Jack In the Box (5)	each $2 set $12
Spider-Man, 2002-Kentucky Fried Chicken (4)	each $1.50 set $5
Disney 100 years, 2002-McDonalds (100)	each $1.50 set $125
Lilo & Stitch, 2002-McDonalds (8)	each $1.50 set $10
Justice League, 2002-Subway	each $5 set $20
Jungle Book 2, 2003-McDonalds (6)	each $1.50 set $8

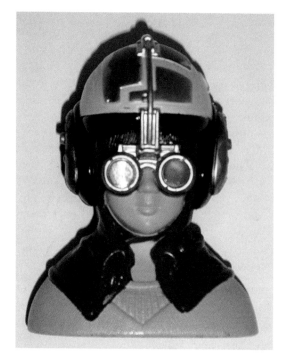

Copyright: LucasFilm
Anakin Skywalker fast
food giveaway.

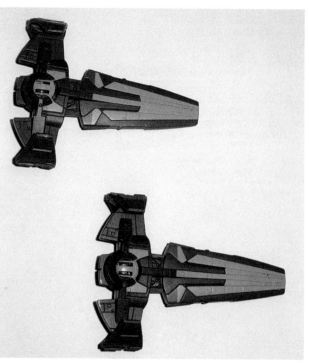

Copyright:
LucasFilm
Empire ships
from *Star Wars
Episode I*
fast food
giveaways.

Copyright:
DC
Crackerjack
premiums
from 1979.

Copyright: DC
Mugs with Batman and Robin
figures as handles.

133

Copyright: DC
Batman and Robin pins.

F. Category: Oddities

We would like to explore all the different types of non-fast food premiums, toys and licensed products that have been produced over the years which we will call oddities because most have not as yet being cataloged or priced in most price guides. In future issues this will be the major focus of our comic related survival and price guide any help with information would be greatly appreciated we have amounted a wealth of information but unfortunately do to space requirement in this issue we are only going to focus on a few.

Superman Wood Doll Ideal 1940: This Superman Doll is fully jointed. It stands 13in (33cm) tall with cape and Superman logo on chest. $695

Batman Bread Wrapper 1966 by Golden State-Harvest Queen Bakeries Inc. $25

Batman Stamp Set 1966
Kellogg's Mail Premium.
Contains 6 stampers and pad-
Batman, Robin, Batmobile,
Riddler, Penguin and Joker.
$125

Batman Periscope 1966
Kellogg's Mail Premium. It is
approximately 11in (28cm) long
and extends to approximately
21in (53cm). It is made of
black plastic. $95

Vari-Vue Batman Flicker
Rings1966: These flicker rings
could have been had for as little
as a penny in 1966 from gum
machines if you were lucky
enough to have it come out
with a hard piece of round gum
resembling a marble. There
were 12 different Batman flicker rings with Batman, Robin,
Joker, Riddler and Penguin on
them and they would flick from
one picture to the other as you
moved it. Each ring had two
pictures. each $25 set $300

Batman Mobile Bat Lab 1975
by Mego Corp. The unit had a
rear Bat-Grappling hook, front-
end foe catcher, revolving Bat-
platform. $250

Corgi Toys Gift Set 3
(Batmobile, Batboat and
Trailer) 1976 Die Cast $295

Corgi Batcopter 1976. Includes
figure in the copter with red
propellers. $195

Corgi Batmobile red tires
includes 7 missiles. $215
Batman and Justice League
Playset by Ideal, consists of:
Sanctuary Mountain/Batcave,
Bat Plane And Launcher,
Periscope and Weather Vane,
Batmobile, A Robot, Batman,
Robin, Superman, Wonder
Woman, Aquaman and Flash.
A few of the characters have
accessories such as Wonder
Woman who has a flaming
hoop and Aquaman with a
knife. There are still details on
this item of which we are
unsure, but this is truly one of
the premium items in comic-
related toys, as complete sets
are very rare, it could sell for
anywhere between $15,000 to
$25,000 in near mint condition.

The PVC characters are around
with most people not knowing
from what or where they came.
Prices for the PVC's range from
$125 to $200 in near mint with
Flash being one of the harder
to find characters. The Bat
Plane sells for about $250,
Robot for $100 and the
Batmobile for $300, again keep-
ing in mind that most people
have not heard of or seen any
of these. You could conceivably
put a set together piece by
piece, but finding the
Batcave/Sanctuary and the box
could be next to impossible.

136

Opposite page:

Top:
Copyright: DC
Batman finger rings in
two different colors.

Middle:
Copyright: DC
Two different
Batmobiles based on
the hit 1989 Batman
movie.

Bottom:
Copyright: DC
Batman and Robin
miniature license
plates from the 1960s.

Above:
Copyright: Marvel
Hulk ornament.

Copyright: DC
Superman pinball game
from the 1950s.

137

Chapter 7

Cartoon List

Not all comic book related merchandise fits nicely into one of the toy categories defined in this book. This does not make them any less interesting and so we are planning to include near-complete lists of some collectibles that fit into the 'other' toy category, but which have had an enormous impact on the sales of comic book related toys. In this edition, we provide a list of Spider-Man (Marvel) cartoons and Super-Friends (DC) cartoons.

SPIDER-MAN Cartoons
* First Aired on ABC from Sept. 1967-69
* Season one had two episodes during its half hour time slot and season two had one episode.
* The third season was released at a later date in syndication. It was produced by Gantray-Lawrence Animation and Krantz Animation in association with Marvel Comics. (Approximately 79 Episodes)

Season 1 had 40 episodes all were made for 15 minute time slots unless stated
Spider-Man
EPISODES
(Not Necessarily in Order of Release)
1- *Never Step On A Scorpion* (Scorpion)
2- *The One-Eyed Idol*
3- *Farewell Performance*
4- *The Terrible Triumph Of Dr. Octopus* (Dr. Octopus)
5- *The Power Of Dr. Octopus* (Dr. Octopus)
6- *The Sky Is Falling* (The Vulture)
7- *The Vulture's Prey* (The Vulture)
8- *Sands Of Crime* (Sandman)
9- *The Golden Rhino* (The Rhino)
10- *Horn Of The Rhino* (The Rhino)(24 min.)
11- *Magic Malice* (The Green Goblin)
12- *The Witching Hour* (The Green Goblin)
13- *To Catch A Spider* (Green Goblin, Vulture, Electro and Dr. Noah Boddy)
14- *The Peril Of Parafino* (Parafino)
15- *Armorer Car Robbery*

16- *Where Crawls The Lizard*
(the Lizard)
17- *Sub-Zero For Spidy*
18- *Electro The Human Lightning Bolt* (Electro)
19- *The Kilowatt Kaper* (Electro)
20- *Fiddler on The Loose*
21- *The Revenge Of Dr. Magneto* (Not Magneto)
22- *The Sinister Prime Minister* (Charles Cameo)
23- *Diet Of Destruction*
24- *Fifth Avenue Phantom* (The Phantom)
25- *The Dark Terrors* (The Phantom)
26- *The Night Of The Villains* (Parafino)
27- *Here Comes Trubble*
28- *Captured By J. Jonah Jameson* (Teddy-Bear Smythe Robot)
29- *Spider-Man Meets Dr. Noah Boddy* (Dr. Noah Boddy)
30- *The Fantastic Fakir*
31- *Blueprint For Crime* (The Ox,Cowboy and The Plotter)
32- *Spider And The Fly* (The Human Flies)
33- *The Slippery Dr. Von Schlick*
34- *Penthouse Robbery*
35- *Fountain Of Terror*
36- *The Menace Of Mysterio* (Mysterio) ½ hour Episode
37- *Return of The Flying Dutchman* (Mysterio)
38- *Sting Of The Scorpion* (Scorpion)
39- *Trick Or Treachery* (Human Flies)
40- *Double Identity* (Charles Cameo)

Season 2 had 20 episodes and were made for a ½ hour time slot

41- *The Origin Of Spider-Man*
42- *King Pinned*
43- *Criminals In The Clouds*
44- *Rhino* (The Rhino)
45- *Vine*
46- *The Madness Of Mysterio* (Mysterio)
47- *Cloud City Of Gold*
48- *Home*
49- *Spider-Man Battles The Molemen*
50- *The Evil Sorcerer*
51- *Pardo Presents*
52- *Blotto*
53- *Neptune's Nose Cone*
54- *Thumble Rumble*
55- *Spider-Man Meets Skyboy*
56- *Cold Storage*
57- *Swing City*
58- *To Cage A Spider*
59- *Menace From The Bottom Of The World*
60- *Diamond Dust*

Season 3 had 19 episodes and were also produced for a ½ hour time slot

61- *Conner's Reptiles*
62- *Sky Harbor*
63- *Trouble With Snow*
64- *Spider-Man Vs. Desperado*
65- *The Birth Of Microman*
66- *Scourge Of The Scarf*
67- *The Vanishing Doctor Vaspasian*
68- *Down To Earth*
69- *The Phantom From The Depths of Time*
70- *Revolt Of The Fifth Dimension*
71- *The Winged Thing*

72- *Up From Nowhwere*
73- *The Devious Dr. Dumpty*
74- *Super Swami*
75- *Knight Must Fall*
76- *Rollaramp*
77- *Specialists And Slaves*
78- *Trip To Tomorrow*
79- *The Big Brainwasher*

The second Spider-Man series was called *Spider-Man And His Amazing Friends* which included Iceman and Firestar as his sidekicks in all of these episodes. There were many guest appearances by many of your favorite hero's and villians such as: Captain America, Sub-Mariner, Dr. Strange, The Hulk, X-Men, King pin, Red Skull and many others. (Approximately 24 Episodes). First Aired-Sept 1981-1984 all were produced for ½ hour time slot by Marvel Productions.

Season 1 had 12 episodes (1981-82)

Spider-Man And His Amazing Friends
EPISODES
(Not Necessarily in Order of Release)
1- *Sunfire* (Sunfire)
2- *Spidey Goes Hollywood* (Hulk & Mysterio)
3- *VideoMan* (Electro Creates Videoman)
4- *Swarm*
5- *The Triumph Of The Green Goblin*

6- *The Fantastic Mr. Frump*
7- *Seven Little Super Heroes* (Capt. America, Sub-Mariner, Dr. Strange, Sheena & The Chameleon)
8- *The Quest Of The Red Skull*
9- *Vengeance Of Loki*
10- *Pawns Of The Kingpin*
11- *The Prison Plot* (Magneto & The Brotherhood Of Evil)
12- *The Crime Of All Centuries*

Season 2 had 4 episodes (1982-83)

13- *Along Came A Spidey*
14- *A Firestar Is Born* (X-Men & Juggernaut)
15- *Knights And Demons*
16- *The Origin Of The Iceman*

Season 3 had 8 Episodes and was renamed

(The Amazing Spider-Man And The Incredible Hulk: 1983-84)
17- *The Origin Of The Spider-Friends* (Tony Stark-Ironman & The Beetle)
18- *The Transylvania Connection*
19- *Spidey Meets The Girl Of Tomorrow*
20- *The X-Men Adventure*
21- *Spider-Man Unmasked!*
22- *Attack Of The Arachnoid*
23- *Mission:Save The Guardstar* (S.H.I.E.L.D)
24- *The Education Of A Super Hero*

The third Spider-Man series came out in 1984-85, Spidey returned to his solo act. (Approximately 26 episodes). Each episode produced for ½ hour time slot by Marvel Productions.

The next Spider-Man series came out in 1993-1998 (approximately 65 eppisodes). It ran for 5 seasons and was also produced for a ½ hour time slot by Saban & Graz Entertainment.

17- *Neogenic Nightmare, Chapter 4- The Mutant Agenda*
18- *Neogenic Nightmare, Chapter 5- Mutant's Revenge*
19- *Neogenic Nightmare, Chapter 6- Morbius*
20- *Neogenic Nightmare, Chapter 7- Enter The Punisher*
21- *Neogenic Nightmare, Chapter 8- Duel Of The Hunters*
22- *Neogenic Nightmare, Chapter 9- Blade The Vampire Hunter*
23- *Neogenic Nightmare, Chapter 10- The Immortal Vampire*
24- *Neogenic Nightmare, Chapter 11- Table Of Time*
25- *Neogenic Nightmare, Chapter 12- Ravages oOf Time*
26- *Neogenic Nightmare, Chapter 13- Shriek Of The Vulture*
27- *Neogenic Nightmare, Chapter 14- The Final Nightmare*

Season 3 had 14 episodes (1995-96)
28- *Sins Of The Father, Chapter 1- Doctor Strange*
29- *Sins Of The Father, Chapter 2- Make A Wish*
30- *Sins of The Father, Chapter 3- Attack Of The Octo-Bot*
31- *Sins Of The Father, Chapter 4- Enter The Green Goblin*

32- *Sins Of The Father, Chapter 5- Rocket Racer*
33- *Sins Of The Father, Chapter 6- Framed*
34- *Sins Of The Father, Chapter 7- The Man Without Fear*
35- *Sins Of The Father, Chapter 8- The Ultimate Slayer*
36- *Sins Of The Father, Chapter 9- Tombstone*
37- *Sins Of The Father, Chapter 10- Venom Returns*
38- *Sins Of The Father, Chapter 11- Carnage*
39- *Sins Of The Father, Chapter 12- The Spot*
40- *Sins Of The Father, Chapter 13- Goblin War*
41- *Sins Of The Father, Chapter 14- Turning Point*

Season 4 had 11 episodes (1996-97)
42- *Partners In Dangers, Chapter 1- Guilty*
43- *Partners In Dangers, Chapter 2- The Cat*
44- *Partners In Dangers, Chapter 3- The Black Cat*
45- *Partners In Dangers, Chapter 4- The Return Of Kraven*
46- *Partners In Dangers, Chapter 5- Partners*
47- *Partners In Dangers, Chapter 6- The Awakening*
48- *Partners In Dangers, Chapter 7- The Vampire Queen*
49- *Partners In Dangers, Chapter 8- The Return Of The Green Goblin*

Copyright: Marvel
*Spider-Man and His
Amazing Friends* video.

Below:
Copyright: Marvel
Spider-Man Insidious Six video.

Copyright: Marvel
*Spider-Man Spider
Slayer* 80-minute
video.

50- *Partners In Dangers,*
   Chapter 9- The Haunting
   Of Mary Jane Watson
51- *Partners In Dangers,*
   Chapter 10- The Lizard
   King
52- *Partners In Dangers,*
   Chapter 11- The Prowler

**Season 5 had 14 episodes
(1997-98)**

53- *The Wedding*
54- *Six Forgotten Warriors,*
   Chapter 1- Six Forgotten
   Warriors
55- *Six Forgotten Warriors,*
   Chapter 2- Unclaimed
   Legacy
56- *Six Forgotten Warriors,*
   Chapter 3- Secrets Of The
   Six
57- *Six Forgotten Warriors,*
   Chapter 4- The Six Fight
   Again
58- *Six Forgotten Warriors,*
   Chapter 5- The Price Of
   Heroism
59- *The Return Of Hydro-*
   Man- Part 1
60- *The Return Of Hydro-*
   Man- Part 2
61- *Secret Wars, Chapter 1-*
   Arrival
62- *Secret Wars, Chapter 2-*
   The Gauntlet Of The Red
   Skull
63- *Secret Wars, Chapter 3-*
   Doom
64- *Secret Wars, Chapter 1-*
   Really, Really Hate Clones
65- *Secret Wars, Chapter 2-*
   Farewell, Spider-Man

Superfriends Cartoons
The Superfriends

Aired Sept, 1973 on ABC and was a Hanna-Barbera Production. Wendy and Marvin and Wonder Dog were introduced in this series.

EPISODES
(Not Necessarily in Order of Release)

1- *The Power Pirate*
2- *The Baffles Puzzle*
3- *Professor Goodfellow's*
   G.E.E.C.
4- *The Weather Maker*
5- *Dr. Pelagian's War*
6- *The Shamon U*
7- *Too Hot To Handle*
8- *The Androids*
9- *The Balloon People*
10- *The Fantastic Frerps*
11- *The Ultra Scam*
12- *The Menace Of The White*
   Dwarf
13- *The Mysterious Moles*
14- *Gulliver's Gigantic Goof*
15- *The Planet Splitter*
16- *The Watermen*

The All New Superfriends Hour:
Aired Sept, 1977 on ABC and Produced by Hanna-Barbera.

Wonder Twins were introduced and replaced Weny and Marvin. Show was one hour in lenth and had four separate cartoons.

EPISODES
(Not Necessarily in Order of Release)

1- *Invation Of The Earthors-*
   The Brain Machine- Joy
   Ride- The Whirlpool
2- *City In A Bottle- Invation*
   Of The Hydronoids-
   Hitchbike- Space Emergency

3- *Will The World Collide-
The Marsh Monster-
Runaway- Time Rescue*
4- *Day Of The Planet
Creatures- Doctor Fright-
Drag Racing- Fire*
5- *Superfriends VS Super
Friends- The Monster Of
Dr. Droid- Vandals- Energy
Mass*
6- *Voyage Of The Mysterious
Time Machine- The Secret
Four- Tiger On The Loose-
The Antidote*
7- *Planet Of The Neanderthals-
The Enforcer- Shark Attack-
Flood Of Diamonds- Flood
Of Diamonds*
8- *The Mind Maidens- The
Collector- Handicap- Alaka
Peril*
9- *The Water Beast- Attack
Of The Giant Squid- Game
Of Chickens- Volcano*
10- *The Coming Of The
Arthropods- The Invisible
Menace- Initiation- River
Of Doom*
11- *Exploration Earth- The
Fifty Foot Woman-
Cheating- Attack Of The
Killer Bees*
12- *The Lionmen- Forbidden
Power- Pressure Point- Day
Of The Rats*
13- *The Tiny World Of Terror-
The Man-Beast Of Xra-
Prejudice- Tibetan Raiders*
14- *The Mummy Of Nazca-
Frozen Peril- Dangerous
Prank- Cable Car Rescue*
15- *The Ghost- The Protector-
Stowaways- Rampage*

16- *Mxyzptlk's Flick- Alien
Mummy- Eruption- Return
Of The Phantoms*

Challenge of the Superfriends:
Aired Sept, 1978 on ABC
and Produced by Hanna-
Barbera. Introduced The Legion
Of Doom

EPISODES

(Not Necessarily in Order of Release)
1- *Wanted: The Superfriends*
2- *Invasion Of The Fearians*
3- *The World's Deadliest Game*
4- *The Time Trap*
5- *Trial Of The Superfriends*
6- *The Monolith Of Evil*
7- *The Giants Of Doom*
8- *Secret Origins Of The
Superfriends*
9- *Revenge On Gorilla City*
10- *Swamp Of The Living Dead*
11- *Conquerors Of the Future*
12- *The Final Challenge*
13- *Fairy Tales Of Doom*
14- *Doomsday*
15- *Superfriends: Rest In Peace*
16- *History Of Doom*

**The World's Greatest
Superfriends**
Aired Sept, 1979 and
Produced by Hanna-Barbera.
Featured two ½ hour Episodes.

EPISODES

(Not Necessarily in Order of Release)
1- *Rub Three Times For
Disaster*
2- *Lex Luthor Strikes Back*
3- *Space Knight Of Camelon*
4- *The Lord Of Middle Earth*
5- *Universe Of Evil*
6- *Terror At 20,000 Fathoms*

7- *The Superfriends Meet Frankenstein*
8- *Planet Of Oz*
9- *The Beasts Are Coming*
10- *The Anti-Matter Monster*
11- *Attack Of The Vampire*
12- *Battle At The Earth's Core*
13- *The Demons Of Exxor*
14- *Rokan: Enemy From Space*
15- *The Pied Piper From Space*
16- *Journey Through Inner Space*
17- *Invasion Of The Brian Creature*
18- *The Incredible Space Circus*
19- *Batman: Dead Or Alive*
20- *Battle Of The Gods*
21- *Terror From The Phantom Zone*
22- *World Beneath The Ice*
23- *Sinbad And The Space Pirates*

Superfriends- Shorts 1980
EPISODES
(Not Necessarily in Order of Release)
1- *Yuma, The Terrible*
2- *Haunted House*
3- *Termites From Venus*
4- *Revenge Of Bizarro*
5- *One Small Step For Mars*
6- *The Make-up Monster*
7- *Rock & Roll Space Bandits*
8- *The Incredible Crude Oil Monster*
9- *The Killer Machines*
10- *Dive To Disaster*
11- *The Man In The Moon*
12- *Elevator To Nowhere*
13- *Journey Into Blackness*
14- *Invasion Of The Gleeks*
15- *Circus Of Horrors*
16- *Circus Gang*
17- *Return Of Atlantis*

18- *Voodoo Vampire*
19- *Around The World In 80 Riddles*
20- *The Ice Demon*
21- *Bigfoot*
22- *Garden Of Doom*

Superfriends- Shorts 1981
EPISODES
(Not Necessarily in Order of Release)
1- *The Warlords Amulet*
2- *Alien Mummy*
3- *Sink Hole*
4- *The Witch's Arcade*
5- *Palette's Perils*
6- *The Lava Men*
7- *Stowaways From Space*
8- *The Creature From The Dump*
9- *Colossus*
10- *Bizarroworld*
11- *The Iron Cyclops*
12- *Three Wishes*
13- *The Scaraghosta Sea*
14- *The Airport Terror*
15- *The Evil From Krypton*
16- *Scorpio*

Superfriends- Shorts 1983
EPISODES
(Not Necessarily in Order of Release)
1- *An Unexpected Treasure*
2- *Invasion Of The Space Dolls*
3- *Once Upon A Poltergeist*
4- *Mxyzptlk's Revenge*
5- *Day Of The Dinosaurs*
6- *Prisoners Of Sleep*
7- *Video Victims*
8- *Outlaws Of Orion*
9- *Playground Of Doom*
10- *A Pint Of Life*
11- *Attack Of The Cats*
12- *The Recruiter*

13- *The Malusian Blob*
14- *Bully For You*
15- *Revenge Of Doom*
16- *Terror On The Titanic*
17- *One Small Step For Superman*
18- *Space Racer*
19- *Roller Coaster*
20- *Warpland*
21- *The Krypton Syndrome*
22- *Superclones*
23- *Two Gleeks Are Deadlier Than One*
24- *Bulgor The Behemoth*

Superfriends: The Legendary Super Powers

Aired Sept, 1984 on ABC and Produced by Hanna-Barbera. It was a ½ hour long show with two cartoons in each show.

EPISODES
(Not Necessarily in Order of Release)
1- *The Bride Of Darkseid, Part 1*
2- *The Bride Of Darkseid, Part 2*
3- *The Case Of The Shrinking Superfriends*
4- *The Mask Of Mystery*
5- *Mr. Mxyzptlk And The Magic Lamp*
6- *No Honor Among Super-Theives*
7- *Super Brat*

8- *The Village Of The Lost Souls*
9- *The Royal Ruse*
10- *The Wrath Of Brainiac*
11- *The Case Of The Dreadfull Dolls*
12- *Darkseid's Golden Trap, Part 1*
13- *Darkseid's Golden Trap, Part 2*
14- *Reflections In Crystal*
15- *The Curator*
16- *Island Of The Dinosoids*

Superfriends: Galactic Guardians

Aired Sept, 1985 and Produced by Hanna-Barbera. No Wonder Twins This time, but More Super Heroes and Villains, most shows were made for a ½ hour time slot.

EPISODES
(Not Necessarily in Order of Release)
1- *The Bizarro Super Power Team*
2- *The Ghost Ship*
3- *The Case Of The Stolen Powers*
4- *Brain Child*
5- *The Seeds Of Doom*
6- *The Wild Cards*
7- *The Darkseid Deception*
8- *The Fear*
9- *Escape From Space City*
10- *The Death Of Superman*

Chapter 8

Toy Gallery

Copyright: Marvel
Big and small Spider-Man
action figures. The big one
comes with a handle that
moves Spider-Man.

Copyright: DC
Life-size replica of a Green Lantern power battery.

Below:
Copyright: Marvel
Mini-busts of Vision, Colossus, Scarlet Witch and Daredevil.

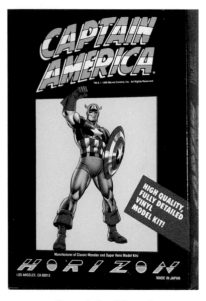

Captain America durable vinyl toy.

Punisher porcelain statue in its original box.

Porcelain statue of the original Iron Man costume.

Copyright:
Marvel
Porcelain statue
of the Hulk.
This is the
scary version,
not the lovable
Lou Ferrigno
rendition.

Copyright: Marvel
Magnificent Magneto porcelain statue.

151

Copyright: DC
Barry Allen Flash
porcelain statue.

Copyright: DC
Wonder Woman porcelain statue.

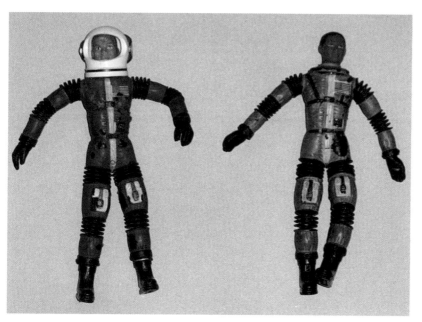

Above:
Major Matt Mason
action figures from the
1960s.

Copyright:
Warner Brothers
Neo action figure from
The Matrix hit movie
series.

Above:
Copyright: DC
Batman porcelain
statue.

Copyright: Marvel
Wolverine porcelain
statue wearing
original yellow
costume.

1st Wolverine porcelain statue wearing his second *X-Men* costume.

Wolverine 1989
The Marvel™ Collection

Wolverine TM & © 1989 Marvel Entertainment Group, Inc.
All rights reserved.

Underside of
base showing
authenticity of
the 1st Wolverine
porcelain statue.

155

Copyright: Marvel
Spider-Man pencil case.

Below:
Copyright: DC
Robin Dragstar.

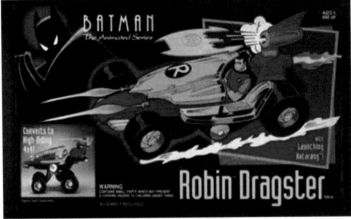

Copyright: DC
Top view of the
*Justice League of
America* play set.

156

Copyright: DC
Side view of the *Justice League of America* play set.

Above:
Copyright: DC
Robin Wallet.

Copyright: Ideal
Captain Action
with Batman
costume dates
back to the
1960s.

Above:
Copyright: DC
Batman action figure
wearing red translucent
costume

Copyright: DC
Batman action figure

Above:
Copyright:
DC
Batman,
Batgirl and
Robin
action
figures.

Copyright:
DC
Superman
action
figure with
detachable
red plastic
cape.

159

Copyright: Kazuki
Takahashi
Yu Gi Oh! action
figure.

Copyright: Kazuki
Takahashi
Yu Gi Oh! action
figure.